Tamsin Bradley is Reader in International Development Studies at the University of Portsmouth. Her previous books include *Religion and Gender in the Developing World: Faith-Based Organizations and Feminism in India* (I.B.Tauris, 2010) and *Challenging the NGOs: Women, Religion and Western Dialogues in India* (I.B.Tauris, 2006).

'In delineating a range of violence against women and girls and its exacerbation in neoliberal times and in its disentangling and problematising of the diverse constructions of such violence – in national and "Western" media, by local and "outsider" feminisms, in activist and academic analyses, in multilateral agency programmes and statements of government persons and in recountings by women who have experienced it – this book is an important intervention in the struggle to understand and resist from a perspective of gender equality.'

Rajni Palriwala, Professor of Sociology, University of Delhi

'Bradley argues that economic liberalisation in India has yet to deliver on its promise to usher in a rights-based socio-political order, especially for women; on the contrary, it has had the effect of increasing women's vulnerability to some forms of gendered violence such as dowry-related harassment and female foeticide. Given the widespread expectation from economic liberalisation to usher in a rights-based socio-political order, Bradley's book constitutes an important and timely warning regarding the ability of entrenched patriarchal structures to resist and subvert socio-economic change.'

Megha Kumar, Deputy Director of Analysis at Oxford Analytica and author of *Communalism and Sexual Violence in India* (I.B.Tauris, 2016)

WOMEN AND VIOLENCE IN INDIA

Gender, Oppression and the Politics of Neoliberalism

TAMSIN BRADLEY

BLOOMSBURY
NEW DELHI • LONDON • OXFORD • NEW YORK • SYDNEY

BLOOMSBURY INDIA
Bloomsbury Publishing India Pvt. Ltd
Second Floor, LSC Building No. 4, DDA Complex, Pocket C–6&7,
Vasant Kunj, New Delhi 110070

BLOOMSBURY, Bloomsbury Academic India and the Diana
logo are trademarks of Bloomsbury Publishing Plc

First published in India 2022
Published in 2017 by I.B.Tauris & Co. Ltd

This edition is published with permission from Bloomsbury Publishing Plc.
50 Bedford Square, London WC1B3DP

A catalog record for this book is available from the Library of Congress.
A catalogue record for this book is available from the British Library.

ISBN: 978-93-56400-79-5

For sale in the Indian subcontinent only

Exclusively distributed in the Indian subcontinent by
Manohar Publishers & Distributors
4753/23, Ansari Road
Darya Ganj, New Delhi 110002
Tel.: 23284848, 23289100
Email: sales@manoharbooks.com, manoharbooks@gmail.com

Typeset in Garamond Three by OKS Prepress Services, Chennai, India
Printed and bound in India by Replika Press Pvt. Ltd.

For Megan Bradley, Ariane and Eira Brown:
You are three beautiful, outstanding young ladies and my optimism that things can be different is in your hands

CONTENTS

Part IV. Harmful Cultural Practices

LIST OF ILLUSTRATIONS

Figures

Tables

LIST OF ABBREVIATIONS

AIDWA:	All India Democratic Women's Association
BJP:	Bharatiya Janata Party
CEDAW:	Convention for the Eradication of Discrimination Against Women
DFID:	Department for International Development (UK)
FGM:	Female Genital Mutilation
FM:	Forced Marriage
GBV:	Gender-Based Violence
GDI:	Gender-related Development Index
HCPs:	Harmful Cultural Practices
HDI:	Human Development Index
ICRW:	International Centre for Research on Women
IPV:	Intimate Partner Violence
MDGs:	Millennium Development Goals
RSS:	Rashtriya Svayam-sevak Sangh
SAPs:	Structural Adjustment Programmes
UP:	Uttar Pradesh
VAWG:	Violence Against Women and Girls
WHO:	World Health Organization

ACKNOWLEDGEMENTS

Firstly, I must thank once more my publisher I.B.Tauris, in particular Baillie Card and Alex Wright for their continuing support in my work and patience as I stretch deadlines. I also thank colleagues and mentors at the University of Portsmouth who have given me considerable support and funding to cover numerous research trips to India. I also acknowledge funding received from the British Council that enabled me to research the anti-rape movement. The data has fed into this volume across a number of chapters. To Richard Bartholomew, I have no idea how you do it but my work could never make it to the shelf without your attention to detail and sheer kindness with your time.

Without the support of my family, my mother and father Ruth and Colin Bradley, this book, as with all my research, would not be possible. The childcare they give my daughter means that I can work in a profession I love. My mother's willingness to take Megan so I can write and conduct fieldwork is incredible and will never be possible to repay but I do love her so very much. To my daughter Megan thank you for giving me the space to write, for letting me go to India and for just being you. My life could never be as full of joy without you.

Friendship and inspiration come from many people, Suti Sahariah and Zara Ramsay: you are amazing researchers but also my friends, together we have had many Indian adventures and long may they continue. And finally to Dave: you give me hope and optimism that anything is possible – thank you.

Finally, to all the wonderful activists I have spoken to over the past few years, you are all truly inspiring and courageous.

INTRODUCTION

The context

The motivation for this volume is the aftermath of the brutal gang-rape and murder of *Nirbhaya* (Courageous One), who was raped on a bus in Delhi on 16 December 2012 and died from her injuries on 29 December. The international spotlight that this incident placed on India and the endemic nature of gender-based violence (GBV) in the country that it has been taken to evidence have sparked national outrage, with waves of protests. However, activists who have been working on violence against women and girls (VAWG) in India for some time argue that acts of brutality such as this are far from exceptional: figures from the National Crime Records Bureau show that, on average, 92 women are raped in India each day.[1]

Although sexual assault has dominated Indian media coverage of VAWG since the gang-rape and murder of *Nirbhaya*, statistics show that intimate partner violence (IPV) is the most prevalent form of VAWG in India, and its prevalence (or at least reporting rate) is increasing. An International Centre for Research on Women (ICRW) study of Indian women found that 52 per cent of those interviewed had experienced IPV,[2] while an even greater number (60 per cent) of male respondents said they had inflicted violence on their partners. The same study found that men who experience economic stress were more likely to have perpetrated violence, either ever or during the past 12 months. According to Sohini Paul, who used national survey data, women in the age group of 25–39 are most likely to suffer violence at home. Of the religious communities, Buddhist women (usually Dalits) are most likely to suffer IPV. Jain women (who tend to be richer) suffer the least violence. Of all 'social groups', Scheduled Caste women suffer most IPV.[3]

More broadly, statistics indicate that South Asia has the highest regional prevalence of GBV: at least 43 per cent of women in South Asia have experienced physical and/or sexual violence at the hands of their partners,[4] and South Asian women fare badly in the 'Mothers' Index' published in May 2015 by Save the Children. The index ranks 179 countries according to the wellbeing of their women, using indicators including the prevalence of GBV as well as maternal mortality, the survival of young children and women's involvement in politics. Women in India and Pakistan (ranked 140th and 149th) have a quality of life only a little higher than those in Afghanistan (152nd) and far behind those in China (61st).

The picture in India is bleak and has triggered renewed determination nationally but also globally to finally tackle and end violence against women and girls. The goal of this volume is that it may contribute, even in a very small way, to the eradication of violence in the lives of women. Additionally, this volume aims to fill a gap in the literature. Very few publications explore in depth the dynamics of different forms of GBV in one specific context. Whilst the data presented above already gives both a country-specific and a regional picture of the prevalence of gender-based violence in India, this volume argues from the outset that if such violence is to be eradicated, its dynamics must be unravelled contextually. In other words, we cannot make sweeping statements or assumptions about why violence persists and how it might be eliminated. One strand to the critique woven through this volume argues strongly against uniform programmes to reduce violence: environments that sustain VAWG differ too significantly to helpfully produce any overarching approaches. However, whilst I argue for the need to take each country individually, I also stress the need to offer regional and global contextualisation so as not to unhelpfully sensationalise violence in one particular case. This volume is an attempt to offer a one-country case study, but the approach and analysis used in compiling it could be drawn upon in the development of others.

A further motivation for this volume is that the analysis of data on violence against women often stops short of delving very deeply into understanding *why* this violence seems to flourish. Patriarchy is not enough of an explanation, because we are still left wondering how, despite the voice of feminist movements, violence manages to dominate the social, political, economic, religious and cultural worlds of human beings across the globe. The reality for women and girls in India and everywhere is that despite advances in gender equality more widely it remains a persistent normalised horror. Women across South Asia now have access to education, healthcare and employment, providing them with a better quality of life and much enhanced opportunities. These positive changes, though, have done little to dislodge the daily violence women across the socio-economic spectrum face.

In this volume I highlight that in many parts of the world, including India, there has been a sharp swing to the right, with the emergence of conservative, fundamentalist religious views that focus on controlling women's bodies in order to preserve the societal status quo; however, I argue that these right-wing ideologies, whilst particularly extreme and blatant in their views on gender, exist alongside the continued normalisation of violence against women within secular and other more liberal ideologies. At several points in the chapters following, I show that the blame for continued and rising levels of violence cannot solely be pinned on the rise of the conservative right, but that the failure of established state structures to make a clear stand through sustained actions against the abuse of women and girls is also responsible. The problem is not just the strengthening and continuation of conservative misogynistic views on gender: some more liberal religious ideologies support patriarchal values without perhaps realising the way in which they render women vulnerable to violence. I argue that, given the visibility of global and national women's movements and the huge advances in relation to women's rights, there can be no excuse for even blind complicity with the violence that patriarchy invites.

This volume attempts to give something of an overview of violence against women in India. As stated above, India will be taken as the main case study, but the conceptual frame applied to analysing violence against women in this country will be presented as universally applicable. By this I mean not that violence takes the same shape and forms across the globe, but that the frame I use here can be applied to draw out the particular dynamics of violence across countries North and South. Essentialising India as the 'worst place in the world to be a woman' is not the intention, but I argue that we are at a significant moment in the country's history of fighting for women's rights. Research presented here shows that there is a readiness across certain liberal sections of the population to delve deeper into critical reflection, asking why violence remains so embedded and normalised in day-to-day life. The new data and methodology to emerge from this volume will have practical implications for the formation of global gender and development policies and national frameworks for the eradication of GBV and for a more nuanced global understanding of why it persists.

The category of 'gender-based violence' is broad and consists of forms of domestic violence happening in the home; in particular what has been coined 'intimate partner violence', which is abuse a husband may direct at his wife. Other forms include rape, whether taking place in private or in public; so-called 'honour crimes' carried out when a woman's behaviour is thought to threaten or tarnish the reputation of her family and/or community; and violence caused as a result of harmful cultural practices such as female infanticide and dowry-related harassment. All these forms will be looked at in different ways through this volume, but it will not be possible to fill the knowledge gap completely. For example, research on the different forms of GBV in India is patchy, with little focus on how, at a local level, people understand (or not) these different forms. The extent to which people identify these various forms of abuse as such is not known, and understanding this issue requires significantly more data of a different kind than that presented here. Through this volume I ask how and why violence continues to be normalised. Violence flourishes because it is sanctioned through dominant codes of behaviour. It is therefore likely that perpetrators do not see it as abuse but as a legitimate means of disciplining. A change in mind-set is most certainly needed in order for people to recognise violence when it occurs; once this happens, then eradication becomes possible. This volume then is intended to explore some of the dynamics of mind-sets around violence and delve into the views and perceptions that need to be changed. To this end the data presented here will explore the interplay between culture, religion, caste and gender. Other factors which may emerge impacting on peoples' perceptions of violence against women include: employment status, age, perceived level of beauty and dress as linked to notions of modesty. Research presented here will explore the possibility that to some, certain forms of GBV (e.g. female genital mutilation) are socially acceptable, even necessary.

The conceptual frame

As discussed above, whilst India is the case study, the frame used here to analyse violence can be applied to other locations. GBV is conceptualised within a web of interlocking factors that primarily serve to maintain a set of power relationships. The study contributes to understanding how norms around violence are supported, legitimised and maintained through and by a web of cultural, religious and societal values and beliefs about the role of women (and men). It will also look at the part that economics, or specifically consumerism, plays in building a material dimension to already harmful cultural practices such as dowry and female genital mutilation that reduce women to commodity objects to be bartered and exchanged through marriage.

The central argument behind this volume is that despite decades of feminist campaigning across India and the national implementation of various global conventions (e.g. the Convention for the Eradication of Discrimination Against Women (CEDAW) and the UN's Declaration on the Elimination of Violence Against Women) and the pursuit of the Millennium Development Goals in relation to women's empowerment and gender equality, rates of violence against women are increasing. We can also see increases in harmful practices such as dowry, which is widely accepted as leading to forms of harassment against young brides, and female infanticide and sex-selective abortion linked to the high cost associated with raising daughters who will ultimately leave home.

In short, it is shown that the contexts in which inequalities exist are shaped by a number of overlapping factors, including the way in which external, even global, responses are understood and implemented. The conceptual frame will allow for a holistic analysis into the immediate context in which women live that seeks to pinpoint key factors that may render some or all women vulnerable to violence. The framework to be applied and developed through this research can then be used in any field site across the globe. It will guide researchers through the process of collecting complex data to give a sophisticated and accurate insight into why GBV occurs, out of which practical responses and policies can be formed.

'Gender-based violence', 'violence against women and girls': What do they mean?

What then do the labels 'gender-based violence' and 'violence against women and girls' actually mean? What are the origins of these categories and are they useful as a way of identifying and recording abuses against women? Whilst it is now widely acknowledged that men also suffer from forms of GBV, this volume is concerned to stress the far greater prevalence of violence directed at girls and women. Hence, in this work 'gender-based violence' is interchangeable with 'violence against women and girls', which arguably is also the case in numerous policy documents. As summed up by UNFPA:

> The primary targets of GBV are women and adolescent girls, but not only are they at high risk of GBV, they also suffer exacerbated consequences as compared with what men endure. As a result of gender discrimination and their lower socio-economic status, women have fewer options and less resources at their disposal to avoid or escape abusive situations and to seek justice. They also suffer [. . .] consequences [for their sexual and reproductive health], including forced and unwanted pregnancies, unsafe abortions and resulting deaths, traumatic fistula, and higher risks of sexually transmitted infections (STIs) and HIV.[5]

It is revealing that it took a long time for international human rights law to accept and enshrine violence against women in its statutes. VAWG only began to be seen as a human rights issue in the late 1980s when gradually conventions began to include it. What this slow pace of change arguably suggests is that up until this point it was globally accepted as a part of women's daily lives.

The UN Convention on the Elimination of All Forms of Discrimination against Women (CEDAW), which forms the major

UN women's rights treaty, in its original 1979 formulation did not contain a provision on violence against women. This gap was not addressed until 1992, at which point CEDAW was amended to include General Recommendation No. 19 on VAW (GR 19). GBV is defined in CEDAW as 'violence that is directed against a woman because she is a woman or that affects women disproportionately.' Crucially here is the link between violence and gender which opened the way for the label GBV. This is now often defined as including 'acts that inflict physical, mental or sexual harm or suffering, threats of such acts, coercion and other deprivations of liberty.' GR 19 of CEDAW also specifies that GBV may constitute a violation of women's human rights, such as the right to life, the right to equal protection under the law, the right to equality in the family or the right to the highest standard attainable of physical and mental health.

GR 19 of CEDAW in turn has influenced The UN Declaration on the Elimination of Violence against Women (DEVAW) adopted by the UN General Assembly in 1993. This is clear, for example, in how it defines VAW as '*any act of gender-based violence that results in, or is likely to result in, physical, sexual or psychological harm or suffering to women, including threats of such acts, coercion or arbitrary deprivations of liberty, whether occurring in public or in private life*' (Article 1). The declaration gives a comprehensive spectrum of GBV including physical, sexual, economic and psychological violence, no matter in which context or setting they occur:

- in the family (such as battery, marital rape; sexual abuse of female children; dowry-related violence; female genital mutilation/cutting and other traditional practices harmful to women).
- in the general community (such as rape, sexual harassment and intimidation at work, in school and elsewhere; trafficking in women; and forced prostitution), and violence perpetrated or condoned by the state, wherever it occurs. (Article 2).

Both CEDAW GR 19 and DEVAW include forms of violence occurring in both the private and public sectors and committed by people in official and unofficial private positions. This was a significant shift; violence against women committed in private was, until this point, excluded from human rights laws and ignored in wider discourses on rights and equality. Different types of vulnerabilities gradually became included in treaties and actions, for example, the Beijing Platform for Action adopted in 1995 expanded on the definition of DEVAW to include: violations of the rights of women in situations of armed conflict, including systematic rape, sexual slavery and forced pregnancy; forced sterilisation, forced abortion, coerced or forced use of contraceptives; prenatal sex selection and, female infanticide. It also mentioned specific groups of women, for example older women, who are more vulnerable to violence and pinpointed particular contexts such as conflict that also render women more open to forms of violence.

The spectrum of GBV now covered by these global conventions is wide, covering all forms of domestic violence: physical, sexual, psychological, emotional and economic.[6] It is also acknowledged at a multi-lateral level that the life cycle plays a significant part in determining the types of violence to which a girl or woman may be vulnerable. In other words, a woman will be open to different forms of violence as she ages. Identifying and acknowledging this reality is an important step in countering violence. However, acceptance of the definition of GBV at this macro level has not translated into policy and mind-set change at national–local level. South Asia is a good example of the patchy, almost half-hearted, way in which these conventions have been translated into policy and practices (picked up again in the conclusion to this volume). This may well be a reaction against the outside pressure to change in line with the decrees of organisations dominated by the West. In other words, the politics of global policy making and its dissemination are complex and a rejection or failure to implement should not automatically be taken as lack of commitment to the issue itself but rather of the imperialist way in which such conventions are framed and then enforced on the Global South. This can be seen in Chapters Two and Five, where tensions between different women's rights organisations emerge. Chapter Two in particular shows how divisions can be seen between those that work within these global priorities and therefore benefit from the funding streams that flow alongside them and those organisations that challenge the relevance of conventions such as CEDAW. Those organisations that challenge the effectiveness of CEDAW state that such uniform legalistic mechanisms cannot possibly respond to the specific climate of abuses women face in the Indian context. However, it is important here to set violence against women in India within the global context of women's movements, as this can help us understand how country-level debates, policies and actions are interpreted and reinterpreted by different actors, often in unhelpful and distorting ways.

In terms of the usefulness of the category of GBV, this volume will argue that there is value in it as a vehicle for embedding a moral reaction against violence across the globe, through a largely instrumental and symbolic use of global conventions. The effectiveness of these conventions is discussed early on in this volume, and whilst the conclusion is that the reach and impact is limited, they do serve as a moral compass making visible the systematic and global realities of violence in women's daily lives. However, the category of GBV has to be contextualised both at national and then local levels in order to pinpoint the particular forms of violence to which groups of women in different places and backgrounds are exposed. This volume highlights that across a region – across a country, even – different parts of the spectrum are more or less relevant in helping to unpack and understand the violence manifesting.

As stated at the start of this volume, there is significant evidence from across the globe that we are seeing rising levels of GBV. This in the context of India can be associated with its economic liberalisation programme, which has brought more and more women into the workforce and seen greater investment in education and health infrastructure, enabling at least some categories of women to assert greater control over their lives and decision-making. These improvements have been met with a violent backlash which accounts for the documented increases in various forms of violence. In Chapter Two I call for stronger acknowledgement of the realities of a backlash againt women's empowerment and a more concerted effort in looking at ways of mediating it. Clearly, changes/improvements in women's lives have not caused a shift in peoples' perceptions of violence as regulatory normality. In a recent UNICEF report it was found that 57 per cent of adolescent boys in India think a husband is justified in hitting or beating his wife.[7] Understanding what underlies this normalisation is vital if patterns of violent abuses against women are to be broken and gender relations positively transformed.

The theoretical frame: A critique of neoliberalism

As the title of this volume alludes, in accounting for these increases in violence against women I apply the critique of neoliberalism as developed by scholars such as Jean and John Comaroff, James Ferguson, David Harvey and Noam Chomsky. None of these scholars talk about gender, instead focusing their critiques on the generalised and global oppressive and marginalising impact of neoliberal capitalism. However, I argue that their commentaries –which convincingly explain why and how power hierarchies have been maintained both globally and nationally and their consequences for populations and groups – can be helpfully developed to provide more far-reaching explanations for women's increased vulnerability to violence. Before I piece together the specifics of the theoretical critique I will be applying through this volume I need to first present the neoliberal critique as it has emerged from these often-cited scholars. I begin with a statement by Comaroff and Comaroff: 'liberation under neoliberal conditions has been marred by a disconcerting upsurge of violence, crime, and disorder.'[8] Certainly when applied to the rising levels of violence against women a disturbing link can be made between the free market, consumerism and women's reduced safety both in private and public spaces. Comaroff and Comaroff state that what they coin the 'ideology of consumerism' has been actively cultivated by Western states under the guise of being in the common good since the end of World War II. Neoliberalism then is the 'the second coming of capitalism in the form of consumerism'.[9] The impact of the neoliberal project is to include (the already wealthy) and to marginalise in unanticipated ways, 'to produce desire and expectation on a global scale; yet to decrease the certainty of work or the security of persons; to magnify class difference but to undercut class consciousness, above all, to offer up vast, almost instantaneous riches to those who master its spectral technologies – and simultaneously to threaten the very existence of those who do not.'[10] All in all this is a pretty damning critique of the neoliberal system but one that bears out in the Indian context. For example, in Chapter Eight I present research that evidences the spread of dowry giving across groups of the population previously unaffected. I evidence that even in a progressive state like Kerala not only are Muslim communities now practicing dowry but the amount given has dramatically increased along with expectations driven by this consumer ideology identified by Comaroff and Comaroff. Dowry, then, has lent itself as a vehicle to both fuel and satisfy this neoliberal consumer frenzy, the legacy of which is the increased vulnerability of young brides and the threat of a lifetime of indebtedness, or at the very least acute marginalisation, for those poor families unable to meet this capitalist appetite. I argue in this volume, however, that neoliberalism has not only introduced the destructive force of consumerism but has also woven a set of values attached to an idealised conceptualisation of what it is to be a 'modern' person. Concepts such as democracy, liberation and empowerment denote this state of being with little regard for the historical, religious and cultural contexts onto which it is projected. Again in relation to dowry, the giving of exuberant gifts and money is seen as part and parcel of what it is to be modern and therefore a respectable person with honour and status. These values lauded by neoliberalism, 'empowerment' and 'liberation', are translated in the most distorted of ways into material expectations that will only ever be fully met by the most wealthy and elite Indians. Claiming the status of being 'modern' brings with it a sense of power over those without; it is necessary therefore to maintain an underclass so as to ensure the elite can secure the mantel of modernity. Neoliberalism then, according to Chomsky (2011) operates not only as an economic system but as a political and cultural system as well, and certainly in the case of dowry we can clearly see how these dimensions intertwine.

Chomsky is perhaps the fiercest of all critics of neoliberalism. He writes:

> The economic consequences of these policies have been the same just about everywhere, and exactly what one would expect: a massive increase in social and economic inequality, a marked increase in severe deprivation for the poorest nations and peoples of the world, a disastrous global environment, an unstable global economy and an unprecedented bonanza for the wealthy.[11]

Chomsky argues a link between neoliberalism and democracy. Formal electoral democracy consists of controlled information flows which curtail the populace from free unlimited access to alternative views, experiences and ways of being. Public forums in which a free flow of information may take place are also restricted within formal democracies. In such a political environment the dominant discourses of power that flourish favour free markets or rather, big business, and through limiting public access to information ensure the electorate complies with the so-called logic of the private sector. Real participatory democracy is not possible within neoliberalism and any allusions to it are just that. This reality then makes a mockery of the core values of neoliberal 'empowerment' and 'liberation', which are not attainable through this brand of democracy.

What I argue in this volume is that neoliberalism ensures not only that consumerism flourishes, but also patriarchy. In other words, I assert that patriarchy should also be seen as a defining characteristic of neoliberalism alongside consumer capitalism, the flourishing of corporations that are barriers to participatory democracy. Neoliberalism essentially is about ensuring populations remain divided so as to guarantee no overwhelming powerbase can erupt that might ultimately shake the very foundations of big business. Gender divisions are the most fundamental of all such separations and lead on to further marginalisation when class, caste and race interplay. Such divisions also serve an additional and important purpose in the neoliberal economy: they ensure a supply of cheap labour, and here again patriarchy is a necessary dimension. The workplace is highly gendered, with most cheap labour being provided by women whose contractual arrangements are precarious and open to their being exploited, both in terms of personal safety as well as economics. In making the argument for the inclusion of patriarchy in the critical understanding of neoliberalism, I hope to usefully develop the work of these important and ground-breaking scholars. Taking India and GBV as the case study, I seek to add compelling evidence to the already convincing mountain of argument. The argument that I am building on here is intended to destabilise neoliberalism as the lens through which even the unaware are forced to see and be in the world and then judge others in accordance with a notion of what it is to be modern. As the feminist activists interviewed in Chapters Three, Four and Five state: neoliberalism has failed to deliver a transformed/empowered life for most women. Furthermore, it has failed to improve the lives of many men, which has only added to women's vulnerability as they become the focus/target for the ensuing backlash as men seek to vent their anger and frustration at the unattainable dream of modernity. Women who have been invited into the workforce look at times as if they are benefitting above and beyond their male counterparts; this is of course an illusion, given the realities of low pay and workplace harassment, added to which employment has increased women's vulnerability at home as family relations are challenged by their new working status and the threat of their financial independence. The reality that this backlash to women's increased access to the employment market reveals is that without the wholesale eradication of the patriarchal ideal on which 'family' is founded the empowerment of women remains far-fetched.

Harvey talks of this when he refers to the creative destruction 'not only of prior institutional frameworks and powers [. . .] but also divisions of labour, social relations, welfare provisions, technological mixes, ways of life and thought, reproductive activities.'[12] He goes on in his critique: 'neoliberalism values market exchange as "an ethic in itself" capable of acting as a guide to all human action and substituting for all previously held ethical beliefs. It emphasises the significance of contractual relations in the market place.'[13] Harvey in his project to write the history of neoliberalism begins by outlining the Keynesian model of economic development particularly prevalent in the 1960s. This model prioritised the development of a large welfare state and was founded on the concepts of individual liberty and social justice. However, as the welfare state grew it became increasingly bureaucratic and under pressure from a buoyant trade union movement that sought to regulate as a means to protect worker's rights. This over-burdening through layers of legislation and regulation led to a crisis in capital accumulation and ultimately to economic stagnation, signalling for some the need to look for a new model. Thatcher and Reagan devised – either by design or default – a shift that began with the rejection of social justice as a core driver of economic growth. Whilst individual liberty was retained as a core value embedded into the neoliberal vision it was interpreted not in terms of political agency and free expression (in other words a buoyant social and trade union sector) but in terms of choice. The freedom to select your preferred option from a number of alternatives from schools and hospitals to goods spelt the start of the modern consumer age already detailed above as the hallmark of neoliberalism.

Harvey identifies two countries as the bookends of neoliberalism: Chile and Iraq. In 1982, Chile was forced by America to pragmatically adopt the neoliberal model and liberalise, rolling back the state to attract foreign investment. A similar story unfolded following the Iraq War in 2003. In both instances the country opened up to privatisation across all sectors – apart from their most prized natural resource, which for Iraq is oil and Chile copper. State control of these key raw materials assures an easier access path to securing supply for the world's richest and neediest countries. However, Harvey also notes that neoliberalism as achieved through structural adjustment was first tested out in the city of New York in 1975, when an indebted city government found itself at the mercy of its bankers. The financiers refused to pour any further funds into the city, taking control of tax receipts. The city government was suddenly left cash-strapped and forced to rethink its model, services were centralised and privatised, assets sold in a desperate attempt to generate revenue from which to rebuild a government powerbase. The workability of structural adjustment programmes (SAPs) was tested in New York and then rolled out across the globe as countries hit financial crises.

The fundamental thrust of Harvey's thesis is that neoliberalism is about the restoration of class power. Elites across the globe from the 1970s under the Keynesian model found their wealth ebb away as emphasis was placed on achieving social justice and equality through a large and expensive welfare system funded largely through taxes, which hurt the wealthiest the most. As economic growth stagnated, the rich saw their profits plummet. In Harvey's analysis, in a number of countries quick to embrace the neoliberal model – Russia and China are just two examples, but India can certainly be added – a small percentage of the population retain the lion's share of the country's wealth, creating huge inequalities with little or no intention of closing the gap emerging from government or the elite themselves. Neoliberalism is a political ideology designed to ensure power structures preserve the position of the elite, ignoring social justice and morality.

The contractual underpinnings of neoliberalism are the focus for the macro strand to the gendered critique I offer in this volume. Despite the now well-documented and highly visible awareness of women's rights, and in particular the persistent problem of violence against women, the global institutions of neoliberalism (IMF, World Bank, UN) have failed to eradicate violence in women's lives. The reason can be dug out from within these critiques: as already stated, neoliberalism is dependent upon societies across the globe maintaining internal divisions so as to protect unchallenged the free market. Gendering the workforce has only served to ensure the ease of this fundamental segregation, drawing women out of the home where they continue to maintain a subservient position into the employment sphere in which they are treated as inferior justifying a lack of promotional opportunities and low pay.[14] The rhetoric of democracy that Chomsky talks about can be seen in the conventions that claim to project values that protect a woman's right to live a life free from an array of violence (as already outlined in the expansive definitions given by the very neoliberal institutions critiqued here), and it is ironic that despite the problem being so directly conveyed in CEDAW and the UN Declaration of Rights, the ideology of neoliberalism that relies upon these global institutions for its very existence (as decreed by the Washington Consensus) has in fact rendered women more vulnerable, and this reality is borne out to an extreme in India today. This argument has been made in a number of feminist texts: for example, Kristin Bumiller writes about the abusive state in which neoliberalism has appropriated the feminist movement for its own subversive purposes.[15] Her critique sits with my own just articulated, in which I argue that the very institutions of neoliberalism are incapable of launching a radical feminist campaign because in order to achieve women's rights the very hierarchal structures on which the whole discourse is founded must be eradicated. The managers of institutions such as UN Women are certainly not about to advocate their own demise. Mary Hawkesworth in her work on globalisation and feminist activism observes that for the past four decades feminist activists and feminist scholars have struggled to make the gendered dynamics of globalisation visible, yet their work seldom captures public attention. She writes: 'relations of concern, affection, companionship, intimacy, sexuality, and reproduction once highly localised and shielded from the intrusions of the market have become objects of global exchange.'[16] This is a similar point to that made by Nancy Fraser, in which she recognises the need for a reinvigorated feminist radicalism to respond to the crisis in neoliberalism. Fraser argues for a feminism that could join other egalitarian movements in struggles aimed at subjecting capitalism to democratic control, while retrieving the core utopian insights of feminism's earlier phases on the feminist movement.[17]

The texts I have reviewed here represent just a few of the wave of recent feminist critiques of neoliberalism which collectively highlight the ways in which neoliberalism working through globalisation runs counter to the principles of equality bound up in the feminist view of the world. The critiques utilise Marxist theory in drawing attention to the ways in which the marketplace has invited – even dragged – women in whilst continuing to oppress and marginalise them. Whilst global markets are now well and truly gendered, this should not be mistaken for women's empowerment. This volume is concerned with how neoliberalism has at its heart retained a violent exercising of patriarchy as a way of maintaining a hierarchal status quo that secures elitism as the driving economic and social force. I argue that this violence needs to be recognised far more widely as the unacceptable reality of a system that has simply not delivered on its claim to offer a better and more moral future. The rhetoric of neoliberalism needs to be de-normalised though an unravelling of the many smokescreens it has created for its preservation.

The focus of this volume is of course India, so this critique will form the perspective through which violence is unpacked and offer an explanation that focuses the blame squarely on neoliberalism rather than 'culture' and/or 'tradition'. Violence in India is not a remnant of a society still not truly modern, but rather is manifest in new forms of systematic abuse exercised to maintain the status quo for the convenience of neoliberalism. This volume, as outlined at the start of the introduction, will apply simultaneously to an account of violence against women the critiques of neoliberalism and post-colonialism.

These critiques highlight the unhelpful and inaccurate representations of Indian society as culturally backward and expose moments when the Indian political elite themselves slip into using this colonial narrative to explain the persistence of violence. The horror of women's vulnerability in India must remain in sharp focus but its eradication requires a more deep-rooted shift in dynamics from local to national and to global than ever previously conceived.

Book structure

The volume is structured in four parts, beginning with two chapters that theorise and contextualise violence against women in India. These chapters will present in greater detail a theoretical critique of how violence against women is accounted for in India, looking at different emerging narratives that offer explanations as to why it persists. Chapter One applies critiques of development emerging within post-development theory alongside post-colonial feminist concerns, to challenge the over-dominance of a white, middle-class voice in the framing of the violent problematic in India. The second chapter reviews the emergence and application of global conventions such as CEDAW in India, looking at how CEDAW has been received by different feminist organisations. This chapter also considers the reality of the backlash to women's improved position as the result of successful decades of campaigning by the women's movement. Combined, these two chapters will set the scene in terms of the reality of violence against women in India and the measures taken to respond to it whilst also highlighting the importance of challenging and critiquing narratives emerging to explain, dismiss or even normalise it. In particular, this section explores the politics of voice, asking questions around whose views are most audible and the impact they have in shaping wider public perspectives about the lives of Indian women.

The second part of this volume will focus on rape. Rape, as stated at the beginning of this introduction, has become one of the most talked about forms of violence in India. Chapter Three reviews two years of rape reporting in the popular Indian newspaper the *Hindu*. The analysis looks at both before and after the rape and murder of *Nirbhaya*, who was mortally injured on 16 December 2012 and died on 29 December;

the analysis seeks to reveal the extent to which the reporting supported the concerns and perspectives of key feminist organisations and activists who are working to eradicate GBV in India. The findings are interesting, revealing that the movement had made significant headway in influencing a surge of reporting of rape cases; however, the reporting is patchy and fails to offer a consistently comprehensive picture of why violence occurs and the barriers to its eradication. The activists interviewed as part of this study voice a mixture of optimism and pessimism, highlighting that India's conservative elements have in fact acted to increase women's vulnerability to violence despite significant achievements in women's rights.

Following on with the analysis of media coverage, Chapter Four is based on a review of around 100 English-language press articles reporting rape in India: no cases were reported prior to the tragic and brutal rape of *Nirbhaya*. The chapter presents a critical analysis of the dominant discourses running through the articles and highlights the extent to which the colonial lens is still present as the main perspective through which India is viewed by outsiders. The chapter highlights how press narratives have constructed a new subaltern, and continued to maintain a second. First, because of the narrow reporting of rape only occurring to middle-class or modern urban women, the daily experiences of low-caste and Dalit women are ignored, their very existence denied. Second, I identify the construction of a 'problematic-male subject' who is labelled deviant, sexually feral and the key perpetrator of all rape violence in India. This chapter in no way denies the reality of violence against women in India – quite the contrary – but argues that the distorting imperialist picture emerging through the press does not support the work of feminist activists in India whose nuanced and complex understanding of the realities of violence must lead the way in eradicating it.

The third part looks at the conflict between the feminist movement in India, which is largely secular and liberal in political orientation, and the influence of conservative and right-wing ideologies. Chapter Five looks at the makeup of the feminist movement in India, offering case studies of some of the most prominent organisations and documenting the views and reflections of some of the people who work for them. This chapter will return to questions asked in Chapter Two over the relative position of these organisations in relation to global organisations and conventions, and the impact of different channels of funding on and for the work they do. Chapter Six looks at the implications of conservative readings of gender on and for feminist campaigning around GBV. This chapter documents the rise of conservative religious organisations in India, not least the implications of the Bharatiya Janata Party (BJP) government on and for the pursuit of women's rights. How do right-wing organisations talk about gender and in what ways does a conservative view of women's roles help to sustain a climate of violence? These are important questions, not least for helping us to understand the backlash introduced earlier, in Chapter Two.

Part Four turns to a critical examination of harmful cultural practices and in particular applies a criticism of neoliberalism, arguing that the consumer society that India now represents has only served to increase the violence associated with practices such as dowry and female genital mutilation (FGM). Chapter Seven in particular will pick up this critique that is the title of this volume and highlight how neoliberal ideology is essentiality materialistic and has woven itself into the fabric of society via certain cultural practices that are in turn linked to marriage. Gifts are exchanged at the point of marriage and tied to the transfer of a young woman from her natal home to a marital one. Practices such as dowry (Chapter Eight) and FGM operate to ensure this transition is tied to the transfer of wealth. The violence associated with the practice is a symptom of the aggressive way in which materialism is acquired by those in control of the process. While focusing on the prevalence of FGM amongst Bora Muslims in India, this chapter also argues that the breadth of HCPs in India is still largely unknown. FGM in India is hardly researched and much less talked about or even acknowledged by those working on women's rights. It remains, so this chapter will argue, a largely invisible but yet extremely brutal form of violence against women. FGM has received a lot of global coverage and is the focus of many large-scale eradication programmes; this chapter then hopes to raise awareness of its existence among communities in major cities in India such as Mumbai. The chapter ends by saying that understanding the extent of violence and digging down into exploring why each form still exists is a vital starting point in the quest to eradicate all forms.

Chapter Eight looks at dowry and argues that it is one of the most prevalent practices that leads to the violent harassment of women, in particular newly married brides. Although the definitions of dowry itself do not allude to its 'harmful' quality, this chapter argues that it should be squarely placed in the category of 'harmful cultural practice'. Dowry reduces women to an economic commodity at the point of marriage; the amount she brings into her marriage is seen as a sign of the honour and status of both her family and that of her groom. Harassment then erupts when the newly married woman is viewed as not bringing sufficient money into her new home; this is taken as a sign of dishonour. The spectrum of harassment experienced ranges from psychological to physical abuse. This chapter presents recent research on dowry and its link to violence conducted in Kerala, supposedly a development success story, and explores a question: why is it that, despite high levels of gender equality in Kerala, with women accessing education, healthcare and employment, dowry is still practised?

The work concludes by returning to the title and outlining the central critique, which is that neoliberalism in fact has done little to support the projection of social justice and women's rights, if anything at all; in India, the situation has deteriorated with GBV persisting and some forms of it even increasing. It ends with a call for a radical new way of approaching the eradication of violence that is reflexive, listening to the voices of those affected and those who have worked tirelessly to end it. This transformation must also be rooted in the grassroots rather than in global organisations that offer money in return for uniform compliance with neoliberalism and knot us in a perpetual cycle of materialistic desire that in turn maintains a climate of violence.

PART I

THEORISING AND CONTEXTUALISING VIOLENCE AGAINST WOMEN

CHAPTER 1

THE POLITICS OF VOICE: UNRAVELLING THE DISCOURSES

Introduction

In this chapter I attempt to unravel the various discourses surrounding GBV in India. My analysis will ask critical questions about whose voice and viewpoint dominates the arena and what the implications of such dominance may be for and on the audibility of others. Here and in the subsequent chapters in Part Two of this volume, I will show how media reports and political speeches focus on creating and conveying a profile of a perpetrator. Less attention is given to presenting an accurate and diverse picture of the types of violence women and girls suffer from across age, class and wealth boundaries. Instead, the public narratives on violence seem to focus on apportioning blame either back onto the victim or onto a particular group of men whose views are seen by India's modernised and growing middle classes as abhorrent. The reality is far more complex and understanding the full extent of violence both in terms of why it happens and the various forms it takes needs a much wider set of voices to reach the public sphere. What I argue in this chapter is that activism to end GBV is being hampered by various public narratives operating simultaneously at national and global levels which play out locally. These narratives construct limited categories of both victim and perpetrator, and these narrow typologies work within a binary that enables those who are currently benefitting from India's economic success to maintain a position of superiority by drawing a line between themselves and those sections of the population still to adopt a global way of life.

In this chapter and throughout this volume I intend to interrogate the ways in which neoliberal ideology has been packaged in such a way so as to entice India's middle classes into a mind-set that requires them to separate themselves from the rest of society. The situation is further complicated by an additional narrative that places the blame squarely on women who transgress gender norms. The middle and elite classes are just as responsible for legitimising violence against women when traditional norms are seen to have been overridden. Tradition in these narratives is not seen as an obstacle to progress but as something that must be upheld. For example, some senior male politicians have been caught on camera and in print either denying that GBV is a normalised and embedded reality, or, even more worryingly, saying that violence is necessary and deserved when it occurs. These views give us a clear guide as to the mind-set underlying the violence which sits alongside India's economic success. It is the uneasy juxtaposition of violence and economic growth that has forced the issue of gender inequality to the surface. The political discourses now being hurriedly formed still carry the hallmarks of patriarchy and misogyny, so a contradiction emerges between two sets of public narratives. The first narrative blames an underclass of uncivilised and backward men for acts of violence no longer tolerated by modern India (see Chapters Three and Four in particular), while a second narrative expressed across the class-caste spectrum accepts violence as necessary when traditional values are ignored by women and girls.

The mix also includes feminist discourses of different kinds, in particular international feminist commentary from outside frames conventions such as CEDAW and shapes the lobbying voice of platforms such as UN Women. These vehicles undoubtedly have power in determining how and where money should be spent, and the problems with this process are deconstructed in Chapters Five and Six. The type of feminist politics behind global development programmes tends to ignore the local and to advocate one-size-fits all programmes which are seen as the most effective way of transforming society into one safe for women. Education, health and employment are key components in these programmes; if these are in place, then violence, so it is thought, will decrease. The theory of change underpinning this prescription is simple; if women are empowered through education, and given access to healthcare and employment, they will seek justice when violence occurs. As I go on to show later, this has not happened; in fact, the reverse can often be seen in the form of a backlash to changes in traditional gender relations. Of course a good education and health system are important tenets of a neoliberal economy, because neoliberalism is reliant both on a skilled and healthy workforce but also on a large labour force. Women's entry, therefore, is necessary so that a neoliberal economy can continue to grow. In other words, the coming together of neoliberal economics with a brand of feminist politics is clear in the operation of the UN and other multi- and bi-lateral organisations, but has not yet delivered the eradication of GBV. The feminist voices behind these programmes contrast with the array of national and local feminist activists and academics who bring a more contextual and closer reading of why and how violence impacts on the lives of girls and women in India. The different type of feminist lens national activists hold needs to be distinguished from those figures, also feminist, but who look in from the outside, commentating often in overly simplistic and unhelpful ways.

The review of these narratives serves a single purpose, which is to draw attention to those voices that are heard and hopefully to allude to the absence of others. We rarely hear from those blamed most frequently for violence against women and girls, namely poor low-caste men from rural areas. If we did hear their views we would perhaps hear that they alone are not to blame (although I am not for a second endorsing the legitimisation of violence, wherever it is voiced). First, their views on VAWG mirror those of the professional elite men caught making public statements accepting VAWG as normal. Second, we may hear in their justifications the echoes of a backlash. Their endorsement of VAWG is the result of a failure of aspirations produced by neoliberalism, in which the poor and marginalised are left chasing the dream of wealth laid out in and through urban markers of success. Also silent are victims or survivors, who rarely find a platform available to them to talk about their experiences. The silencing of subaltern groups such as these serves to maintain hierarches of power and oppression. A political and economic hierarchy represents the necessary infrastructure for neoliberalism and in turn demands women remain inferior. The subordination of women is the first foundation for any system of power and control, and that is what neoliberalism represents.

This chapter is divided into two broad sections: the first will explore what I am terming the 'global architecture' of GBV. I locate within this architecture different types of feminist responses and ask the question, as outlined above: whose voice is heard most strongly? The second part digs into the national context, looking at the discourses emerging from the political elite as they attempt to defend India's image despite the horrific cases of violence that have hit the international media. This section also explores how different groups respond to and explain violence, as evidence for my claim that a neoliberal ideology continues to enforce a set of mythical binaries between 'those who have' and 'those who not only do not have but who succumb to uncivilised and violent behaviour'. This mythical binary is a convenient way for the elite to remove themselves from the root of the problem even though they often clearly hold the same views as the so-called perpetrators on the role and status of women.

The global architecture of programmes and policies to end gender-based violence

Throughout this volume I argue that the failure to get to the root cause of GBV (or VAWG) means it continues to flourish, with certain types (for example sex-selective abortion) clearly on the increase. I advocate that the process of understanding why women continue to be vulnerable to violence requires a critical perspective that views neoliberalism as a negative and divisive force. Neoliberalism has done little to challenge or dislodge patriarchy; in fact, it has worked alongside it and benefits from the power structures it embeds. The reality, that capitalist values have continued to dominate and preserve inequalities, has been masked by the production of a vocabulary that acts to bury the harsh impact of neoliberalism. The language surrounding this ideology projects neoliberalism as a force for positive change, suggesting it holds the potential to spark a transformation to better, more enlightened existences. Feminist discourses have also emerged shaped by this neoliberal bribe, claiming that accepting and even embracing global capitalism will bring women the empowerment that has so far eluded them. These feminist discourses I point to are behind the production of global policies, conventions and frameworks designed to latch on to the power channels opened up and created through and by capitalist markets. Visions of what it is to be a liberated woman underpin the hard sell, as multi-lateral organisations such as UN Women enter into persuasive relationships with leaders across the developing world. Money is attached to frameworks guaranteeing the compliance of national governments, at least as far as paying lip service to the implementation of conventions such as CEDAW is concerned. Ironically, and as analysed later in this chapter, the USA, whose dominance over these multi-lateral organisations is well known, has resisted signing CEDAW. The refusal of the so-called most powerful nation in the world to sign up to what was touted as an important global symbol of the intention to move forward with gender equality suggests that these conventions serve another purpose, which requires a more suspicious and critical reading.

Once a country has signed up to a particular framework, money then flows to support implementation. Once funds are accepted a contractual relationship is in full force that sees a government tied into a weakened position of having to deliver on a programme conceived from the outside.[1] In the mid-2000s a number of critiques of top-down development emerged out of the applied area of the Anthropology of Development. These argue that programmes designed externally, even when modelled to fit the national context, rarely work.[2] The global structures and systems that underlie so-called global development are best referred to as an architecture shaping and determining global governance structures. As Mosse states: 'Today's development policy is characterised by the convergence of ideas of neoliberal reform, democratisation and poverty reduction within a framework of "global governance".'[3] This architecture has been built according to the neoliberal blueprint and dissenters are quickly dealt with, marginalised and excluded from resources. As already stated, the ineffectiveness of top-down development is now well evidenced.[4]

There is now more than sufficient evidence to argue that this approach will not remove violence from women's lives. So where does this question-issue of voice come in? Why do I think it is important to start in the first chapter with a critical discussion of speech and power? The answer is straightforward: the current development architecture, which has been co-opted by the global feminist movement, has been shaped largely according to the views, perceptions and voices of those from the Global North. The post-development critique that I have briefly revisited here has been around for a long time, but what I argue in this chapter is that it can also equally be applied to the feminist movement. This does not imply a homogenous entity, and it may be more accurate to regard the movement as a series of networks that converge strategically around key issues (for example, violence against women and girls). What I am interrogating here is the dominance through these networks of a specific discourse which appears to align itself with neoliberalism through the maintenance of a binary between those who have and those who do not. In the case of women's rights, this means those who are positioned as liberated against those who are considered, in contrast, to be oppressed.

The problematic binary between white Western middle-class feminists and the black women of the Global South they seek to liberate was much critiqued in the 1990s–early 2000s, most famously by Mohanty.[5] What is worrying is the persistence of second-wave feminist thinking, which Mohanty and other third-wave post-colonial feminists such as Haraway[6] blame for the construction of a power hierarchy between women of the North and South. Second-wave feminist rhetoric creates and sustains a category of Southern victim whose lives must be reframed through the transformation of society into something more enlightened. This awakening is determined by the neoliberal vision, which projects images of what it is to be a modern woman made visible through many media, including global marketing and advertising campaigns. Examples of the problematic and continued dominance of such binary thinking will be demonstrated in the chapters to come, in particular through critiques of various interlocking discourses which reveal the coming together of a colonial mind-set with so-called modern capitalist principles of neoliberalism. The convergence between colonial and neoliberal thinking is seen in their mutual reliance on a backward 'other' to justify the dominance of their respective ideologies. Within this heady nexus the voices of women from the Global South, in fact at all levels but particularly the most poor and oppressed, are ignored.

But rejecting universal approaches to eliminating gender oppression and violence leads us to a natural alternative of more localised strategies that attempt to engage with the particulars of each emergent form of violence. Here another set of problems seeps through: in seeking a responsive understanding there is a tendency to reduce instances of violence to matters of 'culture' and 'tradition'. Critiques warning against cultural essentialism are now well versed and have been vitally important in opening up the space for different experiences of violence and oppression to emerge and for a more extensive array of voices to be heard by the academy, development practitioners and politicians. For example, Mohanty and Narayan both produced powerfully important critiques directed at the narrow, racist lens of some Western feminist writings/viewpoints; the importance of their work sadly lives on, and lessons that have not yet been fully learnt will be explored in this chapter. However, in understanding the continuation of GBV in India a balance is needed between not slipping into a cultural critique whilst maintaining a focus on understanding how patriarchy is constructed and projected. Patriarchy is maintained fundamentally through the belief that women are inferior to men, which in turn is embedded in society through various systematic processes that include cultural practices: for example, practices that honour the birth of a son, and marriage practices that reduce women to economic commodities (dowry). However, these cultural dimensions have to be contextualised within a much deeper web of interlocking beliefs and values that ultimately oppress the chances women may have to live a free, safe and equal life; removing particular cultural practices that promote violence is unlikely to magically transform society into being socially equal, but for many feminists it represents a useful starting point.

So whilst some 'cultural' narratives can be critiqued as essentialising a whole tradition based on some problematic aspects, and whilst the project to expose and guard against Orientalist responses to violence in India is necessary, these critiques have not in themselves helped to find ways to eradicate gender inequalities across the region and/or the rest of the world. I posed the question to a prominent Indian feminist sociologist and activist interviewed at length in the chapter to come; I asked her how we can talk about violence against women in India without slipping into a colonial narrative of a 'backward' Indian culture. She replied quickly and confidently to this question:

> But we do have a problem here, there is no point trying to side-step it, violence against women is normalised and embedded and it is holding us back, so I don't worry about the reproduction of a colonial mind-set, we need to address the problem and not bury it in an Orientalist critique.[7]

It is perhaps easier for her to make this assertion than a white, middle-class outsider such as myself, but nonetheless her message is clear: it is time for open acknowledgement that there is a serious problem which has to be addressed with an even greater urgency than ever before.

The issue, however, is not so much a debate over whether there is a problem with GBV in India; indeed, many Indian feminists stress the urgency to act in light of growing concerns over the backlash, but rather more focused work is needed to unearth the full range and extent of violence against women and girls. The reality that we have not yet got to the bottom of understanding the variety of manifestations of violence is highlighted in Chapter Seven, in which I present evidence of how female genital mutilation is an issue for girls in the Bora Muslim community in India. This is a reality that has remained hidden from feminist campaigning in India, but that arguably represents one of the most brutal forms of violence and abuse directed at young girls. The issue rather is one of 'voice', and specifically who should be speaking about the dark horrifying human experiences that violence in all its forms represents. I want this volume above all else to push more forcefully this question of who has the right to speak and who in fact should do more listening. I believe the debates surrounding Leslee Udwin's BBC documentary *India's Daughter* nicely introduces the very discussion I think we need much more of.[8]

Interviews in Udwin's now infamous documentary contain material that sent shivers of horror down the spines of activists inside and outside of India; but whilst there is nothing to dispute in the utterly bleak and disturbing picture painted through the testimonies recorded, there was a problem not with the content but that of the voice, specifically that of the journalist behind it. I am a white, middle-class English woman who has worked on GBV in India for over two decades, and this question/issue of voice, or more specifically who has the right to speak, is one I grapple with constantly. In my head, as I write about dowry harassment, rape or female infanticide in different states of India, I am constantly trying to navigate the thin line between using my scholarship *to give voice and space* to marginalised experiences of abuse, and *speaking on behalf of*. What Udwin did was to *speak for*, and so to silence still further, the subaltern that Spivak first highlighted in the margins of all colonial writing about and on India.

The Indian feminist movement is a coherent and mobilised network. Whilst feminist activists do not speak with one voice and the sisterhood is no more a reality in India than it is elsewhere in the world, they do all strategically unite over the deep-rooted and shameful misogyny that penetrates every corner and class-caste of India's society. They have fought tirelessly for centuries to dislodge the structures underpinning this extreme patriarchy built on power and coercion and have made inroads, not least in raising a vibrant young generation of women and men who will not tolerate even a fraction of mistreatment on buses and pavements or in their homes. And so there is optimism that the tide is turning, but in response to this wave of change the misogynistic thread through society pulls back and an almighty backlash is unleashed. We see this in the public declarations of twisted abuse threatened against and directed towards any woman who dares to challenge and transgress so-called 'tradition'. This is what Udwin captured: the backlash against change symbolised in the mobility of *Nirbhaya*. Udwin, however, was not the first journalist to record such distasteful views; the Indian print press had been doing so already, sparked by the anti-rape protests of December 2012.

India has elected a right-wing prime minister whose roots run deep into the murky Hindu fundamentalist movement. The older generation of feminists recognise a responsibility to highlight the vulnerabilities of those younger feisty women who are claiming the ground they forced open for them. The younger generation of women has already been targeted by the fundamentalist movement, attacked when leaving bars and clubs for acting in ways deemed inappropriate; as one defence lawyer interviewed by Udwin said, he would not think twice about pouring petrol on any female member of his family who dared to behave in such a 'shameful' way. Of course those that are bringing shame upon India are those who carry these misogynistic views, and they exist at every level of society.

India's Daughter has made and will make no contribution to the fight for gender equality; and it has ridden roughshod over the delicate and purposeful determination of many Indian feminists who have shaped my view not just of India but also of gender issues across the globe. She rendered subaltern those whose intellectual understanding of gender runs deep, exposing the web-like complexities of the why and how such views are able to continue wrecking so much damage to and on women. Why is it so difficult for white liberal women to remain silent and just listen, be open to the possibility that they may learn something? There are ways and means through which as outsiders we can contribute to the change that is happening, but a sensationalist exposé (as if the issue is not already exposed) is not the way to do it. The activism of those from the outside looking in needs to be self-reflexive in order to maintain itself as a positive enabling force rather than one that adds another layer of power stifling the voices of those already struggling to be heard. Although that must read like a rant, its purpose is to highlight the difference between giving voice and speaking on behalf. When I write about GBV/VAWG in different contexts it is a line I need to keep firmly in mind, and to invite my readers to judge how well I have trodden it.

National discourses on violence against women and girls

Understanding the relationship between discourses – private and public – and structures of power that render groups of men and women inferior and marginal is a crucial thrust to the critical analysis of violence against women I advocate throughout this volume. The discourses I refer to are not just global; already in this chapter I have pinpointed neoliberalism and forms of global feminism as deeply problematic when it comes to gaining a nuanced and close understanding of how power operates through violence in the daily lives of women. This is because, ironically, these ideologies in fact recreate power binaries between the modern and unmodern, civilised and uncivilised, which shape notions of voice, of who has the right to speak and be heard and who must remain silent until they have undergone a sufficiently modern transformation. I now argue in this section that the analysis into discourse and power must dig into national-level politics. At the national level we not only witness blatant misogyny, visible and audible through the views of politicians and agents of government, but also how deep-rooted neoliberal binaries have seeped down, impacting on how different caste and class groups within India see each other. Newspaper articles and the statements of some upper-class feminist activists indicate that, at times, the violent atrocities to which women are subjected are dismissed, or rather ring-fenced, as the acts of those sections of society not yet modern. Rape, dowry harassment and FGM are seen to be the practices of unenlightened members of society; this discourse of blame conveniently enables a side-stepping and alignment of the upper classes with the global neoliberal project. For example, in a recent conversation with a middle-class feminist activist in Delhi, I asked her about the prevalence of FGM in India; she replied: 'This is only something that affects tribal communities in remote areas. It is not a concern for women living in urban or even semi-urban contexts.' As I show in Chapter Seven, this is not the case; what is interesting in this exchange was the emergence of another discourse that separates different groups of female victims in India according to how modern, educated and ultimately how well they fit with the neoliberal programme.

Let us now turn to a more detailed examination of these problematic discourses and consider the implications they have for GBV in India. It is clear that a very close and sceptical reading is needed whenever politicians speak using the language of rights: in particular, the language of women's rights has been co-opted by groups that maintain a patriarchal perspective yet profess to be actively engaged in protecting and reducing women's vulnerability. The issue of violence against women has emerged as a key global priority, and will represent a strategic area of focus moving into the newly drawn Millennium Development Goals as Sustainability Goals. This has caught the attention of the world's media, which is now reporting on a much broader range of cases than ever before; hence the intensified interest in countries such as India and Pakistan, where violence against women erupts in particularly extreme forms. This media focus influences the rhetoric of political parties, as could certainly be seen in the 2014 Indian elections, during which all the main political parties made pledges to combat violence against women. Both Narendra Modi and Rajiv Gandhi, the two front-runners, made pledges to improve women's safety in public places; however, among feminist commentators these statements were hollow:

> Analysts such as Niranjan Sahoo from the Observer Research Foundation say that even when political parties speak about the lack of security for women, they do not mean that they seriously intend to resolve the situation.
>
> 'It is simple tokenism, which the parties offer,' he told DW, adding that 'parties try to demonstrate that they are sensitive towards women's issues by fielding women candidates – who are often from influential families and therefore receive prospects for a political career – here and there.[9]

The superficial nature of these declarations is clearly evidenced by a series of telling and disturbing omissions by members of the now-ruling party. Not long after the newly elected Bharatiya Janata Party (BJP) took the reins, senior politicians were recorded making statements in which they endorsed violence as a normative unproblematic reality in women's lives. A collection of these statements are given below and need little unpacking as the sentiment behind them is singularly blatant:

- 'Even if we provide one policeman per house we can't stop crimes against women [. . .]. The rise in atrocities against women is due to obscene images used in advertisements,' Mr Patil was quoted as saying by Indian newspapers and websites on Wednesday. (R.R. Patil, home minister of Maharashtra state)

- 'It [rape] is a social crime which depends on the man and the woman. It is sometimes right and sometimes wrong,' Mr Gaur said on 5 June. (Babulal Gaur, home minister of Madhya Pradesh state)
- 'Such incidents [rapes] do not happen deliberately. These kind of incidents happen accidentally,' he said on Saturday. (Ramsevak Paikra, home minister of Chhattisgarh state)
- 'Boys make mistakes. They should not be hanged for this. We will revoke the anti-rape laws,' Mr Yadav had said during his campaign for the recently-concluded general elections. (Mulayam Singh Yadav, chief of the regional Samajwadi Party)
- The chief minister recently reacted angrily when asked about the rising number of rape cases at a news briefing. 'You are safe, why are you bothered?' Akhilesh Yadav asked a journalist. (Akhilesh Yadav, chief minister of Uttar Pradesh state)
- 'If the limit of morality is crossed by women, such cases will happen,' he said in January last year. (Kailash Vijayvargiya, minister in Madhya Pradesh state government)
- 'I have no hesitation in saying that about 90% of the girls consensually go with men and then they end up meeting criminal minds and become targets of rape,' he said in 2012. (Dharamveer Goyat, senior politician in Haryana state)

The problematic comments documented above were in the main sparked by a series of horrific cases of rape and murder in Moradabad district in Uttar Pradesh which took place in May–June of 2014. Mr Patil later issued a statement, saying he had been misquoted by the media and the security of women was the top priority of his government; Mr Paikra also said he had been misquoted, while Mr Goyat issued a clarification, saying he had no intention to criticise women. Mr Yadav's party rules Uttar Pradesh state where a number of recent rape cases have been reported; around the same time, police said they were also investigating another case of a woman found hanging from a tree in Bahraich, Moradabad district.

The passages above highlight not only a lack of any real substantial commitment to eradicate violence in women's lives in India, but also show how vital it is to get behind the rhetoric. Politicians are conscious of the need, if they wish to appeal to their electorate, to campaign on women's rights, such is the success of the women's movement nationally and globally, but real transformation is unlikely to be borne out whilst such misogynistic values remain entrenched among the political elite. So in relation to the gender spectrum I propose in the next chapter, these views are reflective of a viewpoint that must be located on the very right; Modi's public sentiments might appear to support women's rights, but these are not consistent through the BJP and cannot therefore be taken seriously.

Uttar Pradesh state is noted for exceptionally high instances of brutal violence against women. In an attempt to interrogate the societal-political context in which violence flourishes in this region I took a fieldtrip to Moradabad to interview members of the district police force and a cross-section of local people, with the objective of ascertaining what perceptions of violence against women were held. Were these reported cases seen as a usual or daily occurrence? Was the international press right to use these few cases as further evidence of a brutal society in which women are vulnerable to the most extreme forms of violence? And, indeed, were local people even aware of how the national and international spotlight had been shone on their district? Before I present my findings from that brief fieldtrip let us begin with a snapshot of how the Moradabad cases have been reported in the international and national press. The international press in particular picked up on a case involving two teenage cousins who were found hanging from a tree after they were gang-raped in their village in May 2014. An example of the tone and general narrative of the reporting is given below, in the form of an article published in *The Times* newspaper in London. The commentary adds this horrific case to that of *Nirbhaya* (see details on the reporting of that case in Chapters Three and Four), evidencing further the problem which, as documented in Modi's Independence Day speech, has made it difficult for politicians to sweep violence against women under the carpet; however, as already shown, these views should not be taken as concrete commitments to see a wholesale societal transformation towards gender equality.

> RAPE LEVEL SHAMES COUNTRY, SAYS INDIA LEADER MODI
>
> India's Prime Minister Narendra Modi has said the number of rapes in the country is a source of shame and is urging parents to take responsibility for the actions of their sons.

During his first Independence Day speech, he vowed to improve the lives of the nation's poor as he delivered a withering assessment of the ruling establishment.

Although insisting India had much to be proud of, Mr Modi spoke about subjects including sexual violence, religious unrest, farmers' suicides and a lack of toilets, which he said was intolerable in the twenty-first century.

Mr Modi, a right-wing Hindu nationalist, also reiterated his solidarity with the wider South Asian region but held back from mentioning Pakistan, which is also celebrating its independence 68 years on.

'We have to improve our national character and we have to put selfish thinking to one side,' said Mr Modi, 63.

The number of rapes in India had shamed the country, he said, and he urged parents to teach their sons right from wrong, rather than putting the onus on their daughters.

'When we hear about these rapes our heads hang in shame,' he said.

'The law will take its own course but as a society every parent has a responsibility to teach their sons the difference between right and wrong.'

Anger among Indians over sexual violence has been steadily rising over the past two years, fuelled by a series of high-profile assaults, including the fatal gang-rape of a student on a bus in New Delhi in December 2012.

There was also widespread outrage in May when two teenage cousins were found hanging from a tree after they were gang-raped in their village in the state of Uttar Pradesh.

The girls, aged 14 and 15, were attacked when they went to the toilet in a field after dark because they did not have a toilet in their own home.

'We are in the twenty-first century and yet there is still no dignity for women as they have to go out in the open to defecate and they have to wait for darkness to fall. Can you imagine the number of problems they have to face because of this?' Mr Modi, the son of a tea vendor, said.

'People may criticise me for talking about toilets from Red Fort, but I am from a poor family. I have seen poverty first hand. For the poor to get dignity, it has to start from here.'

Mr Modi said India should strive to equip every household with a toilet in the next four years, and pledged to ensure all schools had separate toilet facilities for girls and boys.

Uttar Pradesh, India's largest state, has also been the scene of several recent flare-ups in communal violence between Hindus and minority Muslims.

Mr Modi said the violence was 'stalling the growth of the nation' and had gone on for too long.

Before becoming prime minister, Mr Modi was the chief minister of the western state of Gujarat, where he was in charge in 2002 during one of India's deadliest chapters of communal violence since its independence.

While he was accused by his opponents during the election of being too business-friendly, Mr Modi said his government would take action to allow even the poorest members of society to open a bank account.

Hundreds of farmers have committed suicide in the past decade in a trend that the prime minister attributed to their inability to pay back private loans.

'It's because they have to take money at huge interest rates from the money lenders,' Mr Modi said.

'We will have a prime minister's people wealth scheme so that even the poorest of the poor can have a bank account of their own.'

Mr Modi said the government would set up a scheme to provide farmers with special guarantees in exceptional circumstances worth up to 100,000 rupees.

'Government should be an organic entity, moving in one direction with a common aim goal,' he added. 'I am trying to break down these walls.

'We have to strengthen the systems in order to realise the dreams of the people.'[10]

Modi as the newly elected Prime Minister of India is forced through the reporting of these cases to use the word 'shame' to describe the high prevalence of rape and other forms of GBV – and of course it is shameful – but it was this kind of media reporting, focusing on the statistics and a handful of particularly brutal cases, that forced figures in authority to look for reasons and solutions. However, these explanations, and then responses, do not necessarily get to the root of the problem, in that they usually fail to go far enough and to expose the underlying gendered ideology responsible. Proposals therefore merely scratch the surface of the problem. In this account of Modi's Independence Day speech we hear him talk of the impact of poverty, specifically lack of sanitation, has on rendering women vulnerable to violence. Modi has subsequently made pledges to ensure that all Indian homes have toilets.[11] He also highlights the need for boys to be educated to understand that violence against women is a crime.

Two concerns emerge: the underlying explanation for violence given in Modi's speech is simplistic and does not reflect the complex realities of GBV in India. Violence, as Chapters Seven and Eight show, cuts across caste and socio-economic status; it is not just poor women or those living without an inside toilet that are vulnerable. Gaytri, speaking in an interview (summarised in Chapter Five) is clear: GBV relates to a deep-rooted ideology that sanctions the disciplining of women in the most brutal and oppressive ways. Furthermore, and evidencing this embedded viewpoint, the UNICEF Report Card[12] clearly shows that violence is normalised in the opinions of both boys and girls, so singling out just one gender for re-education will not produce the wholesale mental transformation needed. There is a clear disconnect emerging between the realities of GBV, the nuanced way it is understood by feminist activists and the emergent public-political discourses on violence against women propounded by prominent individuals such as Modi. Clearly, if GBV is to be eradicated the two ends of the gender spectrum need to converge, or rather the political sphere needs to listen to and be informed by those who have worked on this issue for decades.

The Times in its coverage draws attention to the visibility that GBV now has in the public political discourse of India, but the lack of interrogation in terms of the complex realities of how violence plays out in different contexts and across caste-class groups does little to support its eradication. Furthermore, there is a danger in that it presents India as an exceptional case in terms of women's susceptibility to violent attacks, and this present volume in its analysis of GBV in the country is careful not to feed into any such stereotypes but rather to use India as a useful case study to work though more nuanced and complex ways of unpacking the embedded ideology that lies behind GBV. The need for this more detailed analytical frame is apparent in the way in which Indian papers reported the Moradabad cases. In India, papers carried stories on a daily basis focusing attention on Moradabad district and carrying the narrative that violence is exceptionally high in this area and questioning (without offering answers) why this might be. An example is a piece published in the Calcutta *Telegraph* on 12 June 2014:

> THE HORROR OF BODY POLITICS
>
> The social protests of unprecedented reach and intensity that followed the brutal gang rape of a woman in a Delhi bus in December 2012 led to amendments to the law against rape, making it more stringent and inclusive. Since then, women's empowerment and gender justice have tended to emerge as mainstream political issues in the country. However, incidents of gender crime continue to occur at an alarming rate. The most recent instance that has captured the media's attention has been the gang rape and murder of two minor girls in Badaun district of Uttar Pradesh. Understandably, both the public and the media have decried the incident, and the chief minister of UP, Akhilesh Yadav, has agreed to a probe by the Central Bureau of Investigation into the matter. The next step, we can imagine, would be demands by the public and the media for the death penalty for the rapists.
>
> Indeed, capital punishment for rape has been one of the chief public demands made after the December 2012 incident. The amendments to the (anti-)rape law created the scope for sentencing a repeat offender to death, especially if the victim has been killed or permanent physical damage inflicted upon her. In April this year, the Mumbai court that tried the accused in the Shakti Mills twin rape cases put this new legislation into practice by imposing

the death penalty on the three repeat offenders among the accused. For the first time, rapists were handed the death sentence, thereby sending what many think is a sharp warning to potential offenders. The Badaun incident – the two minor victims were killed – is likely to renew public demands for capital punishment.

Gender crimes of such brutality need to be handled with an attitude of zero tolerance. However, there is scope for debate as to what is the best way to go about it. The efficiency with which the Maharashtra administration and the court completed the investigation and the trial in the Shakti Mills cases, for example, was admirable. But sentencing a rapist to death even when the victim has not been killed or dealt permanent bodily damage raises a question. Even without pleading against death sentence per se, it is still possible to wonder if the principle of fairness was smothered by the societal outrage generated by the acceleration of gender crimes in the country.

Besides, the societal demand for the rapist's head underlines a perspective on women, one that equates a woman's 'honour' or physical 'purity' with her selfhood and, ultimately, with her life itself. This is the point of view that sees rape not merely as a terrible accident with criminal implications that befalls a woman but as a life-changing event of irrevocable impact. True, rape, apart from causing grievous bodily harm, is bound to be an intensely traumatic experience for women. It is indeed difficult and time-consuming to undo the psychological damage it inflicts. But often it is the social stigma that is attached to the loss of bodily 'purity' that makes recovery more difficult.

The average rape victim faces insult and neglect at the police station; she faces uncomfortable questions and is the subject of prurient curiosity at the hospital and even in the court; snide remarks and isolation in her neighbourhood and even in her home are also part of the package. In extreme cases, the trauma of the aftermath becomes more painful than the immediate consequences of the assault. In such cases, the victims are even led to kill themselves – like, possibly, the Madhyamgram girl earlier and the woman from Malda in recent times. It is to counter such post-rape torture that the J.S. Verma Commission's recommendations regarding humane treatment of victims in hospitals and courts have been incorporated into the law against rape and the infamous 'two-finger' test abolished. But mind-sets do not keep pace with changes in legislation.

Around the time the Shakti Mills verdict was announced, we witnessed another phenomenon relevant to the understanding of gender attitudes in India. The Samajwadi Party supremo, Mulayam Singh Yadav, declared in Moradabad that rapes take place due to relatively pardonable 'boyish mistakes'. Soon after, his colleague, Abu Azmi, observed that the death penalty should be handed to women who, after having consensual sex, accuse the perpetrator of rape. These might have been constituency-sensitive gimmicks targeted at khap-panchayat patriarchs in UP. But the fact that prominent political leaders, electoral candidates to boot, have the temerity to make such rabidly anti-feminist remarks is an indication of the depths of misogyny in our society.

Indeed, the attitude towards women reflected in these comments is in perfect harmony with that which is pervasive in Indian society. Many Indians, women included, tend to think that a rape victim is somehow accountable for the crime committed against her. Attempts to dilute the gravity of the crime and delay investigations and the framing of charge-sheets reflect administrative laxity that arises out of relative tolerance of crimes against women.

Then there is the tendency to label rape victims as licentious by raising questions about their lifestyle, dress sense and marital status. An MLA in Bengal, who happens to be a former 'star', is only one among many who think that immodest dresses invite rape in urban India. The woman who had been gang raped while returning home from a night club in Park Street faced criticism for staying out late, visiting a night club, and travelling with male acquaintances. There had even been rumours that the victim – a divorcee – was actually a call-girl. The insinuation was that the circumstances extenuated the culpability of the crime. Clearly, as a society, we are unaccustomed to think that adult men have a responsibility to behave sensibly with women, irrespective of their

> dress sense, professions or lifestyles. We are incapable of or unwilling to concede that women have equal rights to personal liberty. We tend to forget that without this right, the right to life itself becomes meaningless for women.
>
> Until we are able to view rape for what is – a traumatic assault that violates a woman's person – and cease to look at it as a fate worse than death, women will continue to suffer and wily politicians will keep pandering to socially entrenched misogyny. Demands for the death sentence for rapists reflect something more than righteous rage: it is a tacit endorsement of the archaic and pernicious view of womanhood that equates a woman with nothing more than her body. It also side-steps the issue of the raped woman's rehabilitation and the State's frequent failure to give her adequate care and protection.
>
> A society in which rape victims get threatened by rapists and are led to suicide and a nation that averages a 26 per cent conviction rate of rapists should perhaps focus on unbiased investigations and, above all, on the protection and rehabilitation of victims rather than on vindictive justice. If anything, sentencing rapists to death would delay the dispensation of justice and may even lead to acquittals. The success of the Shakti Mills case is offset by the Suryanelli episode – 18 long years from crime to conviction. The focus should be on speedy justice rather than on hasty revenge since the impetus to seek revenge arises from a regressive, misogynistic mindset.

The Indian press draws attention to a number of interlocking factors key to understanding why rates of violence against women remain so high: deep-rooted mind-sets right across the socio-economic spectrum, failings of the police and judicial systems and caste inequalities. In the brief time I spent in Moradabad district I wanted to test the extent to which these elements were widely accepted as the root causes of violence against women. I conducted around 20 interviews, mainly with lower and upper middle-class people and business owners but also with those of lower castes – cycle rickshaw drivers and cart pullers – and whilst this number is very small and so cannot be taken as either an extensive or representative sample, it was clear that people viewed this kind of violence against women as an almost daily occurrence. Something interesting emerged in particular from the interviews with those who considered themselves middle-class, which was the view that rape was symptomatic of a 'backward' rural mentality. In other words, that rape was a rural crime that did not impinge on their more developed urban lives. Despite being adamant about the rural nature of the crime the informants, when asked 'why' they thought this was could not come up with an explanation beyond 'they lack education'. Another informant said: 'Rape is an act conducted by the uneducated, they have not learnt how to behave in a modern way'. This image of rape as a rural problem contradicts the evidence that highlights the cross-cutting impact of rape in that it is not restricted to any one specific socio-economic group. It is as much a crime affecting the lives of the urban middle classes (such as those interviewed in this study) as it does Dalit women in villages. Having said that, it is thought that Dalit women are particularly vulnerable to daily instances of rape because this violent act is used as a mechanism for maintaining power relationships (see Chapters Three and Four). This view of rape as a crime conducted by the uneducated and so-called backward does reflect at least one of the narratives I identify in the reporting of the *Nirbhaya* case (given in more detail in Chapter Four), thereby suggesting that as India becomes more 'modern', such violence against women will reduce. This is an argument not borne out in the rising levels of violence that have in fact occurred as India has become richer. The apportioning of blame for violence against women away from the emergent middle classes and towards a male underclass creates a smokescreen that protects those who are benefiting from and seeking to progress neoliberalism. It also absolves many from the need to take responsibility for the extensive normalisation of violence in the lives of women.

As Chapter Four highlights, in the analysis of media reporting of rape in India, one of the criticisms launched at the sudden surge of articles covering rape in India was that they were prompted because the horrific crime was directed at an urban middle-class woman. The normalisation of Dalit rape has until recently been largely ignored, taken as a silent, underreported day-to-day reality for the reasons revealed in the interviews here (because that is what the unmodern 'do'). The misrepresentation in blaming a disadvantaged 'other' for rape crimes supports a critique of neoliberalism that exposes the way in which capitalist values are embedded into the lens through which people see the world. These values present a particular 'modern' way of life as more desirable than others (such as that lived by the uneducated rural classes). Neoliberalisation sells itself still further by attaching value to this modern way of life; living according to this model is seen as aspirational and reflective of a better quality of person. The process of 'claiming' this desirable status of a 'modern' person requires a binary that has positioned in contrast at the other end the 'unmodern'. Emerging from my brief interviews in Moradabad, the newspaper reporting of rape in India presented later in this volume, and also conveyed in the Independence Day speech given by Modi, is an image of the uneducated, low-caste rural populations as representative of this unmodern end of the binary. Indeed Modi himself uses it to depict his own rise to power, highlighting his humble beginnings born to a chai seller, uneducated and illiterate. His retelling of his early childhood acts to mark out his transformation into the modern citizen he is today: he invites the electorate to recognise where he sits now along the linear route of progress. For Modi it was a useful campaign tool; he was able to present himself as understanding the poor and low-caste, whilst in his own journey he makes it clear that striving for modernity is the only option available to the poor (and the rest of society). What the story hides are those left marginalised and even permanently excluded from the path of progress. Their marginality is needed as a symbolic reminder to the rest of what fate would befall them if they do not embrace modernity. And so it is through this neoliberal myth that Modi and many like him across the globe justify their close partnerships with the corporate sector. This model for economic growth does not automatically also involve an agenda of social justice. It is only when horrific cases of extreme abuse garner wide public attention that leaders such as Modi dig into a moral vocabulary and talk of the shameful elements of Indian society which must now be transformed.

The (mid-ranking) police officers interviewed in Moradabad claimed that notions of 'honour' and 'shame' were key factors in both the rapes themselves and then the reactions of families following the crime. For example, one police officer interviewed, claimed in the case covered in the newspaper report given above that the girl was raped because she was thought to have taken a boyfriend from a lower caste; her rapists were relatives who wished to rectify the dishonour she had brought to the family by disciplining her in this most horrific of ways. 'Shame' then emerges as a key concept in how rape at least should be analysed. Shame was used by Modi to describe the scourge of GBV, and is used in a number of media articles analysed in Chapters Three and Four. Rape is underreported because families want to hide it, either because it was dealt out as punishment to a girl/woman whose behaviour was thought to bring dishonour. However, even when so-called 'honour' is not directly involved (in other words, that the girl or woman did not behave, according to the perspective of misogyny, inappropriately) families will hide instances of rape for fear that it might be taken as a sign of dishonourable behaviour. Furthermore, it can also be taken as an indication of a family's failure to protect its women. Whatever the motivation behind shame, it represents a barrier to the eradication of violence in women's lives and needs to be a central focus in campaigning.

The deeply entrenched concept of honour shapes the gendered perceptions of groups across caste/class divides in India. This can be seen in interviews in *India's Daughter* (the documentary problematised above). For example, A.P. Singh, a defence lawyer, on the *Nirbhaya* rape case, stated:

> If my daughter or sister engaged in premarital activities and disgraced herself and allowed herself to lose face and character by doing such things, I would most certainly take this sort of sister or daughter to my farmhouse and in front of my entire family I would throw petrol on her and set her alight.

This misogynistic view is echoed by one of the rapists himself:

> When being raped she shouldn't fight back. She should be silent and allow the rape. Then they'd have dropped her off after doing her and only hit the boy. A girl is far more responsible for rape than a

boy, a decent girl won't roam around at 9 o'clock. Housework and housekeeping is for girls, not roaming in discos and bars at night doing wrong thing and wearing wrong clothes.

Conclusion

In this chapter I have argued that this binary between modern and unmodern, civilised and uncivilised, is unhelpful and even destructive to attempts to eradicate violence from women's lives. It oversimplifies the nexus through which power is exercised over women and serves to render invisible many forms of violence that happen in a variety of contexts from professional workspaces to the home and to women from across the socio-economic spectrum. Whilst certain groups of women (for example Dalits) have been systematically marginalised and ignored and this must be challenged, the violence faced by these women must be analysed through the same feminist critique used to challenge the experiences of other groups; in other words, not simply reduced to a crime committed by the uneducated on the uneducated.

Interviews with a number of feminist activists in India (summaries in subsequent chapters) point to the introduction of neoliberalism to India as a negative turning point in the battle for gender equality. The language of neoliberalism co-opts human rights discourse to promote capitalist economic principles, and in doing so gives the impression that a capitalist liberal vision of society will go hand-in-hand with social empowerment and equality. Instead, we see across the globe that as women have found themselves part of the neoliberal vision they have in fact become more exposed to misogyny. Neoliberal capitalism is not a vehicle for addressing the fundamental structural transformation needed if social equality is to be achieved. Turshen argues that neoliberalism is an ideology of power masked by a language of global development that claims concern for the poor and marginalised.[13] In a review of the success of the United Nations Millennium Development Goals (MDGs). Turshen focuses in particular on MDG 8, which seeks to develop global partnerships for development. Close analysis of the indicators linked to each dimension attached to the goal reveals a lack of sincere commitment to real equitable partnership building. For example, greater access to the pharmaceutical market is one indicator; whilst the big drug multinationals may now be ploughing greater funds into developing medicines to combat diseases suffered disproportionately by the poor (e.g. malaria and more recently Ebola), they refuse to hand over the intellectual property or patents associated with their drugs. Refusal to hand over the patents stunts the possibility of domestic pharmaceutical companies emerging to manufacture drugs for a local market at affordable prices. In fact, such small-scale businesses were wiped out in many developing countries through the imposition of structural adjustment programmes (SAPs). For example, in Nigeria a flourishing drugs sector was squeezed into nonexistence by the insistence on liberalisation imposed through SAPs. Whilst Bill Gates and his foundation claims to champion global partnerships in health he stops short of demanding multinationals such as GlaxoSmithKline release their patent stranglehold. What this critical analysis of MDG 8 reveals is the global smokescreen provided by and through neoliberalism which must, in the post-MDG era, be interrogated before one set of ineffectual goals is replaced with another.

Kabeer argues that inequalities and social injustice must form the central pillars in any newly framed approach to measure development, and that an over-concern with implementing macro policies has meant the way in which they have impacted on peoples' lives at a local grassroots level has been ignored.[14] Furthermore, this lack of concern with the local also explains why and how the gender backlash has so far been almost entirely missed. The challenge to traditional power structures posed by the language of rights-based discourse has yet to be interrogated as a possible trigger for more, rather than less, violence against women. In the chapters to come I will attempt to make something of a contribution to this project of deconstruction.

CHAPTER 2

INTERVENTIONS, GOOD (OR NOT) INTENTIONS AND THE REALITY OF THE BACKLASH

Introduction

This volume from the outset seeks to place violence against women in India within a global context. In the Introduction, I cited a recent UNICEF study on adolescent views on GBV; it shockingly highlighted the extent to which violence is normative in the lives of girls and women and therefore not challenged but rather accepted and even endorsed by both boys and girls. These views expressed by the youth of India are troubling and support the assertions of many of the activists I interviewed for this volume, who state that the problem is deep-rooted and bleakly persistent. Furthermore, the most recent statistics (also presented in the Introduction) reveal levels of GBV in India are in fact rising, beyond what we might expect with better reporting. It goes without saying that getting behind these statistics is crucial if real transformation is to be effected. Working through an applied methodology that supports this vital project is therefore urgent. Sokoloff and Duport argue the need to emphasise the structural underpinnings of abuse, while not denying the existence of real difference among women.[1] Capturing difference in experiences of violence has to be central to any model designed to enhance our understanding of why violence occurs and what therefore might act as an effective trigger for a long tern change in mind-set. Responses emerging from the neoliberal development institutions, specifically UN agencies critiqued in the previous chapter, have a tendency to deny difference, seeking instead to implement a blanket response to violence justified by very narrow theories of change.

Broadly, two main theories of change are currently being applied across the globe in relation to violence against women. The first focuses on empowering women through education, better healthcare and employment, which are seen as key ways of raising their public and private confidence in resisting and protesting against violence. Running alongside this is a second approach that emphasises the need to improve mechanisms for women to access justice. The thinking is that if justice is successfully sought for instances of violence, then the message will be clearly conveyed to perpetrators that they can no longer get away with it and will then desist. Unfortunately, as demonstrated across the globe, these theories have failed to produce the transformation hoped for, largely, I argue, because the environments in which violence occurs are always highly complex, with a number of interlocking factors. Unless we understand the interweaving strands that promote violence in each context and respond to these specifically, violence will continue. Arguably, and as supported in some of my interviews with Indian feminists, many organisations have become side-tracked by these theories, and this has taken their attention and time away from responding to the specifics of the state-region-country context and to diversity in cultural, social and economic environmental factors that shape different forms of violence.

In this volume I am arguing that the strands that weave together to produce and sustain patriarchy differ across regions and contexts, with many more variants interlocking. This diversity explains why certain forms of violence are prevalent in some places and not others. The explanation therefore cannot stop at identifying 'patriarchy'. I here argue that patriarchy has been taken as a convenient starting and stopping point by the big multi- and bi-lateral development players, and used as the explanation for why women are systematically marginalised from education and employment – the factors, so the story goes, that would make them independent. The universal approaches to countering patriarchy are too simplistic, because they assume if the dimensions/ingredients needed to make a woman independent are in place, she will be empowered and be able to resist or respond defiantly to instances of violence regardless of where she lives. However, as I argue throughout this volume, violence in the lives of women and girls is shaped by many factors and can in fact increase even when these dimensions are in place (see the section below on the backlash). The problematic impact of this simplistic viewpoint is that solutions are sold to NGOs and governments, thereby locking them into the global system in a way that renders them beholden to their donors. To unpack this statement a little more, I am suggesting that the failure to develop deeper understanding of why violence flourishes is convenient within this neoliberal world, because it feeds into the construction of yet another market – a market in which global solutions to GBV are packaged, labelled and then sold on to and through the array of NGOs that now work on this issue globally. In other words, the architecture (see previous chapter) that makes up the transnational arena of policies and programmes presented as solutions to and ways to achieve an end to GBV has in itself become a marketplace. It is a highly competitive global space in which providers of solutions, evaluators of progress seek to dominate with their expertise. GBV ironically has become big business for many consultancy firms and international organisations who are now rebranding or orientating themselves to better capture contracts, for example within DFID's What Works to End GBV programme. Critical questions need to be asked about whether this is really the best way of achieving the end goal of a world free from gender violence. Whilst this might appear a horribly cynical viewpoint I believe it is evidenced in the rising levels of certain forms of violence against women and the continuing dismay at lack of progress voiced by activists who have worked on this issue for decades.

This chapter seeks to present two approaches that can be usefully applied to help us understand the negative and unhelpful impact of a global approach to eradicating GBV in India, whilst also enabling interrogation of the various strands that construct and legitimise forms of violence in specific settings and groups (for example, why is female infanticide higher in some parts of India? Why do the Bora Muslim community practice FGM?). A second strand to the approach seeks to explore the roots of different discourses and forms of activism that claims to want to eradicate GBV. As argued in the first chapter, not all public political declarations in support of an end to GBV are grounded in a radical understanding of the kind of transformation that is needed if a world without violence against women is to be achieved. As also pointed out, not every programme implemented is shaped by the local context, but often instead reflects global theories of change projected as universal solutions. I argue that violence is most likely to end when real commitment (mobilised from the grassroots) is combined with in-depth and indigenously rooted knowledge.

The current chapter is structured in four parts. First, I introduce the two approaches, presented as a spectrum so as to interrogate public narratives on VAWG and thereby ascertain how radical and deep-rooted they may be. The second part looks at the unhelpful interference of outsider perspectives that do not sufficiently engage with activists and survivors on the ground but instead attempt to add yet another dominant discourse into what is already a heady mix. This section argues that insufficient engagement with the grassroots is at least in part responsible for the backlash we are now seeing, which has left many women more vulnerable to violence. With these warnings still in mind, the third part outlines the key global conventions on the eradication of GBV and VAWG and looks at how they have (or not) been applied in the Indian context. The last part looks more closely at the work of three large feminist organisations in India, considering how they have positioned themselves within the global architecture of GBV programming and policy making. The conclusion revisits the key arguments of this volume: that neoliberalism has not delivered on its promise of a fairer and more just world.

Introducing the spectrum

In the fight to eradicate GBV in India I believe two approaches are needed. First, and within the specific context of India, there must be a critical gendered deconstruction of neoliberalism. In particular, focus should be placed on how this ideology influences public perceptions of progress, selling particular consumer lifestyles as aspirational, which then often act in a counterproductive way within and against traditional practices and values. Chapter Eight, which examines dowry harassment, certainly shows how the pressures of materialism merely exacerbate the misogyny underpinning dowry: young brides are blamed if insufficient wealth is brought into the home and perceptions of what constitutes too little are now shaped by capitalist consumerist expectations. In addition to recognising the destructive impact that the consumer mind-set has for women's rights, the critique of neoliberalism needs to think through the implications of development's global solutions approach on and for effective measures to remove violence from women's lives. The current top-down approach to GBV, revolving around a number of key conventions, simply acts as a mechanism for locking governments (in this case India) into the capitalist system. Below, I examine the extent to which India's predominantly male political elite has now bought wholesale into neoliberalism, with little consideration as to the damage that close partnerships with big corporations might have on and for social justice and equality. At the root of this drive for open capitalism is a hyper form of masculinity that is power-hungry and devoid of the necessary social conscience to think through the impact of this alliance with big business. The so-called 'modern lifestyle' sold to India's booming middle classes has in fact rendered women more vulnerable to violence. There are many reasons for this increased vulnerability, but two clearly emerged from the interviews I conducted with activists. First, as women enter the workplace, which is necessary if India is to grow its labour resource in order to sustain economic growth, they are susceptible to harassment. This harassment sometimes manifests in very extreme forms of physical harm, while for many it may be the constant psychological battering of poor working conditions and low pay. Second, the material benefits of neoliberalism are not evenly felt, and this has triggered a backlash among those men who feel they have been conned, and who are looking around for someone to blame. As these men have recognised the shift in traditional patterns of gender, women have become the target for their frustration both in the home and also public spaces. What clearly has not shifted as women move into formal work are the patriarchal and misogynistic views that shape the economic environment, both in terms of the mind-set of those running the businesses that women find work in but also at home, where women's move into waged employment is seen as an act of deviance.

Critical understanding of the extent and reasons for violence against women across India – and of potential responses – requires disentangling competing viewpoints on gender, and identifying those that are to a greater or a lesser degree destructive and violent. I here suggest that this can be achieved by positioning different gendered narratives on women's rights, whether conservative or liberal, on what I call a 'gender spectrum'. This makes visible the activist groups working to eradicate GBV, examining what they do and how they go about articulating their activism and assessing the relative impact of what they do; it also helps us see more clearly the competing standpoints and illuminating narratives on and about women's lives that are deeply problematic and that lie at the heart of the continued rise in GBV. Third, the spectrum helps to pinpoint the interventions and campaigns that have had the most impact in terms of triggering long-term mind-set change which reverses the normative patriarchal view that endorses violence against women as a means of disciplining transgression from traditional roles.

The spectrum I propose is designed to interrogate how deep-rooted claims to support a women's rights agenda actually are and to expose the flimsy, opportunistic nature of various statements. Specifically, it is constructed to explore the following questions: Is there a link between public statements and actual concerted action? How far do the views expressed go? For example, is the individual and/or group challenging the patriarchal underpinnings that maintain unequal power structures, or are they merely suggesting that women should not be beaten whilst still endorsing a view that women must retain their traditional gender role? The spectrum seeks to separate out those who are focusing on the fundamental transformation of the structural gendered underpinnings that render women vulnerable, from those who at various distances stop short of this goal. At the other end of the spectrum are those who see no problem with the use of violence as a means to discipline women, and in fact go further saying that the status quo must be retained (Figure 2.1).

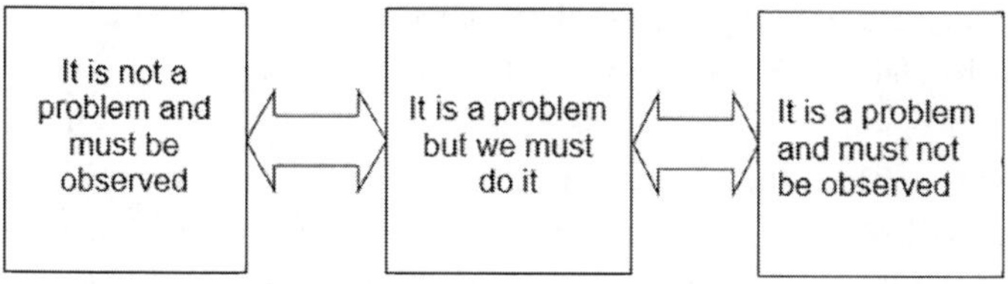

Figure 2.1 The gender spectrum.

The spectrum I propose here differs from other frames, such as Liz Kelly's continuum of different forms of violence against women,[2] in that it seeks in parallel to reveal the roots of abuse and oppression whilst also looking at the reach of different forms of activism. Kelly's continuum approach was indeed ground-breaking, in that it incorporated an intersectional approach to delve into the dimensions that combined to produce violence against women in any given case. Her frame offered a way of producing more nuanced and complex analysis into violence, and what I propose here should be similarly applied alongside an intersectional perspective. As an applied researcher I am keen to see my research make concrete contributions to practice. In other words, I locate my studies within a praxis that seeks to bridge theoretical insights into violence and why it occurs with effective strategies to eradicate it. The spectrum I outline intends to support effective praxis and to measure the reach of different interventions. By 'reach', I mean to what extent interventions trigger mind-set change and thereby reconfigure the gendered construction of society.

India has a long activist tradition and the women's movement in many countries in the region has held a firm strategically essentialist stance in fighting gender inequalities. By this I mean that the fight for women's rights has remained more or less unified despite inevitable differences in perspectives and priorities. Unity is thereby retained through a broad enough focus that can accommodate diversity of stance and outlook. The coherence of the movement is looked at in Chapter Five, but here I want to explore how the impact of the movement might be assessed against the dominance of misogynistic ideologies that maintain the realities of violence in women's lives. This simultaneous analysis is now crucial, as groups within the women's movements are being forced to make the painful acknowledgement that their efforts have so far failed to significantly reverse patterns of violence against women. As Meera reflects in Chapter Five: 'I have to be jolted to see how things really have changed.' So it is important that we stand back and look at the different types of actions and explanatory narratives concerning violence that have been put forward and weigh up their respective impact in dislodging the misogynistic-patriarchal view of gender.

Problematising the outsider perspective and explaining the backlash

A particular gendered ideology is core to all standpoints feeding into, either as cause or reaction to, instances of GBV in India, and indeed in countries across the globe. The secular feminist movement in India, which is also active in other countries not least across South Asia, holds to a liberal vision of women's empowerment and self-determination. This standpoint exposes the harmful impact of the misogynistic patriarchal narratives that dominate so much of public life. In contrast those discourses positioned to the right of my spectrum advocate the strict control of female sexuality as a way of ensuring the stability and so-called 'honour' of future societies. Gender is thereby a consistent component in the analysis of women's lives, patriarchy is a shifting construct in that it is challenged and rejected by those occupying the left ground whose vision of society is founded on principles of equal rights and openly advocated by those on the right who may claim to reject violence against women but hold rigidly to a conservative gendered view of the world. Although a simple frame, it supports the unravelling of a diverse picture of competing views on women, their roles and rights. This diversity is an important point to impress, particularly on those unfamiliar with the Indian context, in order to ensure against the dominance of an Orientalist global narrative on GBV in this region. A narrative that sees the high levels of violence against women as evidence of the civilising project still yet to be achieved (which as the previous chapter highlighted, is voiced by groups internal to India also) and the need for them to work harder to model themselves in the image of the so-called liberal, civilised West. The irony of this narrative can be seen in the application of this gender spectrum to different parts of the so-called West, which are also battling the same tensions between a liberal secular feminist left and a conservative right with many other standpoints in-between. The destructive result of this Orientalised lens is that it fails to point blame at the underlying ideology of misogyny that ultimately is responsible for women's continued vulnerability to violence. Whilst I advocate that this is symptomatic of the conditions of violence against women and girls across the globe, understanding the ways in which it weaves itself into the fabric of an individual society needs to be the first stage in any campaign to eradicate it. Orientalist viewpoints mislead interventions and policy makers because they disproportionately blame culture, suggesting there is something unique about violence that relates to the construction of Indian society. What is needed as a matter of urgency is a more nuanced articulation of the problem in India that sharply avoids a retrograde slip into colonial narratives of backwardness.

Problematising the outsider perspective

Feminists working in India battle on two fronts: manifestations of patriarchy and also the over-simplistic and often reductionist depiction of 'the problem' as seen by feminists looking in (and I recognise myself as someone looking in). Despite Chandra Mohanty's influential and classic essay 'Under western eyes: feminist scholarship and colonial discourses', first published so long ago, it is disheartening to see its continued relevance played out through the reproduction, in perhaps different forms, of the same orientalist discourses she first drew attention to in the 1980s.[3] In her powerful article she holds a number of Western feminist texts accountable for the way they portray an 'ethnocentric universalist' and 'colonial' homogeneous image of the 'average third world woman' – the veiled woman, the powerful mother, the chaste virgin, the obedient wife, etc.:

> This average third world woman leads an essentially truncated life based on her feminine gender (read: sexually constrained) and being 'third world' (read: ignorant, poor, uneducated, tradition-

> bound, domestic, family-oriented, victimized, etc.). This, I suggest, is in contrast to the (implicit) self-representation of Western women as educated, modern, as having control over their own bodies and sexualities, and the freedom to make their own decisions.[4]

Unfortunately, this tendency to essentialise as a means of distancing from the 'other' you do not wish to be associated with continues both on a global but also national stage (as detailed above). The spectrum I advocate must enable these misrepresentations to be clearly visible, and consideration given as to the destructive impact they have on women and for women's lives as they battle to achieve a life free from violence. This spectrum must also guide how instances of violence should be understood, unpacked and responded to. Narayan's (1997) now similarly important critique warns against reducing violence against women in South Asia to a matter of culture. Instead, she urges analysis to focus on the impact of liberalisation, globalisation and capitalism on the emergence of new forms of violence or its resurgence in old forms, rather than simply to identify them as 'cultural traits'. For example, she talks of the relatively recent phenomena of 'dowry murders', which she argues must be situated in the contexts of modernisation and social change (also discussed in depth in chapter eight of this volume):

> The effacement of *cultural change* within historical time [. . .] with the effacement of *cultural variations* across communities and regions [to] suggest a 'Third World culture', which is 'frozen' with respect to both Space and Time.[5]

In line with Mohanty, Narayan has difficulties with representations in which women of Third World cultures are represented as victims of 'tradition/religion/culture', as if these would be unchanging, static complexes. Yet problems in the Western world are never represented in this way. Unfortunately, in this volume it is necessary to apply the critiques of both Mohanty and Narayan to newspaper reporting, specifically as covered in Chapters Three and Four to rape in India. The spectrum then unravels the discourses through which instances of violence are represented, exposing and challenging portrayals that reduce them to exceptional and culturally explainable instances and thereby providing Western actors with further evidence to justify the binary depictions of the West versus the not-so-liberalised rest.

I have identified two problematic discourses that should be located towards the right end of the proposed spectrum presented above (Figure 2.1); whilst the outsider feminist discourse is obviously not an example of misogyny, it is obstructive in that it fails to value the importance of a localised understanding of violence. Failure to take a more sophisticated approach to understanding violence against women in India in fact produces a disturbing marginalising effect, as it disempowers those best placed to give voice to different Indian experiences of violence. Those of us on the outside need to listen to the experiences of those who have survived violence and who work to end it; within these narratives lies a more insightful and complex picture of how and why violence sustains itself.

Explaining the backlash

Bearing in mind these warnings about the perils of an outsider's perspective, I return to a comment made by Meera that was quoted in the Introduction:

> But we do have a problem here, there is no point trying to side-step it, violence against women is normalised and embedded and it is holding us back, so I don't worry about the reproduction of a colonial mind-set, we need to address the problem and not bury it in an Orientalist critique.[6]

The key question for this volume remains: why, despite improvements in women's lives, has GBV remained such an engrained reality? Whilst this question demands perhaps more than one answer in response to a specific country and even regional contexts, and needs to address interlocking factors including liberalisation and modernisation, there is still an urgency to respond to violence. One way to avoid falling into the essentialising trap may be to continue to emphasise that this question is applicable across the globe. History and the specific path through which countries have grown and changed may hold insights in terms of understanding why certain forms of violence are more prevalent in some places than others and also in drawing out competing responses to these instances. However, the picture will always be more complex, still requiring an intersectional web of factors to be applied. What can be said with certainty and perhaps a degree of excusable universalism is that the legitimisation of violence as a means to discipline women remains a reality and is an entrenched barrier to women's complete empowerment and gender equality. This chapter and indeed volume as a whole attempts to dig down into the impenetrability of GBV, exploring a conceptual and analytical frame for the study of it and the activism that seeks to eradicate it – which may in turn prove useful in reframing local, national and global efforts to quell violence against women.

As already stated, and a reality that cannot be overemphasised, in many parts of India, despite significant investment in developing health and education infrastructure primarily targeting girls and women, rates of GBV continue to rise. This picture therefore disputes the validity of the first theory of change, that with women's empowerment will come a change in mind-set that will render women less vulnerable to violence. For example, data presented in Chapter Eight relating to dowry and violence in Kerala suggests that improving women's access to sexual reproductive healthcare and higher levels of educational attainment has not had a particularly significant effect in reducing their vulnerability to violence. In fact, there is evidence to suggest it has made things worse.[7] In particular, it has been suggested that the rise in violence in public spaces could be a consequence of women's increasing mobility in social and public spaces previously occupied only by men, including places of mass transit and business, as well as markets.[8] In an interview with members of the All India Women's Congress,[9] one member stated: 'We have to acknowledge we are now seeing widespread backlash to the advances organisations such as ours have achieved in women's lives, we now must with urgency turn our attention to how we respond to it.' There is a growing consensus that dealing with the backlash is a key priority, but how best to do so remains undecided.

The picture across India and internationally must be placed in the wider global context of efforts to achieve gender equality. Reducing violence against women looks set to be a key goal in the newly reframed

MDGs to emerge in 2015 a sustainability targets. Increased emphasis, at both global and national levels, on the eradication of GBV results from an alarming reality, that improvements in women's lives have not dislodged the normalisation of violence. Whilst women's lives are undoubtedly improved by access to higher levels of education and better access to healthcare, this improvement appears to have had either no impact or, even worse, an adverse effect on the violence they experience. Violence against women remains a normative part of women's lives. The well-documented backlash against improvements in women's lives can also be seen in the analysis of a recent youth survey in India that suggests the more financially independent a woman is, the more likely she is to suffer from violence within the home. This volume must therefore ask the question: what is going wrong in the design and implementation of policies and projects designed to reverse patterns of violence?

Research conducted by Pallikadavath and Bradley (2013) looking at the impact of dowry – taking account of the amount given and whether it is given at all – on women's vulnerability to violence revealed some interesting and challenging findings. The paper used survey data from the 'The Youth in India: Situation and Needs Study' (hereafter: Youth Study) carried out in six states (Andhra Pradesh, Bihar, Jharkhand, Maharashtra, Rajasthan and Tamil Nadu) in India during 2006–07. The study examined dowry, women's ability to exercise autonomy over its use ('dowry autonomy'), and how these associate with domestic violence, using data from a survey of young (15–24 years old) married women. About three-quarters of the women reported dowry at their marriage, and about 66 per cent reported 'dowry autonomy'. Dowry giving without 'dowry autonomy' had no protective value against physical domestic violence. While women's participation in paid employment increased the odds of physical domestic violence, women's education and marriage aged 18 years or above reduced the likelihood of physical domestic violence. Clearly, and as this study reveals, the picture is complex, and so-called advances in some areas, such as in women's employment, do not necessary lead to the sought immediate transformation in gender relations. Two important social changes that led to increased physical domestic violence identified in this study were women's participation in paid employment, and 'love' marriage. In love marriages parents seldom approve the marriage and women retain only limited or sometimes no ties with the natal home. Women who marry for love and are subsequently cut off from their natal families have reduced protection and limited exit options if violence occurs.

However, if a woman has control over the dowry she brings into marriage she is less likely to experience forms of domestic violence. This can be seen when digging further into the survey data for the same demographic group. Various types of domestic violence were considered and overall, about a quarter of the married women in the study aged 15–24 reported physical domestic violence. About 11 per cent reported only one form of violence, 5 per cent any two forms, 3 per cent any three forms, 2 per cent each for any four or five forms, and 1 per cent for all 5 forms of domestic violence (not shown in table 4). Drilling down into the data according to types of violence; about a quarter of women reported receiving a 'slap' from their husbands. This was the most common form of violence among the various physical domestic violence forms examined in this study. Among women who did not practise dowry about 28 per cent reported a 'slap', compared to 23 per cent among those who have practised dowry. Among women who cannot exercise 'dowry autonomy' about 28 per cent reported 'slap' from their husbands compared to 20 per cent among those who can exercise 'dowry autonomy'.

Overall, about 11 per cent reported 'twist' by their husbands: 13 per cent among those who did not practise dowry, compared to 11 per cent who did, and 14 per cent of those who cannot exercise 'dowry autonomy', compared to 10 of those who can. About 7 per cent reported 'push' from their husbands, with a higher rate among those who did not practise dowry: 9 per cent among those who did not practise dowry, compared to 7 per cent who did, and 9 per cent of those who cannot exercise 'dowry autonomy', compared to 6 per cent of those who can. Further, 'punch' was reported by 6 per cent of the group: 7 per cent among those who did not practise dowry, compared to 5 per cent who did, and 7 per cent of those who cannot exercise 'dowry autonomy', compared to 4 per cent of those who can. 'Kick' was reported by 6 per cent of the group: 8 per cent among those who did not practise dowry, compared to 6 per cent who did, and 7 per cent of those who cannot exercise 'dowry autonomy', compared to 5 per cent of those who can. Just 1 per cent reported 'choke': 2 per cent among those who did not practise dowry, compared to 1 per cent who did, and 2 per cent of those who cannot exercise 'dowry autonomy', compared to 1 per cent of those who can.

Given these findings, what then is the way forward? Rao argues: 'It is important that women make incremental gains within the existing social order rather than struggling for wider transformative changes.'[10] Rao seems to be urging caution in not advocating sudden challenges to the status quo because of the reality of the 'backlash'. The levels of violence against women recorded in this study demonstrate the urgency of improving women's position and security within marriage, but radical transformation has not happened quickly and unless the newly formed Sustainability Goals come hand-in-hand with a radical new way of implementing change it is unlikely to suddenly take off now. The study also revealed unexplained community factors at district-level in all forms of domestic violence. These suggest that interventions to improve women's lives need to be responsive to different levels and contexts. Much more research is needed to try to understand the factors that contribute to the diversity in rates and instances of domestic violence. In sum, giving dowry does not protect women from physical violence, but women's autonomy in using dowry could protect them from physical domestic violence; and not giving dowry is more protective than giving dowry that women cannot use. These findings offer a fascinating insight into the dynamics of specifically domestic forms of violence. They also highlight that violence will only be eradicated from women's lives when the underlying gender ideology that legitimises its use is reconstructed according to the values of equality and social justice. Changes in women's circumstances in terms of the opportunities available has not anywhere triggered the kind of reconstructions needed.

The relationship between dowry, gender and violence is picked up again in Chapter Eight.

Global approaches to end violence against women and girls

The data presented in this volume suggests that the shift in gender development policy and practice towards funding women's health programmes and improving access to education and secure employment have not significantly reduced women's vulnerability to violence. That is not to say that these improvements in women's lives are not positive and necessary, but that we need to dig further into asking why, despite these advances, women are still being subjected to high levels of violence. The research presented in the previous section highlights quantitatively how this approach has not worked, and indeed has potentially triggered an increase in forms of domestic violence and work-based harassment that can be described by the term 'backlash'. Violence against women is now recognised nationally and internationally (e.g. by UN Women) as one of the primary barriers to women's empowerment. The spectrum presented earlier in this chapter highlighted how a more complex and nuanced approach is needed. This requires a more holistic analytic frame that uncovers the various strands that weave into and construct the political, economic, social and cultural environments in which violence flourishes. The links highlighted in this chapter, along with the conceptual analytical frame used to reflect on them, are intended to be applied across cultures; violence is not unique to India, it is an endemic problem across the globe.

As discussed in the Introduction, some organisations shifted priorities in line with those of UN Women and CEDAW in the early 2000s, taking a broader approach to empowering women as a means of reducing injustices such as violence; one such was the All India Democratic Women's Association (AIDWA). Thus the focus, until relatively recently, was on how organisations could pursue broader efforts for women's empowerment, rather than on bespoke campaigning on each individual form of violence in the places where it occurs. This approach is in line with the first theory of change related to the eradication of GBV, that if women are empowered through increased opportunities and have a stronger and more confident voice violence will diminish because women will have the emotional and psychological means to fight it. AIDWA, motivated by the findings of its 2003 countrywide survey on dowry, believed that dowry would only be eradicated when women were more holistically empowered. Greater attention was placed, from that moment, on developing women's access to education, healthcare and employment. However, my interviews with AIDWA and other activist groups show that, following a decade of reflection, there has now been a reversion to a more issues-driven agenda, in acknowledgement that a universal approach has not significantly changed things.

Decades of campaigning experience has led these groups to understand that holistic improvements under the banner of 'women's empowerment' have done very little to destabilise or reconstruct gender norms, and this perspective is also supported by the data presented in this volume (above and in Chapter Five). These norms continue to be reinforced in ever more pervasive ways through cultural practices and embedded ideas about the role of women, all of which sit alongside the dark irony hidden beneath the glossy veneer of India's neoliberal prosperity. Despite increased access to education and more career paths opening up, women's roles are still defined according to tradition and demarked by the roles of wife, mother and domestic servant; as discussed already, any shifts in these roles spark a backlash. Interviews with activists from AIDWA reveal their frustration that the 'old' issues on which they had been campaigning for decades have fallen away from national attention, and have instead been replaced by a more universal approach that the activists I interviewed felt is not working. The problem, as one activist argued, is that it is very hard to secure funding for campaigns that focus on what are seen as being 'old' issues:

> The issues that we used to focus our energy on, for example dowry and female infanticide are seen as old and out of fashion, yet we know they are even more of a problem than before. One reason for this reluctance at government level to acknowledge these issues is because the political elite are still observing them secretly, dowry at least, but also strangely they don't want to admit they are still being observed because of the potential damage they could do the global image of 'modern' India.[11]

Dowry and the abuse of widows are two issues picked up by a number of the activists interviewed for this volume as common instances of abuse that fail to receive the attention needed if they are to be eradicated. Instead, media attention is drawn to the more global and, as one activist put it, 'trendy' instances of violence, which capture not just the coverage but also funding. For example, the trafficking of women has received significant attention recently. The interviews presented in the chapters to come certainly highlight the need for responses to emerge out of specific local contexts, in terms of the type of violence to be addressed, the root cause of that violence and the resource capacity already in existence which could be harnessed to eradicate it. Clearly, what the research presented here suggests is that the key barrier to women's empowerment is not a lack of access to education and healthcare but patriarchal constructions of gender that seem to be rendered more invisible by the language of so-called progress, which seeks to deny the widespread and deep-rooted existence of violence. Improving these dimensions of women's lives, whilst important, does nothing to destabilise patriarchal norms about the respective roles of men and women. Violence in fact re-emerges through a backlash as a key mechanism through which patriarchy is maintained. So in terms of effective interventions, more focus needs to be spent on how to destabilise normative ideas about gender, and, as I argue later, engaging men in this process is critical. The spectrum introduced at the start of this chapter needs to highlight if and how interventions are addressing this important aspect of behaviour change.

Multi-lateral stakeholders and their influence on national organisations

Central to the argument presented in this volume is a critique of neoliberalism, which I argue has had an adverse impact on national campaigns to end GBV in India. In the Introduction I looked at the global architecture of aid and suggested that an international brand of feminism has emerged that utilises the processes of globalisation and its infrastructure for the delivery of transnational programmes, and through which it projects specific ideas on how women in the South should be empowered. In other words, the global institutions of development and the channels created through chains of organisations and actors, when it comes to issues of gender, are used by a Northern feminist lobby to project still largely ethnocentric perspectives on how women of the South should live their lives. I have deconstructed this ideology as problematic because of its power binary, which still marginalises the activism and experiences of women in India (and elsewhere). The reality, however, is that huge sums of money are distributed globally by large multinational agencies such as the UN to national organisations who are then tasked with carrying out the remit of empowering women to resist violence. The way in which this money is allocated reflects the dominant views held by these organisations on what the key challenges facing women are. Violence has now risen to the surface as a key problem preventing gender equality, and so money is finally being prioritised for programmes dedicated to eradicating it. However, there is uniformity to how funding decisions are reached, and views on the type of programmes best placed to eradicate violence in turn rest on narrow and often over-simplistic readings of the complex terrains in which GBV flourishes. An Action Aid report from 2013[12] describes through seven linked elements what it views as the best way to approach programming to end GBV. It is summarised as follows:

1. Context is critical: successful interventions are those that are tailored and based on rigorous analysis of the particular factors affecting violence against women and girls in a specific context;
2. The state has primary responsibility for Actions on Violence against Women and Girls. National government should therefore be held ultimately responsible for implementing laws;
3. Holistic and multi-sectorial approaches are more likely to have impact;
4. Social change makes the difference;
5. Backlash is inevitable but manageable;
6. Women's rights organisations create and sustain change so need to be supported;
7. Empowering women is both the means and the end.

It should be noted that while the first dimension above stresses the need to understand the specifics of violence in each given context, I argue that this stage is commonly overlooked. Instead, emphasis is placed on national governments as the key for creating a transformative environment that will achieve the social change necessary – a proposition that is unrealistic in many highly conservative contexts, such as India. I have already detailed the views of many of the male elite who support the use of violence to maintain tradition or who deny it is a problem altogether, and therefore should be located to the right of my spectrum. Commentary in the the *Economist* draws attention to the problem:

> India's bachelor leader, Narendra Modi, struggles with the opposite sex. Last year he tried to be seen to revere his mother by rushing to her side after his big election victory. But then he failed to invite her to his grand inauguration. He has talked, admirably, about the need to respect women. But he defines 'our mothers, daughters and sisters' by their relationships with men and as treasures to protect. It does not help his reputation that, until he was running for the prime ministership, he refused to acknowledge that he has an estranged wife, whom he was forced to marry as a teenager and has not lived with since.[13]

This passage once again highlights an unwillingness to challenge the structural roots of a gendered ideology that is behind violence against women. The reality of a backlash seems to be accepted, but I am not convinced it is so easily managed in contexts (and this will be most instances) in which violence is normalised by a mind-set held by many at every level and stage of life, both male and female. How can it be possible to manage a backlash when defence lawyers are themselves claiming they would not hesitate to use violence if their daughter dishonours them by transgressing traditional gender codes (see Chapter One)? The focus here is clearly on empowering women as a means to change mind-sets and push for change. Legislation is seen as an important route to achieving this, but this again means placing faith in national governments whose own conviction in the need to see such change is questionable. There is an expectation that this shift will be supported and enacted by women's organisations, but while activism is a crucial element in the drive for social change, what I am arguing here is that it needs to be informed and shaped by local knowledge. The activists I have interviewed feel their room for manoeuvre is severely hampered by the approach taken and imposed on them by global institutions.

In short, a global conceptualisation on why violence occurs and how it should be dealt with cannot achieve the first objective outlined here, which is to respond to the specific context. By applying a criticism of neoliberalism to the transnational structures that communicate this global vision of change I draw attention to a number of disconnects that currently hamper the likelihood of achieving the eradication of VAWG. Why is it that despite this acknowledgement that context is everything, the system continues to funnel policy and interventions through a narrow linear concept of change? When placing responses onto the spectrum set out earlier, one consideration is to ask to what extent global solutions/policies/programmes identify the gendered constructions of social relationships as the trigger for violence against women. In other words: to what extent do they get to the structural underpinnings of inequalities that my spectrum demands all approaches and theorising must do as the starting point for triggering social change? The answer first requires a review of the key global conventions designed to shape the programmes implemented at national level, followed by reflection on how influential these conventions are in terms of shaping the work of activist organisations in India and beyond.

The global conventions

There are numerous global conventions that enshrine a commitment to eradicating violence against women and girls, the best-known of which are the UN Declaration on Human Rights (1948) and the UN Committee on the Elimination of Violence against Women (1992). It is not necessary to go through all these conventions individually, since at a global level they converge in the principles and approach they advocate. I will therefore focus on the Convention on the Elimination of All Forms of Discrimination against Women (CEDAW, 1979 and in force from 1981). As briefly reviewed in the Introduction, many national governments, influenced by CEDAW, have undertaken to meet legal human rights obligations to combat gender inequalities. CEDAW is viewed as a key international treaty for women's rights – indeed, it is sometimes referred to as the international bill of women's rights.

Ratified by 185 UN member states, CEDAW encompasses a global consensus on the changes that need to take place in order to realise women's human rights, which include protection against violence. It consists of a preamble and 30 articles, in which it defines what constitutes discrimination against women and sets up an agenda for national action to end such discrimination. It defines discrimination against women as

> any distinction, exclusion or restriction made on the basis of sex which has the effect or purpose of impairing or nullifying the recognition, enjoyment or exercise by women, irrespective of their marital status, on a basis of equality of men and women, of human rights and fundamental freedoms in the political, economic, social, cultural, civil or any other field.

Under CEDAW, governments are required to eliminate the many different forms of gender-based discrimination women confront, not only by ensuring that existing laws do not directly discriminate against women, but also by ensuring that all necessary arrangements are put in place that will allow women to gain equality. A committee monitors the implementation of national measures to fulfil CEDAW obligations. The committee also makes recommendations on any issue affecting women to which it believes the state parties should devote more attention. For example, at the 1989 session, the committee discussed the high incidence of violence against women, requesting information from all countries. In 1992, the committee adopted General Recommendation 19, which requires national reports to the committee to include statistical data on the incidence of violence against women, information on the provision of services for victims and legislative and other measures taken to protect women against violence in their everyday lives, such as harassment in the workplace, abuse in the family and sexual violence. As of the end of 2007, the committee issued 25 general recommendations.

UN Women is the UN Entity for Gender Equality and the Empowerment of Women and is responsible for improving women's human rights by providing support to national governments and civil society to implement CEDAW. The focus of UN Women support is threefold:

- facilitating the development of national human rights frameworks in line with CEDAW, such as constitutions, laws and policies;
- supporting the implementation of existing human rights frameworks to help ensure impact and rights realisation;
- putting special emphasis on particularly vulnerable and marginalised groups, such as poor or indigenous women, so that national frameworks become more inclusive of and responsive to the full range of women's rights concerns.[14]

According to the UN Women website, CEDAW focuses on six areas: violence against women, peace and security, leadership and participation, economic empowerment, national planning and budgeting, and Millennium Development Goals. The UN Women annual report for 2011–12 identifies six 'priority areas of intervention': increasing female leadership, creating economic opportunities, ending violence, creating sustained peace, ensuring social equality and strengthening partnerships for development. For UN Women, 'This fundamental violation of women's rights [i.e. violence] remains widespread, affecting all countries. Women need strong laws, backed by implementation and services for protection and prevention.'[15]

UN Women measures progress to address GBV in terms of the number of countries which have legislation on GBV. However, what they fail to recognise is that although a country may have legislation, it is not necessarily ratified or acted upon. For example, CEDAW has not been ratified by the USA. So, the value of such global policies as mechanisms for lasting change is limited. However, they do act as funding leverages, in that donors peg their resources to them and set markers and indicators of success accordingly. A more sceptical reading on CEDAW might suggest that, given the USA's reluctance to sign, its benefit is not a global consensus but, rather, that it operates as a mechanism for tying poorer and less advantageously positioned countries into the global system, ensuring compliance to wider neoliberal goals. In other words, these global treaties map out the infrastructure of the global system and are the architecture referred to in Chapter One of this volume.

How has India implemented CEDAW?

Mehra documents the implementation and ratification path India has taken in relation to CEDAW.[16] India signed CEDAW on 30 July 1980, but did not ratify it until 9 July 1993 and then it did not agree to a number of the statutes, including the need for all marriages to be formally registered. It was argued that customs and cultural practices around marriage in India are highly diverse and that policing such a requirement would prove impossible, but, as Mehra argues, leaving statutes out left women open to continued abuse in marriage. This refusal to accept CEDAW in its entirety suggests a lack of commitment to achieving gender equality. India was also slow to make the legal changes necessary to demonstrate commitment to gender equality in any form. For example, the legal need for a third of all parliamentary seats to be reserved for women and the establishment of a National Commission for Women to monitor CEDAW were only introduced in the 1990s. Mehra aligns the sudden action in relation to CEDAW to India's initiation of SAPs, which were put in place in 1991 in order to meet aid conditions set by the World Bank and the International Monetary Fund. It does not appear to be coincidental that CEDAW was ratified in India in the same year; instead, it is reflective of India's desire to claim its place in the newly emerging neoliberal world order. Further evidence of this is India's Protection of Human Rights Act, passed in 1993. Signing up to these commitments meant that India became answerable to international standards that required the creation of national commissions to oversee their implementation.

India's ratification of CEDAW then fed into the build-up to the Fourth World Conference on Women in Beijing in 1995, ten years after the UN Decade for Women (1976–85). Mobilisation across India saw attempts to garner activists from the grassroots as well as those positioned at a national level. This network was arguably already in existence as a legacy of Gandhi's emphasis on community development, and the grassroots approach to political and social change which in turn has been hugely influential in shaping the feminist movement in India (Bradley 2010 and Chapter Three in this volume). However, the UN Decade for Women signalled a more visible coming together of different groups of activists. Following the Beijing conference, UNIFEM (as UN Women was called then) insisted more strongly that India comply with CEDAW and invest in developing the technical knowledge and resources needed to oversee it. UNICEF worked with the National Ministry of Women and Child Development to oversee CEDAW, and this relationship proved important for the determination of donor funds, how much should be given to India and how they should be spent (e.g. on what specific issues).

CEDAW, as with all global conventions, is the product of a neoliberal global order. Global conventions represent instruments through which national governments become tied into an architecture that demands conformity. However, and as the continued and persistent levels of GBV in India prove, their ratification does not signal actual government commitment to see gender equality; they should instead be viewed more critically as a necessary stamp of modernity which India desires in order to further its economic success story. The comments documented in Chapter One clearly highlight this lack of consensus over the importance of women's rights. Applying the spectrum model to the implementation of CEDAW highlights a patchy commitment to the principles of social justice it is supposed to enshrine. Gaps or failings in the implementation of CEDAW also point to gaps between different levels of actors, specifically differences between national commissions, government departments and grassroots organisations who respond on a daily basis to very specific forms of violence shaped by the contexts in which they work. Global advocacy campaigns tend to link first to national governments helping with the drafting of legal frameworks and national action plans, which then become the responsibility of governments to feed down to the grassroots. In other words, in the case of CEDAW, UNIFEM helped to craft the legislation needed to see it embedded in the judicial system, but expected and passed on the responsibility to government departments and civil servants to link into and mobilise activism at the grassroots. This linking into the grassroots is crucial, not least so that women across India can in fact access the justice it prescribes as their rights.

Arguably, gender inequality cannot be changed by law alone; nowhere in the world have women's rights been magically transformed by the implementation of even the most robust legal frameworks. If gender equality is to be achieved, mind-sets need to shift and behaviour that legitimises violence needs to be challenged and marginalised as deviant rather than normative. From 2012, UN documents have increasingly included text that acknowledges the need for underlying gender constructions to be restructured, in particular in relation to male attitudes. This can be seen in the dimensions that feed into the theories of change given above. Additionally, UN Women's *Handbook for National Action Plans on Violence Against Women*[17] under the heading 'Social and Cultural Norms' recommends that National Action Plans on violence against women should carry out '"attitudinal change" campaigns that promote positive, respectful and non-violent masculinities; challenge gender stereotypes'.[18] Further, under the heading 'Men and Boys', it states that National Action Plans should 'engage men and boys in challenging gender stereotyping and discrimination, and promoting equitable, non-violent masculinities'.[19] It continues:

> Engaging men, adolescents and boys to play a role in preventing violence against women has been recognised as a critical component of prevention efforts. Men and boys can promote positive masculinities and help shape respectful, gender-equitable attitudes and behaviours among peers and friends. Prevention programmes can engage men and boys in challenging constructions of masculinity that contribute to violence against women, including male dominance or control of wealth in relationships; masculine orientation or sense of entitlement, and weak support for gender equality. Programmes where men are the main participants – such as fatherhood programmes – can provide an opportunity for men to build skills in respectful and equitable relationships, and should include content on gender equality and prevention of violence against women.[20]

Yet, considering the key to reducing GBV is to change male attitudes towards women, it is surprising that engaging men and boys as a means of prevention is buried in the *Handbook*, on page 40 of a 75-page document, and not systematically embedded into change theories. Attitudinal change still seems to concentrate on empowering women to acknowledge their rights to claim public roles and financial independence. The onus therefore is on women to change the views of men. It seems unrealistic and even unfair to expect a woman who has suffered violence from her husband to challenge his actions to an extent that leads to him successfully rethink his behaviour. Again, the real and actual commitment to change must be questioned specifically when it comes to implementation. A question I will consider next is the extent to which these global conventions actually have an adverse impact on the work of national organisations. How constraining is it for feminist organisations in India to be forced to implement global conventions rather than to run bespoke projects across the country?

Trickle down or not? The influence of global policies on the work of national-level women's organisations

There are many activist organisations in India that operate at a national level and through a series of field offices. They campaign on broadly the same issues, giving different priorities to specific projects and focusing efforts in different states/locations. Here, I quickly introduce a number of these, and return to the national infrastructure of the women's movement in India in the next chapter. The purpose here is to consider how these organisations position themselves in relation to global conventions such as CEDAW.

The All India Democratic Women's Association (AIDWA)

AIDWA was created in 1981 as a national-level mass organisation for women, since when it has grown into a network of linked groups. It projects anti-imperialist and pro-working-class values, making it essentially a left-leaning and secular women's organisation. It has an organisational presence in 22 states in India, and a current membership of nine million. AIDWA uses language on their website such as 'achieving democracy, equality and women's emancipation'. AIDWA believes the emancipation of women in India requires fundamental systemic change. It upholds secular values and challenges and resists cultural practices demeaning to women. Recommendations emanating from the UN have clearly influenced the work of AIDWA. As with UN Women, AIDWA also highlights 'women and violence' as a key issue of concern. Under this heading AIDWA states:

> Violence against women takes various forms as a result of contradictions created by age old patriarchal values on the one hand and modern consumerist culture on the other. Increasing poverty and insecurity have worsened the bargaining capacity of poor women. However, there is little attention paid to this most wide spread yet highly invisible form of violence based on economic inequality. Global media has only increased the commodification of women that further encourages violence.[21]

Activists working for AIDWA, in line with the critique made in this volume, believe that neoliberalism has in fact provoked rising levels in forms of violence, and especially in work-based harassment.

However, a note posted on AIDWA's website on 28 January 2009 highlights the difficulty the organisation has experienced in trying to side-step the global system. It seems that in this instance AIDWA has adopted the recommendations made by UN Women and CEDAW, which can be seen in a focus on legislative change:

> The growth in violence against women merits three types of urgent measures from the government:
>
> - formulating new laws
> - amending deficient old laws
> - ensuring effective implementation of existing laws.[22]

Interviews with activists working for AIDWA highlight how reluctant the organisation is to take money from big organisations, especially those positioned outside India. They strongly affirm that local solutions are needed to instances of GBV, which ultimately are shaped by the specific contexts in which they emerge. However, and as shown in Chapter Eight, on dowry, AIDWA have been influenced by global policies on women's empowerment, switching their strategy in early 2003 from focusing on specific forms of violence to a holistic programme of women's empowerment. Arguably now, and given the widely acknowledged backlash, AIDWA is moving back to a stance that responds to the specific context in which forms of violence emerge; e.g. working in states where female infanticide is high and campaigning on that specific issue rather than pursing a broader empowerment campaign.

The Lawyers Collective

In contrast, the Lawyers Collective, which was founded in 1981, has positioned itself as an important actor in the implementation of CEDAW in India, and in 2008 the executive director was elected to the UN Committee on the Elimination of Discrimination against Women. This collective is a feminist organisation that seeks to use legislation as a means to embed women's rights and social justice into the fabric of the judicial and political system. CEDAW, in the view of the collective, has provided an important high-profile mechanism to support its work. Although it might seem that this organisation has been co-opted into a global system, because of its support for and work with the UN, the specific feminist focus of the organisation is to raise the visibility of women's rights issues in India and exert pressure on government to adhere to the principles of social equality enshrined by CEDAW. The Lawyers Collective believes that developing a robust legal framework is an important stage in the transformation of gender relations across the country. The work of the Collective is clearly different from that of AIWDA, and whilst they do focus on specific issues (e.g. HIV/AIDS and dowry harassment), their view is that the empowering of women needs to start with ensuring that there is access to justice and that the routes to justice are functioning. I return to the work of the Collective in the next chapter, and consider where it fits within the network of feminist organisations across the country.

The All India Women's Conference (AIWC)

The All India Women's Conference was founded in 1927 and registered in 1930 under the Societies Registration Act XXI of 1850. According to its website, it is 'an organisation dedicated to the upliftment and betterment of women and children'. The overall vision of the organisation is the 'Emancipation, Education and Empowerment of Women'. As with AIDWA, AIWC operates through field offices across the country and takes a broad approach to empowering women which conforms to the global theory that change will occur once women are educated and financially independent. AIWC projects focus on providing educational opportunities, including literacy classes and vocational training, funding micro-enterprise projects and improving women's gender wellbeing through better sanitation and healthcare. The organisation provides shelter for women suffering from domestic abuse and lobbies for changes to enshrine women's rights in the legal system.

These are only three of many large women's organisations working across India, and whilst there are similarities there are also differences in how they position their work and feminist politics. AIDWA is perhaps the most left-leaning, focusing on community-led campaigns with a critical view of interference from outside. The Lawyers Collective obviously has a concern to ensure the legislative framework operates as a symbolic marker for the way society as a whole should regard and treat women, whilst also looking to ensure justice is rightly delivered. Finally, the AIWC is one of the oldest – if not the oldest – women's organisations in India, emerging from the colonial period, and it utilises social media effectively and seems to see itself as part of a wider social movement. The specific projects pursued would suggest it is working in line with commonly accepted priorities in the global world of gender and development. It is not my intention to evaluate or judge the work of these organisations - they are all highly important and the activists within them tireless - what my analysis seeks to do is understand how they have each positioned themselves within the neoliberal world order. To what extent are they tapping into resources available through multinational agencies such as UNICEF and WHO, and what implications does this have for the vision of the organisation and the specific programmes they implement?

Conclusion: Applying the spectrum

Applying the gender spectrum to the work of these organisations, it is clear that activism in India has focused very much on making women's oppression and vulnerability to different forms of violence more visible and using this to push for changes to the legislative system. At the same time, many activists (for example, the Lawyers Collective) also recognise the need to make the policing systems work better. The continuation of dowry shows that despite the existence of laws rendering it illegal since the 1960s, without effective enforcement of laws, shifts in harmful behaviour simply do not happen. The examples of feminist organisations given here are concerned in their approach to get to the root cause, and this positions them to the left of the spectrum. If we contrast this with the approach so far advocated by Modi, there is a lack of understanding about the underlying and problematic ideology that shapes the gendered outlook of boys and girls, men and women. The interventions emerging from his narrow perspective fail to acknowledge the extent of violence in women's lives, and will therefore fail to make any significant transformation. We might therefore place his efforts, along with those of national government (including previous administrations) towards the right of the spectrum, along with some of his peers, whose conservative views on gender have been captured in the press. Moving forward, I have argued here that when responding to the issue of violence we must apply a critical approach at various levels, from the global down to the national and then local, taking account of how the gender ideology at each level has influenced attitudes and the approaches to gender taken. In addition, this perspective makes it possible to identify specific discourses on gender that may not be regarded as helpful by feminists working at the national level. For example, the conservative views of the Hindu Right in India are shaped by a discourse that advocates the maintenance of a status quo, which is hugely problematic for women's rights. However, I have also critiqued the continued influence of a feminist outsider perspective that applies a culturally essentialist reading in explaining the position of women in India. This second discourse is unhelpful because it perpetuates a power binary that maintains Indian women in a category of backwardness. Change is more often than not sparked by change agents from within the context under scrutiny who are best placed to identify and understand the triggers behind violent behaviours. Devolving, as global institutions do, the responsibility for change to national governments will also not work, especially in an India in which Hindu conservativism is flourishing (see Chapter Six for further discussion).

PART II

NARRATIVES ON RAPE

CHAPTER 3

'TWO FEET FORWARD AND ONE BACK': REFLECTIONS ON THE IMPACT OF THE ANTI-RAPE PROTESTS IN INDIA

Introduction

This chapter explores the impact of the now infamous Delhi rape case, in which Jyoti Singh Pandey, who has since been given the posthumous name *Nirbhaya* (Courageous One), was gang-raped in a moving bus on 16 December 2012, causing her death two weeks later. The incident sparked massive protests against the authorities in Delhi, and this had a ripple effect in the form of countrywide campaigns led by activists who, with the help of social and mainstream media, galvanised broad and wide-ranging public support for pressurising the government to take concerted measures to make Indian society safer for women. This chapter provides a critical analysis of several discourses that are currently playing out within the anti-rape movement: first, that of the media, whose portrayal of rape victims has significant influence in shaping public opinion on violence against women; second, that of activists, whose largely feminist discourse on GBV continues to shape and frame a complex understanding of why violence persists; and third, the pervasive impact of right-wing *Hindutva* ideology, the involvement of which in the anti-rape movement should not be mistaken for a shift away from conservative *Hindutva* views on gender. Each of these has produced narratives on rape, in terms of what constitutes rape, perceptions of who victims and perpetrators are and views on the legitimisation of violence against women. This chapter will argue that these narratives intertwine in simultaneously helpful and destructive ways within the anti-rape movement. Working a coherent path through to the creation of a clear vision of social equality will be vital if India is to eradicate violence against women.

The chapter begins with a discussion of rape-reporting in the *Hindu* newspaper, in order to examine the lens through which this highly popular and influential newspaper views rape. It then presents a number of open-ended interviews with a cross-generational sample of activists, many of whom were involved in the recent anti-rape protests and who now work within the emergent movement. It will be shown that rape-reporting in the *Hindu* contained considerable inaccuracies in how it portrayed violence against women (type and profile of both victims and perpetrators), when considered alongside the knowledge and insight of activists and the academics who work with them. These inaccuracies influence the construction of a public narrative on violence that fails to capture its diversity, in terms of what constitutes rape or other forms of violence against women. The reporting often lacks any explanation as to why violence against women happens, and where accounts are given they are often overly simplistic. These inaccuracies also pose challenges for activists campaigning to end all forms of GBV; the activists interviewed here fundamentally agree that violence will only be eradicated through a drastic change in attitudes towards gender relations. Accurate and nuanced reporting is therefore crucial, and inaccurate reporting is harmful.

However, the research does also highlight that, despite this gap, the press to some extent is sensitive to and responsive towards the strong voice of activists: journalists at the *Hindu* seem to have recognised a new wave of activism around anti-violence against women prior to 16 December 2012, and the second key finding from the review presented here is that in the year leading up to the gang-rape and murder of *Nirbhaya*, the number of articles on rape published in the *Hindu* had increased significantly. That number shot up again following the case of

Nirbhaya, but a groundswell of protests already existed. The *Nirbhaya* case acted as a consolidating moment for a movement that had already self-organised and co-ordinated, and there is hope that the momentum generated may be sustained through the new networks that have been built.

Although some of the feminists interviewed as part of this volume are not optimistic that the movement will maintain its current energy, this chapter argues that, given the extent of changes already in place since December 2012, there is cause to believe that a lasting transformation of sorts is underway. However, the last section of the chapter acknowledges the negative and destructive impact of the conservative *Hindutva* ideology which acts to maintain the patriarchal status quo, the source of women's inferiority and vulnerability to violence. Extreme strands of this discourse promote the use of violence to discipline women who stray from traditional gender norms. Whilst feminist voices are stronger than ever in India (supported by and through social media, which has enabled wider social mobilisation across sections of the public), their lasting reach will be limited unless the mainstream media is captured and used more effectively as a vehicle for promoting a much-needed shift in attitudes towards gender.

An analysis of rape-reporting in the *Hindu*

The research looked at the rape cases that were reported in the *Hindu*, India's national English-language newspaper, over a period of two-and-a-half years. The research was divided into three time-periods: December 2010–December 2011, January–December 2012 and January–April 2013. The study also looked at editorial and opinion pieces published immediately after the *Nirbhaya* trial verdict. The reports were collected from a day-by-day search from the internet archives of the *Hindu*. They were chronicled in a tabular format with the date, place and headline of each report, along with a summary. Colour-coding was used to categorise rape cases into four types, reflecting the narrow range reported: rape of minors, rape of adult women not identified specifically as Dalits, rape of Dalit or tribal women and gang-rapes.

Findings

Table 3.1 Rape-reporting in the *Hindu*, December 2010–April 2013.

	Rape of Minor	Rape of Adult Woman	Rape of Dalit Woman	Gang-Rape
Dec. 2010–Dec. 2011	10	26	4	5
2012	31	78	15	23
Jan. to Apr. 2013	31	62	16	27

Quantitative analysis presented in Table 3.1 shows that in 2011, there were 45 rape-related articles in the *Hindu*. This shot up to 147 in 2012, including around 50 rape-related stories in the final 14 days of 2012; this was as expected given the high profile of the *Nirbhaya* case, but if these are excluded the increase in reporting is still significant and represents a 100 per cent rise year-on-year. This upward trend then continues into the next year: in the first third of 2013 (up to 21 April), there were 136 rape-related articles in the *Hindu*.

The general nature of the increase can also be seen in the different categories of rape being reported: whilst in 2012 the number of rape cases pertaining to minors was 21 for the whole year, in 2013 the figure is 20 in just four months. Similarly, across all other categories there is a considerable increase in the number of new cases reported from all across the country. Even prior to the Delhi gang-rape, it can be seen that the media, perhaps responding to pressure from civil society groups, increased its reporting of rape cases. This undoubtedly helped to put pressure on the judiciary to deal with rape cases more efficiently and sternly. For example, a report in the *Hindu* for 4 November 2012 stated that in Kerala, 715 complaints had been made in the first nine months of 2012. Quoting police crime statistics, the article explained that:

> The number of rape cases till September this year [2012] was much higher than that registered during the whole of 2009 (568 cases) and 2010 (634 cases). According to the data, 1,132 rape cases were registered in the State in 2011 and 432 among the victims were minors.[1]

The *Hindu* also published similar reports of increasing numbers of rapes being reported to the police from elsewhere in the country. A *Hindu* report from 15 December 2012 noted increasing number of rapes in Punjab, and that the National Commission for Women had called upon the Punjab government to produce an action report on all rape cases filed in 2012. Clearly, activism was already making a difference prior to 16 December; this can be seen in both the press reporting of rape and the wider socio-political changes that were beginning.

In a number of articles, the newspaper also took notice of the anxieties of activists, reflecting their concern over the high number of rape cases. On 15 October 2012, it ran an editorial condemning the Haryana government for making regressive statements proposing that early marriages could act as a remedial measure for combating the growing number of rape cases in the state; the following month, it ran a series of personal accounts of street harassment and violence in Delhi, which once again highlighted widespread uneasiness about the growing number of incidents of rape and violent crime against women. The horror of 16 December 2012 was the last straw that eventually caused anger to spill onto the streets, and which launched the current anti-rape protest movement.

Review of opinion pieces

Over the period of reporting under review in this study, a number of opinion pieces were published which attempted to reflect on the deep-rooted socio-cultural issues that sustain and promote violence against women in India. Collectively, these articles draw attention to the problematic normative views towards women which render them objects to be controlled, as well as to the unprofessional attitude of the police, who fail to support women who report rape, and to the moribund legal system that contributes to women not getting justice in the event of rape or any other form of violence.

One piece in the *Hindu* presented an analysis of reported rape cases across India, arguing that a murderer is far more likely to be convicted than a rapist – an indication that the criminal justice system still does not take rape seriously.[2] This is an argument that feminist activists have been making for decades. The same newspaper published an article by Ratna Kapur exploring what lies behind these high incidences of rape; in her view, the steady emancipation of women in the last few decades had challenged the 'sense of superiority and entitlement of the traditional Indian male'. She argues:

> This idea of a woman, as a fully formed human subject remains a difficult concept to embrace.
>
> Even those who are ostensibly in favour of women's rights such as the National Commission of Women and the Department of Women and Child Development, continue to refer to women as vulnerable objects and discuss the issue of violence against women in highly protectionist language.[3]

An analysis of editorials on the subject in the *Hindu* is important, because they acknowledge that the problem of rape in India is huge and highlight the collective failure of social, legal, economic and political instruments to protect women from violence. They also strongly advocate measures such as legal reforms and efforts to change societal attitudes. In the articles reviewed here the media clearly resonates with the views of activists, reinforcing the gravity of the problem of rape in public consciousness. However, these sensitive and more detailed pieces are few, with the majority of rape-reporting taking the form of individual descriptive case profiles.

However: one step back

On the one hand, it can be argued that the reporting of rape in the *Hindu* can be seen to both respond to and support activism on women's rights; however, a deeper analysis of the types of cases reported reveals there has also been 'one step back'. A critical analysis of the narrow categories of rape into which reported cases fall reflects a limited definition of the crime used by the paper in determining which and what types of cases to publish. Rape cuts across all age and socio-economic groupings; given that only four categories can be identified, this is clearly not reflected in the cases published. Studies into rape in India highlight the high and normative rape of low-caste and Dalit women, and although some such cases are reported by the *Hindu*, the low number given for this group is not reflective of the realities of how vulnerable this group of women is to rape. Also, whilst the rape of minors is a particularly shocking and disturbing crime, it should arguably come under a separate category of child abuse, and therefore be reported using different and more specific language reflective of its abhorrent nature. The conflation of child abuse with rape serves to hide the extent to which adult women are vulnerable to rape, suggesting that it is young girls who are disproportionately the victims of rape, when the research does not bear this reality out. The underreporting in the press of the rape of different groups of adult women perhaps also reflects the extent to which rape within marriage is not recognised as a crime, and so, as such, remains normative and not newsworthy. In short, the reporting of rape unhelpfully endorses and projects a narrow and overly simplistic definition of rape which hides the darker realities.

The analysis of media reporting of rape given so far reveals an internal contradiction: whilst the main daily reporting of rape cases distorts the realities of who gets raped and the prevalence of the crime, the opinion pieces increasingly offer a nuanced and well-argued position supporting the views of dominant feminist activists. The support of the media is obviously key in building a sustainable and effective movement for change, but this -- albeit small-scale and focused – analysis of one paper's reporting reveals that progress is a matter of two steps forward and one back.

Two steps forward: What has changed?

The outpouring of anger and grief following the rape and murder of *Nirbhaya* gave rise to hopes for change in India. The government responded with the passage of several new sexual assault laws, including a mandatory minimum sentence of 20 years for gang-rape, and six new fast-track courts created solely for rape prosecutions. As an indicator of the scope of the problem of rape prosecution, the *Nirbhaya* case was the only conviction obtained among the 706 rape cases filed in New Delhi in 2012. Between 16 December 2012 and 4 January 2013, Delhi police recorded 501 allegations of harassment and 64 of rape, but only four inquiries were launched. However, it appears that the *Nirbhaya* case has had an effect on the willingness of rape or molestation victims to report the crime: police records show that during the final nine months of 2013 almost twice as many rape victims filed a police report and four times as many allegations of molestation were made. A report released in 2013 by the National Crime Records Bureau shows that 95 per cent of the cases brought to the police were classified as a crime. However, there is a large backlog of cases: fewer than 15 per cent of those charged in 2012 were tried within 12 months.

The Views of the Activists

In an attempt to understand the dynamics of the anti-rape movement, a number of key activists were interviewed to capture their views on the prevalence of GBV in India and the likely sustainability and impact of the anti-rape movement.

An academic

A leading Indian feminist activist and academic highlighted that underlying misogynistic views on women have shifted very little:[4]

> I think that often we can see that there is a backlash because more women are speaking out, even Dalit women, yet there is increasing violence against Dalit women, and widows especially. Widows are supposed to remember they should be quiet and not speak out. So there is a dual thing: women are speaking out on the one hand but facing the backlash, in some cases entrenched views and insecurities that come out.

She went on to explain that the failure of liberalisation to dramatically improve people's lives has meant that, if anything, women have become more vulnerable to violence, as those men who were promised a better life which has not emerged vent their anger:

> With liberalisation many promises were made of better lives but many have not seen things get better, so who are you going to blame? So I think it is not just violence against women which has increased in the Indian context; the cases of violence against

> Dalits, against widows, particular sections of women, have increased. For someone like me, I really have to be jolted to see how things have changed. As a young woman travelling by bus I would experience those things every day walking along the street – now, it is very rare that I am on the street so I don't see it, I am in a position of power so I don't experience that now, but I experience humiliation in other ways.

Asked why violence against women remains so entrenched, she argued:

> We are not addressing the underlying gender ideology, that is true, but it is goes back to: are we going to stop rapes through having a good law? We know nowhere in the world is rape stopped through having a good law, but I think that through the discourse around it and the discussion which takes place there is a bit of gender ideology that gets challenged and dislodged. And I think part of the way violence is challenged is in different ways of being and thinking and acting.

She was then asked how, in her view, things could change:

> There needs to be a realisation that we are not going to address women's gender oppressions unless we address all inequalities, unless we address class inequalities, all these various different things. And this is becoming more and more stark, and of course making it more and more difficult, because it is almost impossible to get an overarching constituency which will campaign on all these issues. So what can we do? We have to keep addressing each of these things by themselves as well as the gender ideology embedded in them.

For this activist-academic, changing attitudes is clearly at the root of the continued normalisation of violence against women:

> To some extent it takes time, but we don't want to be waiting for another 100 years. As soon as you raise this people say these are

> mind-sets and mind-sets take 1,000 years to change and my response is these are not mind-sets for a 100 years that are going to go on for another 1,000 years; no, these are ways of thinking that are constantly being remade through the way government policy moves, through the way media moves and so we have to address those. This idea that it takes so long for mind-sets to change we should not worry about it.

In relation to the press reporting of violence against women, the distortion comes through in an over-emphasis on some forms of violence and a lack of holistic coverage across the abuses women suffer:

> Almost any issue in relation to women is framed in terms of gender violence, yet there are many more forms of violence that do not get recognised, and issues such as dowry, sex selective technologies, discussion around the anti-rape law. Since the last decade rape became the major issue focused on in relation to violence against women and it became a major issue of reporting in the papers. I think some of us were getting sick and tired with the fact that, ok, every day there are going to be three cases reported on the front pages and the on the inside pages, and you know it is good that the media is focusing on it, but is this the way to focus on it? But along with it was a whole discussion which came up with the Verma Committee and with the changes in law and the discussion which is now going around which is: can law prevent violence against women? Which is actually part of the wider debate in terms of: can discussion on violence against women prevent violence against women?
>
> The rape brought people onto the streets, which was marvellous, and the cases of the last few months people have commented, "where have we got?", and some of us say, "no, young people are coming out and campaigning, and they would not have done so before this means we have got somewhere." On the other hand I remember feeling a huge sense of *déjà vu* because to some extent it was the same issues having to be raised again, the same discussion taking place again, and to some extent again the

> same discussions: 'will law make it worse?', and this has made me angry the last few weeks. Comments that the laws are going to make free and easy relations between the genders impossible, people saying I can't hug and kiss you for fear of being accused of sexual harassment, with young people coming through it is highlighting the need for old people to recognise that their ways have to change. Also, if we look at the Verma Commission we have definitely made progress. And part of the progress is: we are enabling people to speak out. The problem we had before was that very few women would speak out, it depended on them very quickly being able to find a solidarity group, and this still remains the case but there seems to be a greater possibility of them searching for this solidarity, getting that group and then being able to speak out.

Younger activists

A second interview was conducted with a younger activist, who has a leading role working for the All India Democratic Women's Association. She spoke about how difficult her organisation finds engaging with the media:[5]

> It is hard to reach the media, and we feel the media is more interested in newer issues, which is excellent: the issues of smaller sections also need to be reflected, but what we are saying is that the large majority are still stuck with issues of violence and sexual assault that happens in more marginalised sections – poor women and Dalit women – and as far as the media is concerned they are looking for a story and ready-made press releases, which we as women's organisations find ourselves pretty incapable of providing them with. We would love to influence them in covering the issues we are interested in, we would give them ready-made material around it.

As with the academic-activist, feelings expressed here suggest that the media is not reporting a holistic picture of violence against women, but rather focusing in on a narrow range of cases. This was borne out in the analysis of rape-reporting also given above, and indicates that these scholars and activists at least feel the press is not supporting their work and perspective on violence against women. The activist from AIDWA also voiced similar views to those of the academic-activist in relation to the negative impact of neoliberalism on women's rights:

> Nothing has changed, in fact it has become worse: India has opened its markets to neoliberalism and that has only made the situation worse. The sex ratio has gone down, so there is an insane amount of pressure on women to work and so the entire landscape is changing. So, before, men wanted to marry a girl who would not go out and work, who would sit at home and look after the household chores; however, now they want the lady to work and they want the woman to bring in money into the house, so there is additional pressure on these women to work in these horrible places where the wages are not equal to men, where there is an insane amount of sexual harassment and they cannot complain against it, so it has made their situation worse.

Again as with the academic-activist above, the activist also raised the issue of the narrow focus on certain types of violence, as conveyed not just by the media but also in policy coverage at national and global levels. This was seen to ignore even some of the most common and persistent forms, such as dowry harassment:

> Dowry has been out on the back burner – UN Women, for example, constantly shifts the issue; dowry has become a boring issue so to say, that organisations and NGOs avoid getting into direct conflict with communities but when working on issues such as honour crime you have to get into confrontation with certain people. And so then for an organisation like ours we find ourselves pretty lonely even though there are so many organisations working on women's issues we find ourselves completely isolated.

The activist also raised the issue that certain groups of women such as Dalits are more vulnerable to violence. She responded: 'So, with sexual assault you cannot ignore the fact is faced by Dalit women more aggressively than any other section, and they may not want to talk about caste so that's the problem.' I went on to ask her: 'what are your views about the anti-rape protests which happened last year?' She responded:

> Well, the feeling is that I myself have started participating in the women's movement so much more than I used to before that, and there are a lot of young girls in this country today that have really joined the movement or associated themselves with women's organisations after that incident, thinking that this is really the only hope for us now. The problem is that this new onslaught of neoliberal policies in India, there is this massive difference between the issues of one section of women and the issues of this other section of women sitting in poorer rural areas and who are facing all kinds of violence from all sides. Awareness of their rights, legalisation of their rights where there is just the smallest section of women that are educated from urban areas who have been treated by their parents as equal to their brothers and have grown up with a certain amount of equality inside them, and outside as far as they have been educated; now, the problem is that when these women step outside of their houses, and their aspirations are big of course, because they have been treated as equals to their brother, and when they step out onto the street and they see that the ground reality is no different, you know, that is when it hits them that maybe this society is not equal towards us. So where their aspirations are big and they want to do these big things in life the ground reality is completely different and there are lots of contradictions and so it hits them hard.
>
> So then, these young women are more guided by a sense of personal outrage at how things are unlike their earlier counterparts who would come into the movement thinking that we have to change the world for everyone. So after that 16 December protest that happened in Delhi and around the country I feel that a lot of young people came out and participated in the protests, but again I mean that there has to be a look at the wider landscape when looking at women's issues, there has to be a little

> more linkage between what is happening in more urban areas to what is happening in the larger rural areas of the country. So we are really trying to strike that balance somewhere which is a challenge right now.

In earlier interviews with two activists and community development workers in Delhi,[6] an optimistic view emerged on the lasting possibilities of the movement and the changes it has already brought about. Both agreed that the anti-rape protests signal a shift in police protection but also local mobilisation, particularly among women, to report and shout out when abuse occurs. Each police station in Delhi now has to have a GBV committee with local people on it. The committees are called Aawaz Uthad (Raise Your Voice Against Violence). One of the community workers interviewed believes that the police have become more responsive to complaints made and that they are much more visible patrolling the community, and that this has increased women's sense of safety. According to both of them, speaking out is key to creating a transformation: 'If you don't speak out nothing can change, things just stay the same.'

They both went on to explain how the protests extended to the streets in Sarvada, where violence is a big problem. Both were also optimistic that this shift is not temporary, but that it represents a real moment of change: social-networking sites are being used to push for this across many forms of GBV, from acid attacks to so-called 'Eve teasing'. Both talked about a link between anti-corruption protests and anti-GBV, since with high levels of corruption the legislative system will not be effective. There has been a surge in protests in relation to both these issues.

As argued in the first section, it is clear from the analysis of media reports that the press to some extent has responded to this groundswell of opinion and now reflects these concerns in its rape-reporting. However, the reporting is patchy and fails to give a holistic or sophisticated perspective. Activists working in rural areas draw attention to this unevenness: the AIWDA activist stressed that the context and nature of violence differs in rural areas when compared to urban areas, while a director of a women's organisation located in Himachal Pradesh stated that in rural areas violence is much less talked about publicly, but that it is a big problem – in particular, domestic violence, but also high levels of female infanticide. The rape protests did not make a huge impact on rural communities, mainly because not all families have TVs; they are more likely to have radios, and whilst some notable discussion took place as a result of the national reporting, it was not enough to trigger a sea change. Also, illiteracy, particularly among women, is high, so campaign literature is inaccessible to them.

The director of the Himachal Pradesh women's organisation did highlight that the Delhi protests managed to unite the left and the right, all of whom, despite very different ideologies, came out to protest against the rape of women. The success of this unity was down to the fact that

> the girl was perceived as having done nothing wrong, she was dressed modestly, not out late and with her fiancé. If this had not been the case, then the right at least would of said she provoked the attack, that she was a loose woman. This is the point public outrage for many was triggered: by the fact that this happened to a nice girl who did everything right. If she had been seen not to be nice then such mobilisation would not have happened. The problem in terms of changing gender-based violence is it needs a paradigm shift in how women are seen. The increasing influence of right-wing fundamentalist views on gender is actually causing a shift backwards and this is not helped by capitalism, which just further embeds power differences and hierarchies of all kinds.
>
> The protests have, however, achieved some changes and redrafting of legislative provision on rape. This is very positive. Gender inequalities cannot be eradicated until caste is. Caste is inherently gendered and embeds divisions that then give some the power over others; rape is a means through which these hierarchies of power are maintained.
>
> The other issue is one of governance: without good governance nothing will change. With corruption so high how can we expect things to change? We have legislation in place but of course it has to be enforced. This is the problem with capitalism; the elite are only interested in making money, in using their position to get

> richer and richer rather than to see justice done and equality achieved. Therefore in order to see women truly empowered and patriarchy dislodged we have to challenge and change these power dynamics.

The recurring themes resonate in this transcript also: the adverse impact of neoliberal capitalist development, the need to reverse entrenched inequalities related not just to gender but also caste, and a degree of positivity over legislative changes, which offer symbolic hope that transformation is possible.

An interview with a young activist at the Lawyers Collective, a leading organisation of feminist legal professionals, once again highlighted the importance of the rape protests as a trigger moment prompting consciousness-raising in relation to rape. Women, the interviewee felt, are now less likely now to tolerate rape. The main difference, she went on to say, with these protests is that they are across the middle classes, and not just the feminist movement. This signals a mind-set change as regards views of rape, with increased sensitivity towards rape among the general middle-class population. The beginnings of a process of mainstreaming the problem of rape has been triggered by the anti-rape protests, although she cautioned it is still

> one step forward and then two back, for example positive changes to legislation which see rape made illegal but the age of consent increases from 15–18 and marital rape is still excluded from law. This also extends to a woman who has divorced a man, if he then rapes her it is not regarded as rape [...].
>
> The whole system is fundamentally chauvinist. It is difficult to implement these laws within a chauvinistic system and there remains an underreporting of rape, mainly due to an ineffective police service. More training and capacity-building within the police is needed. Also, we need more female police officers to whom women can report.

These interviews highlight scepticism about how much of a transformation is possible given the depth of power inequalities and patriarchal attitudes, but optimism is clear in the witnessing of significant political mobilisation across gender and social groups. These responses can be seen again in an interview with a leading feminist activist and publisher. She stated:

> There is no doubt in my mind that the protests acted to trigger a wave of mobilisation that has brought the issue of rape to the fore. This was also helped by the level of press attention it received. I hope it will last, this current wave, but I am unconvinced that it will, I have seen it numerous times before, what seems like sudden enthusiasm of an issue, almost an excitement that then just burns itself out.[7]

In an attempt to document a cross-section of different activist voices I interviewed some of the male protestors involved in the anti-rape movement. In talking about his organisation, one male activist explained:[8]

> We have some objectives. When we established the objectives, the rape of women – that is the worst crime that happens in India, it keeps on increasing, doesn't slow down. Even after *Nirbhaya* nothing has changed – the rape count hasn't come down. For me if I have to make an official statement, it is on the increase, or at least the fact the levels remain the same. The problem is that the mentality hasn't changed – it is not that the uneducated are raping, educated people are also raping. Take for example Kerala, that has 100 per cent literacy; but Kerala has as many rape cases as Delhi. It's not really about the education, it's the mind-set – it's all about the sickness and the mind-set.

So an engrained misogynistic normative mind-set emerges as the key factor accounting for high instances of rape. This mind-set emerged in a few of the opinion pieces published in the *Hindu*, but is not reflected in the distorted coverage of cases and limited account of GBV in the paper more widely.

He was also asked about the protests after the Delhi rape:

> So what happened was, why *Nirbhaya* case caught our attention was because it was different from other cases, given the brutality of the case. The main reason why we got instigated to try and protest in full strength and to get something done by the government, because that is where we are also lacking in a big way.
>
> So it all started with a friendly chat – social media, Facebook in particular. People started discussing and then venting their anger and then we thought, 'how will venting our anger on the social media going to change things?' That is when people said 'tell us what we should do' [. . .] There was a group of students who wanted to protest [. . .] We acted as a catalyst to organise it on 22 December, 2012 – let that be first day. Five or six groups like ours, but mostly college students, got in touch with each other and the social activist groups in colleges. They agreed to come forward and we decided to push. Let me tell you, we were not controlling it at all – it went beyond our control. It gained its own momentum: the students really came out, even the school students came out. The electronic media played a major role. When they started showing anger among the public. The electronic media came up with the fact that there are a lot of groups that are going to come out on 22 December. It was then people decided to participate.

Further comments were taken from a second male activist, a prominent anti-trafficking activist. He stated:[9]

> Only when we change the mind-set of the people both in rural and urban areas [. . .] in a positive way, where we respect women, where we respect our children and family [. . .]. India as you know is a family-oriented society. That has changed [. . .], we are going more towards nuclear families even in rural areas, so that problem is rising. And you know, years of negligence has brought up at this point because we never spoke against violence on women, we never understood the types of problems women face [. . .]. Neither our central government was speaking. We have Women and Child Ministry but they never took up these issues on a priority basis. Violence was happening in houses – it was hidden.

Activists such as all those documented here are pushing for a fundamental attitude change. This second male activist added:

> Gender inequality it is very deep-rooted. It is so deep-rooted that, despite being educated the choice or decision is not hers, it's her husband's and his family that matters. If a girl is making her own choice, she is branded as someone wrong. They don't respect the family and even the husband starts abusing. Because the husbands think that the wife should respect the family of the husband. It's a tradition that you have to do. But as girls more educated they have their own choice. They want to do their life happily and a few very girls walk away [. . .]. It's very tough to walk away.

The engagement of men in fighting gender inequality is not often recorded, but clearly vital if this kind of attitude shift is going to occur:

> When men come into fight, talking about issues like violence against women, the whole community comes forward. The whole world is talking about violence against women. We have to bring into the fold more men, and the more we talk the more will change. I am happy that more men are coming in and men are changing. Men who were abusive are changing. They are more softer on women. Women needs a helping hand. The more polite you are with a woman, a better woman you will see.

Reflections on the movement and the curse of the right

Clearly, these interviews from a cross-section of different activists reveal that the women's movement in India has expanded and that a number of different networks and configurations exist, increasingly involving men. These interviews also reveal that if lasting, transformative social equality is to be achieved, the movement needs to maintain a collective momentum. A common focus among groups is clear: that whilst legislation is symbolically important, it is the deeply entrenched and patriarchal attitudes that need to be challenged and eradicated if violence against women is to be reduced in any real sense. The media, then, has a role to play here in exposing the views that prevent this transformation from occurring, as well as a role in ensuring that a holistic picture of GBV is recorded that challenges normative constructs of violence. A broader range of cases needs to be included in press coverage, both in terms of the demography of the victims, but also as regards the types of violence, from dowry harassment and female infanticide through to rape. Further, activist organisations need to forge closer allegiances with the press in order to encourage the media to report the causes they work on. However, in India a dark reality threatens to hamper any real progress, as has been already stated: the *Nirbhaya* case occurred against a backdrop of increasing levels of violence against women and within a society that has become more conservative as it has got richer.

Ironically, and as the director the women's organisation in Himachal Pradesh highlights above, conservative groups were also part of the anti-rape protests. Why this apparent unity was possible was because *Nirbhaya* was viewed by the conservative Hindu Right as a woman who had done everything right. She was not out alone, but accompanied by her partner; she had maintained her honour and conformed to what is expected of a 'good woman'. The Hindu Right, as we know, has been behind numerous brutal attacks on women who challenge the oppressive and constraining parameters of womanhood prescribed by *Hindutva* ideology.[10] These attacks, as the media has reported in detail, have targeted women who transgress the conservative religious codes of female modesty and subservience, including women who drink alcohol in pubs and bars or who go to nightclubs, wear Western clothes, and have multiple sexual partners. *Nirbhaya* did none of these things, and in the eyes of the *Hindutva* movement this is why the use of brutal violence against her was illegitimate.

The outcries from the left of the spectrum defined in Chapter Two and as captured in the interviews above were motivated by very different reasons from those of the *Hindutva* groups: they saw this rape as yet another sign of the misogyny lying at the foundations of Indian society. The brutality of the rape was merely a sign of how little progress has really been made in reconstructing dominant images of female sexuality in a more liberal frame. Further motivation for the protests has come from how uncomfortably this violence sits against the backdrop of the country's apparent economic success, although most of the activists interviewed blamed this success for the rising levels of violence against women. The world's media have not been slow in picking up on this ironic contradiction – economic success considered the result of a liberalising agenda hides what has been termed a 'dark underbelly'.[11]

The recent anti-rape protests reveal once again the way in which women's bodies remain the battleground for competing discourses on gender and sexuality in India. Scholars have written extensively on the gendered thread running through *Hindutva* ideology, and on the implications for women's rights of a *Hindutva* organisation that seeks to educate women '"in the right image" as a way of ensuring India remains true to the golden age of the Vedic era'.[12] Control then over female sexuality is crucial in ensuring women conform to their role as procreators and nurturers of the next generation. Female sexuality is associated with the status of the whole nation. Hindu role models such as Sita are used to enforce the image of a good subservient woman. The impact of *Hindutva* on and for the eradication of VAWG is picked up again in Chapter Six.

Conclusion

This chapter has reviewed three different dimensions/discourses on GBV, exposing the media's partial support of the feminist movement in critical editorials, but also highlighting its generally narrow and unhelpful daily reporting of rape crimes. It has also presented different activist views that reveal the diversity of the women's movement but also unity within it, and drawn attention to the 'step back' threatened by the continuing prominence of the right-wing *Hindutva* ideology. Ironically, the anti-rape protests brought together groups who seek to challenge a rigid conservative depiction of gender with those who promote it. These tensions are being played out across India in homes, public spaces, law courts, workplaces, local councils and parliament. Understanding the complex web of factors at work is of paramount importance if women's rights and those of other oppressed groups are to be secured. The pessimism expressed by many of those interviewed regarding the likelihood that lasting transformative change is really just around the corner is understandable, given the strength of right-wing discourses in India. And so whilst the coherence and growth of feminist networks in India – supported and responded to, albeit in a limited sense, by the media – represent significant steps forward, unless an effective and direct challenge to *Hindutva* is launched, steps back along the way will be inevitable.

CHAPTER 4

THE REMAKING OF SUBALTERNS THROUGH WESTERN NEWSPAPER NARRATIVES OF RAPE IN INDIA

Introduction

Gayatri Spivak, in her highly influential article 'Can the subaltern speak?', argues that 'the ideological construction of gender keeps the male dominant. If in the context of colonial production, the subaltern has no history and cannot speak, the subaltern as female is even more deeply in shadow.'[1] In this chapter I argue that, thanks to the work of Spivak and Mohanty and many other feminist post-colonial scholars,[2] as well as the work of activist movements in India, there is now a greater consciousness around the ways in which women are systematically abused, oppressed and ignored both at the level of discourse and also practically in day-to-day life. However, research reveals that despite these inroads a subaltern Indian woman still exists, in and through the ways in which the Western media reports rape in India. This female subaltern was first publically recognised by Roy, who in response to the Delhi anti-rape protests argued that the spotlight had fallen on India because of the middle-class and urban nature of the case. In particular, she noted that the normalcy of rape for rural low-caste and Dalit women who confront it in daily life fails to get comparable media attention, and certainly, as our research highlights, it has not been covered in the international press. The marginality of different groups of subaltern women is currently appreciated in post-colonial scholarship, and analytical attention has been drawn to those groups still rendered silent in public media and political discourse. A challenge, however, remains: despite this academic/theoretical identification of the subaltern position of many Indian women, atrocities against them have not diminished. In fact, according to many the situation has worsened because the outrage sparked by the Delhi case caught the eye of the international press.[3] Rape in India prior to December 2012 was not reported in the international press; since that date there has been a surge in the number of pieces, but focusing on the protests and recording only a narrow selection of cases. Out of 100 articles collected for this study, only four different cases were covered, including the Delhi case and that of the Mumbai gang-rape of a photo-journalist. In both these horrific cases the women can be described as middle-class and/or 'modern' urban. The other two cases recorded were rapes of Western women.

The narrow selection of rape cases covered enforces the marginality of other groups of women; further, it presents an inaccurate portrayal of who gets raped in India, potentially provoking international responses to GBV in India that are founded on unhelpful stereotyping rather than lived experiences. There is a clear disconnect between two groups of actors; post-colonial theorists and grassroots activists, and the international press. Post-colonial theorists have through their deconstruction of a subaltern Indian woman highlighted the epistemic violence caused by discourses that ignore and thereby silence groups of people, while grassroots activists tirelessly respond to this 'episteme violence'[4] by raising the audibility of different groups of women whose oppression is deep-rooted and normalised. The international press is working counter to both these groups; reinforcing, and reconstructing through their rape narratives the subaltern female subject, ensuring the marginality of many Indian women remains intact.

Whilst there may be nothing new in the way in which Western media invokes a subaltern Indian woman, my analysis highlights the emergence of a subaltern male subject, presented and labelled as deviant. This group, once deconstructed, represents an even more silenced and marginal group than oppressed rural low-caste and Dalit women, mainly because they have no public advocates highlighting their marginality and no resources or capital directed at empowering and strengthening their voices. Poor, rural male migrants newly arrived in India's big cities have become the focus for Western press narratives in their clumsy attempt to explain why rape is such a problem for women in India. I argue that these men are constructed as subjects through media reporting. In this volume, the label 'problematic-male' is used, which sums up the way in which they are represented through and by the Western press. Whilst the men found guilty of the Delhi rape can be located in this poor and low-caste socio-economic group, and their crime was hideous and evil, the projection of a problematic-male subject serves to construct a stereotype through which all men in this demographic group will come to be judged. This stereotype will shape how others see this group of men, define their character and embed deeper their marginality, making more distant the possibility that they may claim a different, more prosperous, life for themselves. Doubtless within this group, as with all social groupings, and as both the Delhi and Mumbai cases attest, lie men who fail to curb their objectification of women and feel justified in utilising violence to control, possess and defile them. However, the realities of the rape statistics both in India and across the globe highlight that men who commit rape against women exist across the socio-economic-political spectrum;[5] the construction of a narrow problematic-male subject fails to acknowledge this reality and will therefore take us further away from eradicating rape in the lives of women.

This current chapter, then, will examine how different subaltern groups of men and women have emerged in the last few years through Western press reporting of rape in India, through an analysis of Western English-language newspaper reporting on rape in India. Although five years of reporting were surveyed, going back from October 2013, rape cases in India only appeared in the print press following the Delhi case in December 2012. Across the English-language press a total of 100 articles were reported, as noted above, these concerned two cases in which white Western women were the victims, while the remaining articles either focused on the Delhi and Mumbai case or took a broader perspective, highlighting the problem India faces not just with rape but also other forms of GBV and insinuating that India is increasingly unsafe for women. A significant number of articles looked to offer an explanation for why rape is prevalent, presenting a common narrative that highlights the poverty and low-caste status of rape perpetrators, who target middle-class and/or modern educated women in urban centres. As stated above, this narrative is inaccurate in the sense that perpetrators cut across socio-economic and geographic boundaries – as do the victims of rape. The fact that such a constructed image of a rapist has emerged needs to be interrogated and critiqued; it is, I argue, unhelpful in developing a nuanced and accurate picture of GBV and how it manifests not just in India but across the globe.

In the first section of this chapter, the theoretical frame will be presented; in particular, a summary of Spivak's work on gender and the subaltern adapted for the purpose of analysing masculinity and femininity. This section will also reintroduce Narayan's 'death by culture' critique introduced already in Chapter Two and highlight how this can clearly be seen in the Western reporting of rape in India.[6] The following section will explore the ways in which particular groups of Indian women have been rendered marginal through and by international press reporting, and here Roy's arguments will be used to frame and reinforce the argument. The implications of this silencing for feminist activism both inside and outside India will be considered. The third section will pull out key press articles that feed into and help to construct a male-problematic subject position. I show that the masculinity of low-caste rural men who have migrated to a city is projected as deviant and a threat to 'modern' women. Once again the implications of this subject framing for a nuanced and accurate understanding of GBV will be discussed, as well as the impact of this category for on the prospects and 'voice' of this masculine subaltern.

Death by culture

> For something is happening here, anger is overtaking fear. The dam has burst. The debate the politicians want is one of law and order, but the radical one is about how to *change the culture itself*. And because this is India we are talking about a myriad of

> cultures. Somehow, though, through the shock and the trauma, *this country is examining itself and its much-vaunted modernity does not look so modern.*[7]

The 'death by culture' narrative running through the passage above is reminiscent for many of us working within post-colonial theory. Narayan, in her much cited 1997 work, highlighted how the focus on culture in trying to explain violence against women in non-Western countries is problematic:

> I intend to argue that when such 'cultural explanations' are given for fatal forms of violence against Third World women, the effect is to suggest that Third World suffer 'death by culture'. I shall try and show that fatal forms of violence against mainstream Western women seem interestingly resistant to such 'cultural explanations', leaving Western women seemingly more immune to 'death by culture'. I believe that such asymmetries in 'cultural explanation' result in pictures of Third World women as 'victims of their culture' in ways that are interestingly different from the way in which victimisation of mainstream Western women is understood.[8]

Western media reporting gives the clear impression that Indian culture itself is the dimension found wanting and deficient in morals, and that thereby triggers and endorses violence against women, including rape. Rape has arisen as a particular horror not because it has newly emerged as a problem in women's lives in India, but because it is seen to pose a specific threat to India's claims to modernity. As the quote from Suzanne Moore in the *Guardian* given above states, 'this country is examining itself and its much-vaunted modernity does not look so modern.' The constructed, fabricated nature of these narratives is clear: Moore's article is an example of why Narayan's critique must be brought back to highlight the exceptional way culture is being blamed as the problem in India. However, Indian feminists argue that GBV is caused by a patriarchal gendered ideology that systematically devalues women at every level,[9] and patriarchy is an ideology that be identified in all contexts in which violence against women flourishes to some degree or another. Whilst I am in no way seeking to gloss over the horrific nature of GBV in India (quite the opposite), I argue that patriarchy and misogyny rather than culture should be the focus, as the key dimensions feeding into a gender ideology dominant the world over that devalues and renders women vulnerable to many forms of violence – and that this is what was played out in a truly horrific and extreme way on a bus in Delhi.

Given the world-wide realities of violence against women, it is reasonable to ask why 'culture' is so prominent in media explanations of rape in India. Out of 100 articles collected in our search, 70 directly refer to Indian culture as a key factor in the construction of the problematic-male perpetrator. Spivak offers a way of understanding the politicised nature of Western media reporting, in her observation that 'some of the most radical criticism coming out of the West today is the result of an interested desire to conserve the subject of the West, or the West as Subject.'[10] This can clearly be seen in the binaries underpinning the reporting of rape in India. Common themes call into question the legitimacy of India's claims to modernity, contrasted against Western societies who do not need to make such claims because they automatically reflect the civilised values of a progressive, enlightened world. These binaries cruelly deploy the power to manipulate the ideology of capitalist modernity in order to maintain Western geo-political superiority over India. The tone and hierarchy established through colonial narratives on India is long-established; in the nineteenth century, for instance, they were deployed in writings about the practice of *sati*. Richard Hartley Kennedy, a surgeon in the Bombay Medical Service, published an account in 1843, in which he wrote:

> Let us hope that a new day had dawned on India, and that these wretched sacrifices may be spoken of by future generations as things that were, before British dominion enlightened India.[11]

This binary hierarchy is retained and re-exerted in current Western press reporting on rape in India. There is also a stark lack of self-reflection in the narratives; for some scholars, the inequalities highlighted in the social demographic of India's urban centres can be traced to the Raj's systematic and symbolic embedding of a class-elitism into the very heart of the Indian social system, utilising the divisions already present through caste but carving still deeper trenches between layers of the population. This process has been identified as representing the greatest barrier to human development in India today.[12] The newspaper articles reviewed for this study lack any such awareness or sensitivity to this colonial history, and are in fact utterly ahistorical in their accounts of the rise of rape.

The imperialist project Spivak talks of in her analysis of *sati* accounts clearly resonates in these accounts of rape in India. She identifies a catachresis in the narratives she reviews that deliberately misreads alternative narratives or interpretations, distorting historical accounts for the purpose of adding strength to the imperialist project. This imperialist narrative is formed around 'a deviation from an ideal that is irreducibly differential'.[13] So that leads us to Spivak's key question and the subject of the next section: can the subaltern speak? In her critique of the colonial narrative in which she identifies the silent subaltern woman, Spivak frames the politics of imperialism as 'white men are saving brown women from brown men', and echoes of this can be seen in the reporting on rape in India, both in the ways in which groups of women are silenced and rendered subaltern through and in the pages but also in the construction of a male-problematic, from whom Indian women need saving. The question remains: saved by whom? Given the volume of articles that highlight India's inadequate claims to modernity, it would seem that the greater influence of Western values and morality will reverse the growing rape trend in India. However, modern values are for the most part seen as reflected in the neoliberal capitalist vision that is largely the product of the minds of a few white elite Western men.[14]

There are various ways in which the subaltern woman remains subaltern in press reports about rape.

The missing women

Arundhati Roy gave various television interviews in response to the Delhi rape, in which she made the following point:

> But the problem is that, why is THIS crime creating such a lot of outrage? It's because it plays in to the idea of the criminal poor, you know the vegetable vendor, the gym instructor, the bus driver, actually assaulting a middle-class girl, whereas when rape is used as a means of domination by upper castes, by the army or the police, it's actually not even punished. [. . .]
>
> I think that [this protest] will lead to some laws, perhaps an increased surveillance but all of that, I will repeat, all of that would protect middle-class women. But in other places, we're not looking for laws. There ARE laws but when the police themselves go and burn down villages and gang-rape women, I have personally listened to so many testimonies of women to whom this has been done. [. . .]
>
> But the other thing is that there IS this widening gap between the rich and the poor. Earlier at least the rich did what they did with a fair amount of discretion. But now it's all out there, on television, you know, all the sort of conspicuous consumption. And there is an anger and a psychosis building up, and women at the top, in the middle and at the bottom ARE going to pay the price for it.[15]

Eighty-five articles written on rape in India focus solely on documenting the Delhi and Mumbai cases, with a further two focusing on the rape of Western women in India. The voices and experiences of poor, rural, low-caste women for whom rape and other forms of GBV represent a structural reality are not only ignored but their subalternality deepened by this reporting; their existence obliterated by the focus on these two cases, which whilst brutal and oppressive, fails to acknowledge the many others. Those articles that do seek to highlight how widespread the occurrence of rape is fail to identify these others to whom this violence happens and to give them a subject position from which to speak for themselves their lives and struggles. For example, the passage below gives voice to the case of a Swiss woman brutally gang-raped, but the article then moves to on the Delhi rape. In between the two cases it cites countrywide statistics on rape, but no mention is given to who these other 24,200 women raped are. These two women suffered vicious and brutal experiences, but they were chosen for this article because of their privilege and status: in one case, because she was an affluent Western woman, and in the other as an example of the possibilities open to women whose families can scrape together enough money for a decent education. The article is thus an example of the kind of thing that concerns Roy (emphases added):

> An Indian court has sentenced six men convicted of the gang-rape of a Swiss woman to life imprisonment, a lawyer in the case said.
>
> The 39-year-old Swiss woman was raped while camping with her husband in a forest in the central Indian state of Madhya Pradesh in mid-March. Three months earlier, a student was gang-raped and beaten in a moving bus and thrown bleeding on to the street in a case that triggered mass protests.
>
> 'It was a good judgment. It came early,' said Rajendra Tiwari, a lawyer for the government.
>
> The National Crime Records Bureau says more than 24,200 rapes were reported across India in 2011 – about one every 20 minutes. Police estimate only four out of 10 rapes are reported, largely due to victims' fear of being shamed by their families and communities.
>
> The gang rape of a 23-year-old woman on a bus on 16 December in New Delhi sparked a global outcry over the issue and brought thousands of people onto the streets to demand better policing to prevent sex crimes. The trainee physiotherapist later died from her injuries.
>
> An American tourist was gang-raped by a group of men in a hill resort in northern India in June. In March, a British woman jumped out of her hotel balcony in Uttar Pradesh state to escape a feared sexual assault.[16]

A significant number of the articles (35) subsequent to the Delhi gang-rape on 16 December 2012 also highlight a case of rape against Western women; once again, the focus on these cases, whilst revealing utterly horrific instances of rape, masks the realities of violence for so many other groups of women in India by silencing them through a failure to acknowledge their experiences:

> A British tourist in India leapt 20ft from her hotel window fearing that she was about to be sexually attacked after a man allegedly tried to burst into her room.
>
> The incident has put a further dent in India's reputation as a relatively safe place for female travellers, coming days after the gang rape of a Swiss tourist.
>
> Last Friday night a Swiss tourist was raped during a cycling holiday with her husband in Madhya Pradesh, about 125 miles from Agra. Six men charged with gang rape appeared in court on Monday.
>
> [...] The Foreign Office updated its advice for female travellers this week, warning them to use caution when travelling in India.[17]

The last sentence of this article is interesting as it highlights the revised UK Foreign and Commonwealth Office travel advice given to British women thinking of travelling to India, which alerts female travellers to the need to take extra care.

In reality, India has not suddenly become a more unsafe place for women, and neither, when the global statistics are looked at, is it significantly more violent towards women then other places for which a similar warning is not given. The FCO is clearly responding to the hysteria generated by the cases reported in the press and, although understandable, it feeds into and supports this construction of Indian culture as not yet civilised, not safe enough for British women to travel in.

In the next article, *sati* is presented alongside rape as if it too is widely practised. A number of scholars have written about how colonial accounts of *sati* were manipulated to provide evidence for the civilising project of the Raj, and one example of this is given above.[18] The conflation of *sati* and rape is unhelpful for various reasons. Only a handful of cases of *sati* were reported in the 1990s; it certainly was not widespread, and scholars argue it never in fact was. Rape is not unique to India yet the positioning of rape alongside *sati* suggests there is something uniquely Indian about it (emphasis added):

> *Extreme violence against women may be nothing new in India, where sati, or widow burning, was practised as recently as the late 1990s.* But the

> number of reported cases of rape and, in particular, gang rape, appears to have increased sharply in recent years. In 2011, there were more than 24,000 reported *rapes in India*, a 9.2 per cent rise over the previous year. The real figure is almost certainly far higher, as so many cases go unreported.
>
> However, Kaimini Jaiswal, a feminist lawyer, says there is a simpler answer. 'This has always been going on in India – but rape never used to be reported. Women just suffered in silence. These days, it is getting reported much more and women are coming out and talking about it.'[19]

Further parts of this article, published in *The Times*, are critiqued and analysed below.

The subaltern male

I now turn in this section to the how, through these newspaper articles, a problematic-male has emerged, which has the effect of creating a subaltern out of all men who potentially classify under this label. Specifically, the category refers to poor men recently migrated from villages to an Indian city. The following article in particular sums up the category as it emerges in a significant number of reports (emphases added):

> *Indian cities are awash with feral men, untethered from their distant villages*, divorced from family and social structure, fighting poverty, exhausted, denied access to regular female companionship, adrift on powerful tides of alcohol and violent pornography, newly exposed to the smart young women of the cities, with their glistening jobs and clothes and casual independence – and not able to respond to any of it in a safe, civilized manner. *This is the world of women under siege, the medieval world of the walking undead, the rise of the zombies*, targeting females rich and poor. For women, at least, winter is coming.[20]

This passage, and 55 out of the 100 collected, clearly constructs a 'problematic-male subject' who, because of his poverty and low-class caste and educational status, is both marginal and subaltern within

India's wider booming society. This male subject-other is the face of this most heinous rape case which in turn is presented not as an exception but as revealing a dark and immoral secret about the realities of violence against women in India. And so, through these articles exploring the lives of this subaltern man, an image emerges of an uncivilised other within India's now civilised and modern interior; a convenient focus of blame as India feels the pressure to find an explanation acceptable to the outside world.

Common threads through the narratives that project this 'other' are descriptions of a character that is volatile and untamed, as indicated by the phrase 'feral and untethered'. These descriptions present the moral characters of these perpetrators through descriptions of their environment, for example in the passage below (emphasis added):

> Two of the killer-rapists came from a squalid slum colony of New Delhi called Ravi Das colony, one of dozens in the national capital, and thousands across the nation. While there are productive and even 'dynamic' slums, such as Dharavi in Mumbai (Asia's largest), which has thriving industries in its midst, many if not most slums are *hotbeds of despair, alcoholism, drug abuse and lawlessness* where police do not bother or dare to even enter.
>
> A lot has been said about the need to change Indian males' centuries' old misogynistic attitudes and backward mindsets towards women.[21]

The phrase 'hotbeds of despair, alcoholism, drug abuse and lawlessness' could serve as keywords for a number of articles; they paint a vivid picture of the environment from which the perpetrators emerge, and the reader is left with no doubt over the likely character and moral dysfunction instilled through such places. Other passages go further in offering explanation for how this moral underclass arrived in India's shinny metropolis, highlighting how out-of-place and ill-at-ease they must be surrounded by modernity and 'civilisation' (emphasis added):

> Delhi itself has a particular problem because tens of thousands of newly urbanised people, from villages still almost *medieval, live*

> *alongside modern workers* including liberated women. Many young men consider 'Eve-teasing' (the disgustingly coy subcontinent euphemism for sexual harassment and assault) as their male birth right. The rapists in this case were, we are told, from this demographic; their victim a medical student whose parents sold their land to pay for her education.[22]

The backwardness of this 'male-problematic' is once again highlighted above and constructed against the advanced 'others' of India's cities. The word 'medieval' clearly resonates and reflects the kind of language used by the colonisers in describing the urgent need to civilise a culture whose difference they presented as backwardness. It is not much different from the words of the American writer Katherine Mayo, published in 1927:

> Take a girl twelve years old, a pitiful physical specimen in bone and blood, illiterate, ignorant, without any sort of training in habits of health. Force motherhood upon her at the earliest possible moment. Rear her weakling son intensive vicious practices that drain his small vitality day by day.[23]

A further strand to this narrative emerges here, that tells of India's progress in women's rights and the opportunities available to women, in contrast against the statistics on violence against women. The word 'liberated' is used to describe the status of urban professional women; a loaded term which carries implications of a negative, oppressed life lived before a transformation occurred which saw women lifted from the shackles of a backward society. In other words, we understand the meaning of 'liberated' because it is contrasted against a picture of an unliberated or backward state of being. Feminist discourses around liberation emerged out of second-wave feminist theory, influenced in particular by the writings of white, middle-class scholars such as Mary Daly.[24] This feminist thought has been heavily critiqued, most famously by Chandra Mohanty in her much-cited work 'Under Western Eyes' (also discussed in Chapter Two), in which she identifies a category of liberated white, middle-class Western woman that is contrasted against the oppressed state of women in the so-called 'Third World'[25]. The mission for liberated women was to release other women from their backwardness. This narrative can clearly be seen running through many of the articles collected for this study. Rape is depicted as an act of backlash against the progress Indian women have made towards liberation. In other words, the rape of modern, Westernised Indian women is seen as an attempt to pull them back and reduce their freedom. The articles infer that something must urgently be done to stop this backlash before it reverses the inroads made by many Indian women. However, before action can be taken an explanation must be reached. The explanation given through these articles for this persistent abuse is the existence of a 'male-problematic' that now, the articles suggest, must become the focus of a new civilising project. Fifty articles stress that India's women are well on the way to liberation, as is clear from the opportunities of which the rape victim herself was able to take advantage (albeit through her parent's indebtedness and hard work rather than being born into a middle-class family). The message is clear: if you are prepared to work hard and make sacrifices it is possible to progress to a modern prosperous status. This progression is understood in terms of a shift not just in wealth status but in subjectivity, marked by a move away from backwardness. The male-problematic, then, has emerged as the end marker of the spectrum of backwardness against which all other Indian subjects are measured. This can be seen again in the next passage, in which the rampant, uncontrolled nature of male sexuality is again constructed and projected as problematic (emphasis added):

> In a country where reported sexual violence is increasing – despite heightened attention to the problem – many say the women-only spaces are a welcome *refuge from lewd looks, groping and unwanted male attention*.[26]

Returning to the article from *The Times* discussed above, this problematic-male is presented as newly created in the passage below, emerging as an unwanted by-product of rapid urbanisation (emphasis added):

> A variety of explanations have been offered up, from a widening gender imbalance, to rapid urbanisation, which has left huge

> *numbers of rootless young men, often with little education and few opportunities.*[27]

A second aspect of the male-problematic is a rampant sexuality that is rendered wild by the sight of young Indian women displaying their liberation and Westernisation (so it is suggested) by wearing Western clothes. So the story unfolds in these articles of a male-problematic emerging as the enemy to modern Indian women, lusting over their bodies, resentful at the success they seem to have achieved:

> Such men see successful and ambitious young women on their way to work in short skirts, laughing and holding hands with boyfriends. Cue scorn, anger, envy and lust. I put lust at the end of that list, because rape has always had an element of contempt, a desire to put uppity women in their place. Ask any prison psychiatrist: serial rapists often hated their mothers or were rejected by girls.[28]

The second half of this article broadens its proposed explanation of rape in India by pointing to the whole of Indian culture as problematic and uncivilised when contrasted against the civilised world of the West. The blatant negativity woven through this narrative is again a jolt back to the tone and language of colonial writings (emphasis added):

> But India can't pin the whole atrocity on a few bad boys. The current healthy protest – long may it last – demands a wider change. A benign cultural earthquake is necessary if the country, one of the world's four big boom economies, can be allowed to *hold its head up in the civilised world.*[29]

One of the most sensitively written pieces, much heralded on social media for offering a so-called 'balanced' picture of the wider context leading up to the Delhi rape, was written by Jason Burke of the *Guardian*. Yet even his more nuanced focus presenting in-depth life histories of the perpetrators feeds into and fuels further the creation of a problematic-male subject (emphases added):

For Ram and Mukesh Singh, 34 and 26 years old, Ravi Das Colony had been home for most of their lives. Ram earned a living as the driver of a bus that, albeit without the necessary permits, carried schoolchildren. Ram's brother, fired from a dozen jobs, intermittently drove a taxi.

The two had grown up on a small homestead in Karauli, a remote eastern part of the state of Rajasthan, five hours by train from the capital. They attended a local school with few facilities and an often absent teacher, playing in the fields and dried riverbeds. They came to Delhi in 1997. India was then beginning to boom after the reforms of the early 1990s injected a new capitalist energy into the sclerotic, quasi-socialist-quasi-feudal economy, and their landless labourer parents decided to try their luck in the capital [. . .].

Though they left local girls alone, the *Singh brothers were known among their neighbours for drunkenness, petty crime and occasional, unpredictable violence.*

Both the 17-year-old, known as *Raju, and Thakur had their own troubled histories. Their paths had taken them through a side of India that has less to do with the emerging economic powerhouse of international repute and more to do with a tenacious, older India riven by conflict, poverty, chaos and random violence.*

The eldest of five children, Raju was born to a destitute day labourer with mental health issues and his wife in a village 150 miles east of Delhi, in the vast northern state of Uttar Pradesh which has 180 million inhabitants and socio-economic indicators often worse than those in sub-Saharan Africa.

As in rural Rajasthan, where the Singh brothers came from, *women in the countryside of Uttar Pradesh suffer systematic sexual harassment and often violence. Rape is common and gang rape frequent.* Victims are habitually blamed for supposedly enticing their attackers. Many are forced to marry their assailants; others kill themselves rather than live with the social stigma of being 'dishonoured'. Police rarely register a complaint, let alone investigate.[30]

The narrow nature of the article unhelpfully continues to perpetuate the colonial narrative, with a final paragraph quoted above commenting on the wider social-cultural environment highlighting the normalisation of violence against women in the daily lives of these perpetrators. The article's content does reflect some of what feminist activists argue about the normalisation and legitimisation of violence against women, but rather than encouraging a more sophisticated and critical insight into GBV, it establishes more firmly this view that India has still not civilised. Not only are problematic-male subjects allowed to exercise their unleashed sexualities, fuelled and motivated by their poverty and marginality, but violence itself is seen as woven into the very heart of the culture.

This article is novel in its approach and attempt to get close to the perpetrators and to understand the social-cultural-economic contexts from which they come, but the piece does not give space for any man fitting the problematic-male profile to speak for himself about his life experiences or to comment and reflect on the brutality of those accused who share their upbringing and lot in life. In a similar way, the poor rural women identified as rape victims are not given a voice, but their existence is at least acknowledged even though they are not given space to challenge for themselves and on their own terms the violence they face.

To reiterate once again, in this chapter I am not for one moment suggesting that violence is not an embedded reality in women's lives; rather, I am arguing that it is not exceptional to India, and furthermore that efforts to eradicate it will not be helped by negative stereotyping which serves to condemn and further marginalise those already oppressed whilst contributing to the silencing of other subaltern groups whose experiences are rendered invisible by the dominance of a few high profile cases. Even attempts to interrogate the normalisation of violence feeds into an image of India as having a problematic culture by suggesting certain global trends are specifically Indian. This can be seen in references to pornography (emphasis added):

> Secondly, (and even more important than the highly sexualized music videos) studies show that among the biggest watchers of

> pornography are boys between the ages of 12 and 18. *The constant bombardment of pornographic images filled with abuse and violence* (supposedly enjoyed by these women) ingrained on these young minds goes way beyond sexism. Little wonder they don't see the problem of chanting a song about underage sex.[31]

Similarly, the passage below suggests that pornography renders women vulnerable to a society filled with rapists (emphasis added):

> Others cite the spread of the internet and *its access to pornography*, and evolving social attitudes, which mean women are more visible in the workforce – and more *vulnerable to rapists*.[32]

Pornography, feminists argue, objectifies women's bodies in a way that renders them vulnerable to violence and abuse, but the sex industry is global and has grown propelled by technologies that support its expansion into markets previously less influenced by it. Pornography therefore is a global problem with global consequences for women's rights. The way in which it is presented in coverage such as the above suggests it is fuelling violence against women in India in a unique way, feeding the view that the culture is backward.

In the passage below again the impression is given of a country filled with sexually unleashed men, and doubt is cast over India's ability to rectify this injustice (emphasis added):

> *Considering research showing that one in four Indian men has committed sexual violence at some point in their lives*, is India serious about pursuing bloody barters in still more cases? The answer is unclear, but the eye-for-an-eye sentiment that has permeated public discussion has allowed a great wrong to be addressed inadequately and perhaps unjustly. Indeed, it is unquestionable that at least three crucial learning moments are slipping through India's fingers.[33]

This male-problematic has become a useful subject onto which to pin the blame for rape, and indeed other forms of GBV. The reality that rape perpetrators cut across socio-economic and caste lines is missed and this in itself produces an epistemic violence which further marginalises and problematises a particular group of men who already struggle to carve out a dignified existence. As Spivak states in relation to the colonial construction of a subaltern woman:

> Yet the assumption and construction of a consciousness or subject sustains such work and will, in the long run, cohere with the work of imperialist subject-constitution, mingling epistemic violence with the advancement of learning and civilisation. And the subaltern woman will be as mute as ever.[34]

And so this story of imperialist subject-constitution remerges yet again in the creation of this male-problematic, which does nothing more than provoke a resurgence of feeling and sentiment further rendering silent those who struggle in their daily lives to find a voice. This male-problematic is now feared not just in India but globally, as an image lodged in the imagery of outsiders that supports this notion of blame pinned to this male-problematic. For example, in the passage below:

> This week in Singapore, a young woman told me how she had put off a long-dreamed of trip to India.
>
> I'd been hoping to go for a spiritual retreat but then there was all that stuff with the rape case, she said. So instead, I planned a trip with my family to Thailand. On Tuesday, she hopped on a plane to Bangkok.[35]

This passage highlights the influence and impact press reporting clearly has – as if we didn't know – in shaping public perspectives which in turn influence behaviour. And here is the danger that lies behind the distorted and twisted manipulations of how violence manifests itself in India. The narratives we have presented clearly do more to support the continuation of an imperialist project than they contribute to the feminist campaign in response to the violence women face in their daily lives across urban–rural and caste boundaries.

Conclusion

This chapter has presented an analysis of Western English-language press reporting of rape in India. The findings reveal that rape in India was not reported prior to the Delhi case of December 2012. In reviewing the cases, a worrying narrative can be seen, resonant of the colonial discourse depicting Indians as uncivilised and not yet enlightened. This rape case, although undeniably brutal, has opened up an uncomfortable reality, highlighting that the colonial lens is still the dominant perspective through which India is viewed in Western public discourse. These negative colonial narratives are seen across the broadsheet and tabloid press, some with shocking blatancy in their directness in accusing India of barbarism and backwardness. The word 'uncivilised' is used in numerous articles to characterise the society in which this rape case occurred. This chapter certainly does not deny the realities of violence against women in India, but it argues that distorted and negative images of how GBV manifests itself in India does not support the work of feminist organisations, who have campaigned on this issue for decades. The complex nexus of violence in India, as across the globe, is lost in the oversimplification and demonisation of a relatively small section of the population – added to which, only a small group of Indian women are acknowledged as victims, leaving the plight of many who face brutal atrocities of sexual, physical, psychological and economic violence on a daily basis marginalised and ignored.

Ironically, in maintaining this colonial narrative in the reporting of rape the press itself commits an act of violence, not directly physical but epistemic, recreating an illusion that masks and hides lived experiences that may help us understand what is really happening in India. There is no doubt that GBV is a problem in India, but the false representation of a singular category of 'perpetrator' neatly demographically defined does not bring us closer to unravelling the gendered web that supports many forms of abuse and injustice against women. This chapter urges critical reflection on the part of the media, which needs to go further in deconstructing the imperialist lens through which it views and represents India.

PART III

THE FEMINIST MOVEMENT AND ITS STRUGGLES WITH THE RIGHT

CHAPTER 5

THE CHANGING FACE OF THE FEMINIST MOVEMENT IN INDIA

Introduction

In this chapter I offer a brief overview of the dynamics of the women's movement. There has never been a singular women's movement in India; what exists today could perhaps be described as an overarching collective in which gender politics is articulated, converging at points on key issues such as GBV. In other words, a number of different organisations operate separately but come together to form strategic networks; however, these networks are momentary and should not be mistaken for universal agreement on a particular type of gender politics. I will consider how some of the earlier organisations, such as the All Women's National Conference,[1] are still working across India alongside much newer networks that operate increasingly through the use of social media. Some of the youth-led initiatives that mobilise around particular issues perhaps characterise a new turn in movement politics in India. At the same time, there is an array of grassroots organisations, many still influenced by Gandhi, that largely work in rural settings, empowering women to set up micro-businesses and self-help groups. This chapter, then, will offer a historic overview of the emergence of a simultaneously cohesive and fractious movement. It will offer case studies of specific organisations of different types, drawing on interviews with activists who work for them. Themes that emerge across those interviews highlight agreement that GBV is the most pervasive and urgent issue that needs to be addressed. Many also talk about a backlash against modernisation that has made the situation worse for many women. There is some disagreement over whether engagement with global women's networks is a useful way of achieving specific goals in India; this chapter will also discuss the increased role that men play in the feminist movement and consider how this shift relates to prospects of reducing GBV.

This chapter is divided into two broad sections. The first offers a brief history of the women's movement, while the second presents a summary of views collected through various activists working on women's rights in India. The activists interviewed are cross-generational, allowing for subtle differences to emerge. The interviews specifically focused on the relative success and longevity of the anti-rape movement.

A brief history of the women's movement in India

During the era of the British Raj a number of women's organisations emerged; they were arguably influenced by the rhetoric of the colonial administration, which used instances of atrocities practised against Indian women as evidence of the need for their civilising influence.[2] As outsiders, they could claim the role of protector of Indian women, interceding on their behalf against brutal patriarchal practices.[3] The Raj set about introducing a social reform movement, encouraging the emergence of a new Indian elite who looked upon atrocities performed against women as a minor obstacle that needed to be overcome in order for India to move forward and modernise. A number of women's organisations emerged influenced by this colonial ideology: these included the Brahmo Samaj in eastern India, the Prarthana Samaj in western India, the Arya Samaj in northern India and the Theosophical Society in southern India. These groups were run by elite men and did not challenge the structural underpinnings that rendered many oppressed and marginalised by the caste system and gender ideology, but a small group of elite women were alleviated through access to education and political roles, and achieved positions from which they could begin to highlight women's issues more effectively – albeit from their position of privilege.[4]

However, some women who had not received a formal education were nevertheless still able draw attention to their conditions. One example of this is Rassundari Devi (born around 1809), who was entirely self-taught and who wrote the first autobiography by an Indian woman:

> I was so immersed in a sea of housework that I was not conscious of what I was going through day and night. After some time the desire to learn how to read properly grew very strong in me. I was angry with myself for wanting to read books. Girls did not read [...]. People used to despise women of learning [...]. In fact, older women used to show a great deal of displeasure if they saw a piece of paper in the hands of a woman. But somehow I could not accept this.[5]

Sen offers a useful account of key figures and moments in the history of Indian feminism.[6] In 1910, Saraladevi Chaudhurani created the Bharat Stree Mahamandal (Great Group of Indian Women) in Allahabad, because she felt there was a need for women to have their own associations that were not just adjuncts to male-led organisations. As a result of this first association others emerged – mostly called Mahila Samitis – which were locally focused and supported small-scale activities such as skills training. These smaller associations set the way for larger national associations to emerge which were also influenced by the first wave of nationalist agitation: the Women's Indian Association (1917), the National Council of Indian Women (1925) and the All-India Women's Conference (1927). As Sen observes: 'Both the Women's Indian Association and the National Council of Indian Women claimed to represent all Indian women, but they were far removed from the masses of women whom they confidently sought to benefit.'[7] The All-India Women's Conference, however, was perhaps more successful in offering national representation to women through an alliance with the Indian National Congress. It was able in its first ten years to make progress with legislation to protect and promote women's rights, for example the Hindu Child and Marriage Bill (1927). Other important early women's movements included Bharat Mahila Parishad (1904) and the Kasturba Gandhi National Memorial Trust (see case study below).

Leading on from the establishment of women's associations, women's participation in political campaigns was legitimised. The Indian National Congress reached out to peasant and women's movements at the grassroots, in an attempt to generate support for a mass movement. However, and as Sen[8] points out, whilst the movement opened up to women of any socio-economic status, only elite women were able to occupy political and publicly visible positions. Gandhi has left a lasting legacy on the women's movement: he arguably feminised the nationalist movement through his emphasis on *Satyagraha*, which focused on non-violent protest and opened up a space for female activism. He stressed that men could learn from the self-sacrificing nature of women, stating that this lay at the heart of his vision for a non-violent movement. As a result, Gandhian ideology has influenced many significant feminists, such as Madhu Kishwar, founder of the feminist publication *Manuski*, as well as an array of grassroots organisations such as the Gandhi Memorial Society in Pune.

The Gandhi Memorial Society

The Gandhi Memorial Society is housed in what is now called the Aga Khan Palace in Pune, which has become a national monument of India's freedom movement. Following the launch of the Quit India Movement in 1942, the British colonial government interned Gandhi, his wife Kasturba and his secretary Mahadevbhai Desai in the palace from 5 August 1942–6 May 1944. Kasturba and Mahadevbhai both died during their internment and their *samadhis* are located in the grounds. Not surprisingly, the place has become a national and international place of pilgrimage. After his wife's death Gandhi requested that the palace be developed into a place of emancipation for women. On the centenary of Gandhi's birth in 1969, H.H. Prince Karim Aga Khan donated the building to the nation as a mark of respect for Gandhi and his philosophy; on 15 August 1972 a Gandhi museum was inaugurated and in 1980 the Gandhi Smarak Nidhi transferred the museum's management, the *samadhis* and the palace campus to the Gandhi National Memorial Society in New Delhi (the Gandhian movement's main headquarters in India).

The primary goal of the society is to offer vocational training and education to enable rural women to seek employment or set up their own businesses. At the heart of this approach is the belief that the best way to empower women is through access to education and training. In 1988 the Gandhi Memorial Society set up the Kasturba Mahila Khadi Gramodyog Vidyalaya, the first women's training centre in India. Initially, it only taught weaving, but it now offers a choice of 23 trades to around 1,500 women each year.

I have previously interviewed the director of the Gandhi Memorial Society of Pune.[9] In particular, I asked her about her vision of female empowerment, and what the term meant to her. She described the process of empowerment in terms of being an 'awakening and a knowledge of rights.'[10] The work of the Gandhian Memorial Trust is rooted in Gandhi's own notion of empowered womanhood:

> My contribution to the great problem [of women's role in society] lies in my presenting acceptance of truth and *ahimsa* in every walk of life, whether for individuals or nations. I have hugged the hope that in this woman will be the unquestioned leader and having thus found her place in human evolution will shed her inferiority complex.[11]

However, despite the acknowledged influence that Gandhi had on Indian feminism, he is not without critics. Sen summarises Forbes' critique of Gandhi's claim that female demonstrators and nationalist leaders included the participation of all women, when in fact upper- and middle-class Hindus dominated the movement. The limitation of Gandhi's political idiom was the elitism of political participation: he used feminised icons like Sita, Savitri and Damayanto in an attempt to resonate with women of all castes but in reality these images project a hyper-patriarchal vision of femininity and so do little to really undermine the status quo given that even women themselves manipulate associated narratives into more radical visions of the world.[12] As Forbes further points out, Gandhi also continued to exclude Muslims from his movement.[13]

In summary, throughout the history of the women's movement in India women mobilised to protest violence, discrimination and rising prices, and agitated for better living conditions through higher wages, the prohibition of liquor and the provision of drinking water.[14] These women represented a wide range of castes, classes and communities, rural and urban, but as over time differences among these women grew, solidarity – if it ever existed – fractured. This was particularly apparent in 1986, when the developing tensions were exposed and fuelled by the Shah Bano case. Shah Bano, a 62-year-old Muslim mother of five had been divorced by her husband in 1978. She filed a criminal suit in the Supreme Court, in which she won the right to an allowance from her husband and his relatives. However, under pressure from Muslim groups, the ruling Congress Party caved in and reversed the judgement. Discrimination against women in personal law had been on the women's movement's agenda since the 1920s, but the Shah Bano case catapulted the issue into a crisis of national proportions. The case intensified a process in which nationalist ideology, religious fundamentalism, communalism and caste tensions were pitted on the site of gender. These tensions played out in the women's movement, which resulted in it losing its fragile unity and broad identity. In this first phase of the movement, differences and diversities were contained in order for concerted political engagement to take place, but the end of this period is marked by the loss of this unity.

Moving into a more contemporary period, women's movement organisations such as the All Women's National Conference have had close links with the Congress Party, and as such do not challenge male political leadership structures but instead pursue a mainly welfare orientated agenda. As such, there has been no demand from within the women's movement to radically restructure the underpinnings of society in a way that would make gender equality possible. Under Indira Gandhi in the 1970s more localised struggles emerged, which helped to solidify a grassroots culture of activism, but still, when it came to gender issues, campaigns were not radical enough to pose any real challenge to the patriarchal status quo.

The Shifting Activist Perspective

The key question moving forward for the shared goal of eradicating GBV is the extent to which the catalyst for change will come from within the historical and established movements or out of the emergent youth movement, which is drawing on social media to promote its campaigns. Many feel that the recent anti-rape movement represents a new era in the history of the women's movement, committed and strategically focused on a single issue: the eradication of violence in all forms from the lives women and girls. When comparing the views of younger activists to those of the older generation, an optimism is present. For example, interviews with three young post-graduates training to be community media activists revealed agreement amongst their peers that the rape protests signalled a shift in youth attitudes.[15] They themselves felt, as a result of the Delhi-based protests, an increased sense of mobilisation to improve gender equality. Their efforts have included a Facebook campaign, in which photos of individuals from different professions and stages in life are posted alongside their opinion on violence against women. They also urge those who have suffered any level of abuse to post on Facebook immediately, in order to highlight the prevalence of abuse and as an attempt to shame perpetrators, and they believe that the younger generation of activists has initiated many similar social media campaigns. They are optimistic that change is possible; as one of those I spoke with told me: 'It isn't a question of "will things change?" They simply have to, we cannot continue to tolerate any form of gender-based discrimination.' These interviews highlight how successful the anti-rape campaign has been in terms of offering and even creating youth platforms. Social media has enabled new forms of activism to emerge that can tap into transnational networks. Those whose activism includes the use of social media seem to have a greater sense of optimism, perhaps nurtured by online discussion forums and access to wider networks of politically vocal people. Social media certainly seems to act as a catalyst for sustained psychological determination. My interviews with different activists aimed to reveal the extent to which views are shared between activists from different backgrounds and ages.

As stated at the start of this chapter, understanding the current dynamics of the women's movement requires not just a historical perspective, mapping shifts in formation and emphasis, but also an examination of generational differences. I have so far in this chapter, and also in the chapters of Part Two of this volume, captured the views of young (late twenties) community and legal activists and a director (mid-forties) of a rural women's organisation. These views can be contrasted with those of an activist who has been involved in the movement for a number of decades and is now in her sixties. Here, I have given her the name 'Gaytri'. Given her vast experience of working in the women's movement, the interview is longer than the others discussed in this work, and I present it more or less in full so that her voice clearly comes through.

> Circumstances just sort of tip the scales and a lot of us think really that that's what and it just became the time what it was just something you read in the papers and thought it's another one of those terrible instances. Partly the brutality and partly the fact that it was so brazen in that it was 9.30 at night, partly the fact that no-one stopped to help, not that many people do. But everything just came together and made a huge impact; what was very different this time is the general outrage, it wasn't just women's groups, it wasn't just activists, not just people who have been talking and agitating about it for a long time but a huge swathe of society that I think was just galvanised into being vocal and for a long time, I mean it continued a very long time after this poor woman died. It led to the justice [...] commission which really did issue some very stringent guidelines.
>
> *Do you think they will make a difference?*
>
> I am not sure that legislation alone can make a difference, it seldom does anyway. What it has done is shine a light, a very bright light, on the police force, on the judiciary and on the general acceptance levels of society at large, and that I think has come in for a bit of a jolt. So there is a response across the board, where people cannot excuse it anymore, you can't pass the buck by people – I mean the authorities the police the criminal justice

system the justice system – the remind all of that and the legal implementation no can really get away with saying the case was badly framed or evidence was omissible, all those alibis which have been used for a long time to somehow minimise its gravity so that is difficult to do now, so in that sense it has been a very big change in terms of social perception, societal awareness, the fact that there was such a big outcry and that people at large were involved lots and lots of college-going students because this kind of vulnerability every woman faces, every college-going student, simply because the public transport system isn't secure and hasn't been very long time; as I was saying, where earlier it was something that you lived with and you somehow tried to protect yourself against, now there is an insistence that public security be provided. So I think in those terms there has been a difference but I am not sure how long it is going to last.

How sustainable are the protests?

I am not sure it is going to be so easy to brush it under the carpet anymore. So whether it makes for a sea change in the way that the police and the criminal system deal with it is one matter but the fact that they are being cavalier about it is picked up very quickly by the media now. There has been a huge increase in the reporting of crime, particularly rape – it is not easy to see where these reports are coming from because that information is not easily available to us; of course, if you go to the national bureau you can get profiles of people and see the kinds of social class, the economic class, of the complainant and also of the perpetrator, you would probably be able to get a picture, but one can't say without doing a serious kind of breakdown of all of that it's very difficult to say, it's not easy to generalise on that. But of course it is true that very few middle- or upper-class women would report a rape even if it were to happen [. . .] and that needs to change, but marital rape is not a crime so far so even if you were to report it that would never figure.

I would say that perhaps this would enable perhaps the younger generation small towns where the stigma is huge – its huge everywhere but what I am saying is that it is much more damaging in other contexts so perhaps it will encourage women to speak up, but whom? It's a very fine line between speaking out and then being ostracised.

What do you think about the global reporting on rape?

There is a tendency towards giving the impression that everyone is a potential rapist, that it is a really terrible place and all women are a potential victim and it has no meaning so one just stripes the page frankly [. . .] and there are travel advisories [. . .] and they go back to widow burning and dowry deaths and everything will get conflated and it becomes part of one terrible reality or continuum, there is not breaks, no differences, no real understanding of these very different crimes. It is very reductionist and is the way the other is demonised. This reductionism will not shift for as long as Orientalism is still around, it has just reshaped in light of the end of colonies, the language is still around and the Orientalist perspective is constantly reinforced and plays to a stereotype and the second thing which I think is equally important is that as long as in this case the Western press and the academy is not listening to the work that is done by academics, activists by social civil society, how will that perception change? If it is still a process of observing this strange and odd culture within its own frame of reference how will that change? It is not possible so it is not surprising as it is an issue of voice and whether there is anyone to listen to that voice. There is a vocal enough voice here, I mean it's not as if there is no voice, it is not a mute object but someone has to be listening [. . .] and who do they (the media) think are legitimate voices to present? Where do these reports come from, who are the correspondents? Which are the news agencies?

Huge criticism of billion raising, which was big here, but to do something for only a day, I don't know how truly transnational that is, it happens across the world but what does that mean? Because I don't see any sustainability in what is happening. Certainly the movement here is so preoccupied by its own compulsions activism even across South Asia is much less co-ordinated than it used to be. On the whole the South Asian women's movement is not as active across borders as it used to be. It's partly a phase, partly that the early generation of activists are much older, they are into other things, institution building, writing they are not the kind of vigorous activism that used to be the case 20 or 25 years ago and a younger generation of activists uses very different forms and they do very different things so there may be a lot of interaction and change issues of sexuality, but not necessary in issues of work, there may be a lot more cross-border engagement and activism on conflict and on peace and not as much on violence. So here the ground has shifted a little and the issues have shifted and people were very active a while back on issues of fundamentalism and personal laws and so on, its more or less zero now, so it's a combination of all of these things, not just one prolonged projected conflict across the region, means a lot of village groups and activists are working on that across the subcontinent because every single country is experiencing it. So I think that there is, you know, activism around gender-based violence is much more national and internationally I really not see anything at all.

Has social media had an impact on feminist activism?

I don't know what the evidence is for the impact of social media, feminist India, is a popular social media group, there are 50–100 exchanges a day but I don't see them as international or even national, they are a closed group and individual members or groups may have very active links with some groups somewhere else but that is the extent of it and those links are not necessarily activist, do you know what I mean? We are not campaigning for them, they are not campaigning for us, at the most there will be a signing of a UN document and at the most there will be exchange on trafficking on issues that really do cross borders on a daily basis but I don't really see an internationalism anymore.

Is that worrying?

We have seen a huge rightward shift across the world. And when that happens economically and socially I don't think it is very easy for women to mobilise. And that's something you will find. Where is European feminism for example? Where is American feminism? They are only active on black feminism; I mean they are rolling back on abortion faster than they can say the word. Where is the mobilising around that internationally? It's a huge issue, it's as big an issue as violence, but I don't see any activism and that was the criticism of one billion-rising; frankly, I think it is much more of an event [. . .], I can't see anything being that effective internationally frankly, as far as all those international conventions and seminars and international instruments are concerned those will continue and that kind of internationalism is at an institutional level not the activist level even though it is activists who are pushing for it and who are very often part of it, but that is a very different kind of internationalism that is the UN, it's like the UN peace mission of the trade commission, it's that kind of internationalism when you need to take 200 governments along with you it's a very different thing you are addressing the governments after all, you are not addressing civil society, you are not addressing other women's groups, you are not necessarily working with activists everywhere, so that's very different but I actually don't see too much coming together internationally very easily, because the movements are not as strong. In Europe where is the movement, how does that internationalisation happen? I mean, a few human rights groups and networks but there is huge difference in perceptions and strategies between those. So there isn't as there is a consensus over how to mobilise, so what is it that you do even if you come together. There has to be some consensus, on this Delhi rape for example there was a huge support but there was no way that strategy was going to be decided internationally on what to do that had to be something local, national, sure that support is welcome, but that's support is not going to have an impact on the situation here how can it? So I think international mobilising is very important at the consciousness raising stage its very important when it comes to institutional instruments in support, but what for example impact has been achieved by me being active on FGM in Africa? We cannot participate in the actual strategy to eliminate it. Even if we agree on certain structural and violent underpinnings we might agree that those occur across cultures but how do you account for the specificity of this? Even if one was to say it's structural, it's patriarchal, it's reinforced by family structures, but there are very specific manifestations of it so how does one mobilise in an effective or meaningful way?

What do you make of the category 'gender-based violence'? How useful is it?

That's the habit UN agencies we should actually be wary of being reduced by that because it's an easy way of categories very different and difficult manifestations.

I don't give too much importance to those UN categories frankly because as an organisation it hasn't been terribly effective. Co-option of funds has been going on for a long time, donor agencies too using their money to exert influence over the agenda, it has been going on for a very long time. Now consultancy management firms are being used to pressurise organisations not conforming to a particular model of accountability and they want outcomes and business plans and all sorts of ridiculous things and it is part of the trend to corporatise everything, after all what lies behind co-operative social responsibility [...], it is blunting the analytical and activist edge because a lot of institutions are dependent on that kind of funding and might find they have not choice but to change their priorities or reorientation. Its happening a great deal that is another kind of problem and dilemma [...], well you see the thing is but if local groups are raising very difficult and uncomfortable questions then the best thing to do is to neutralise critical dissent. But there are questions that must be continually asked around injustice and atrocities. Governments are very much in line with this neutralising impulse so they are very happy to be part of what – how shall I put it? – cover up. Because they are implicated in it and they don't want to hear these uncomfortable questions – they are not going to be able to neutralise it forever and that's part of their anxiety actually, they can't supress it indefinitely. The shift in legislation is to show they are responsive and it is also to protect themselves against and everyone knows that legislation is only as effective as its implementation. With reports they just take out what they don't

> want, so they seem as if they are responding immediately but they just take out what they don't like that's what they do and I suppose what we do is continue to expose them. They find some kind of accountability, be it regionally or nationally whichever is doable mostly.[16]

The views expressed by Gaytri here pick up a number of themes already discussed in Part Two of this volume, and also lead into the discussion in the next chapter. She is pessimistic that the movement will be sustainable, feeling that she has seen similar surges of mobilisation, for example around anti-dowry legislation in the 1960s and 1970s. She also reiterates concerns introduced earlier in this chapter that global conventions do not respond to the complexities of how women experience violence in local contexts. Her pessimistic outlook is also supported by the views of Meera given in the Introduction to this volume; Meera said that she had to be jolted into believing things had actually changed. There is unsurprisingly a disconnect between the generations of activists: younger voices, when compared with those at other points in their career experience, clearly express a less cautious view. However, all those I interviewed agree that there is now an acute urgency that gender-based violence must be tackled and eradicated once and for all, and that activism has to be informed by the grassroots. Whilst views differ on the value of conventions such as CEDAW, all again agree that campaigns must be shaped and run by those who are in touch with the contexts in which abuse occurs, either because they have experienced it directly or work with those who have, or both.

Conclusion

This chapter has offered a brief, concise overview of the history of the feminist movement in India. It has looked at the emergence of associations informed by colonial thinking that stressed the need for Indian society and culture to civilise. The movement entered a second phase under the influence of the nationalist movement and in particular Gandhi, who in turn sparked the creation of grassroots organisations much more in touch with rural communities. Gandhi also introduced a notion of feminised activism, which arguably did little to challenge traditional gender identities but did support women's visibility as political leaders, albeit more at a local level. The movement then moved into a phase in which the global, international arena became much more important. The first UN Decade for Women saw a more outward-looking feminist movement that perhaps gained a stronger voice through being able to tap into a network beyond India. However, the universal and unified nature of the movement has always been questioned, and that is still the case today. The various associations and organisations that operate through a feminist perspective are still fractious and often in disagreement over emphases and priorities; however, the anti-rape movement has brought a moment of strategic unity which, hopefully, moving forward will be recognised as a significant period in the history of Indian feminisms.

CHAPTER 6

THE RELIGIOUS RIGHT AND VIOLENCE AGAINST WOMEN

Introduction

This chapter picks up the theme introduced at the start of the volume and again in Chapter Three, in which the realities of a violent right-wing backlash to women's empowerment were acknowledged and highlighted as deeply problematic. Feminist activists are fighting for social equality in a conservative climate in which their achievements are often met with resistance, frequently articulated in acts of violence against women. The conservative values that shape this backlash have their roots at least in part within religious ideas about gender. Whilst the link between religion and this violent backlash is not obviously direct, it is apparent. Right-wing Hindu organisations promote strict gender codes that demand women conform to a traditional set of domestic responsibilities, upon which is said to depend the stability of society. This ideology is at the very core of *Hindutva* thinking. Dominant strands of Hindu society arguably have become more conservative as India's liberalisation process has continued. Partly, this swing to the right, the increased visibility of right-wing organisations and political parties, is a reaction against foreign influence and a concern to ensure that economic development follows a path controlled and determined by India and not outside pressures. It is also true to say that the Hindu-Right movement operates transnationally, with considerable funding from successful business figures who have achieved prosperity in the West, particularly the USA.

This has enabled the *Hindutva* vision for India to gain prominence, and the goal of this chapter is to frame the battleground on which women's rights in India are being fought, highlighting the tension that activism must navigate. The challenge for feminists remains considerable, despite its achievements: neoliberalism has supported the growth of the right through the provision of global technologies, which means that the communication of ideas and the transfer of funds can happen with ease. Neoliberal economics has also provided opportunities for a few elite figures in the movement to accumulate huge wealth that is now used to fund the dissemination of the conservative ideology that ultimately restricts the freedoms of women.

This chapter will consider the role that religious leaders play in promoting patriarchal interpretations of gender that in turn legitimise the strict control of women, leading in many instances to violence. Whilst religion is not being presented in this volume as the sole explanation for the normalisation of GBV, the ways in which certain religious narratives increase women's vulnerability to violence is under-argued in national feminist discourse. Religious leaders are symbolic of male authority and of 'claims to know' and understand how society should be structured. Gender, along with caste, is a key organisational dimension structuring Indian society embedding hierarchal and oppressive relationships. This chapter will review the rise of conservative interpretations of religious ideas that are inherently gendered and offer a case study of one such male-lead religious organisation whose teachings and worldview alarmingly perpetuate and help to normalise oppressive gender norms.

The chapter is divided into four parts. The first introduces Hindu nationalism and *Hindutva* organisations, whilst the second offers a case study of a nationalist organisation. The third explores the link between conservative ideas of gender and violence against women, and the final part considers the how feminist activism must now navigate and challenge this growing conservatism.

Hindu nationalist organisations

Conservative Hindu ideologies, and in particular the growth of far-right *Hindutva* groups, have had an impact on struggles for gender equality, and as such demonstrate that wider competing tensions between a web of diverse standpoints – secular, religious, liberal and conservative – are often played out through and on women's bodies and by governing sexual relationships in general. By 'Hindu nationalism', or the 'Hindu Right' (terms I use interchangeably), I follow McKean's view:

> The Hindu nationalist movement is by no means a monolithic entity. It is supported by a spectrum of leaders, groups and individuals whose ideological positions range from moderate to militant and whose projects vary from charitable work and religious education to political power, hatemongering and communal violence.[1]

The best-known and largest group in this category is the Rashtriya Svayam-sevak Sangh (RSS). Tomalin outlines how K.V. Hedgewar, a Hindu Mahasabha member, formed the RSS:

> The RSS is not a political party and instead considers itself to be a cultural organisation with an emphasis upon militaristic style training for men, women and children. M.S. Golwalkar, successor to Hedgewar, took a broader understanding of 'who is a Hindu'. He distinguished between culture and religion, taking religion to be a 'private' matter. Thus, although the public culture must be Hindu, people's private faith was a matter of religion.[2]

Today the RSS is one wing of the so-called *sangh parivar* (family of organisations) alongside the VHP (Vishva Hindu Parishad, founded in 1964) and the BJP (Bharatiya Janata Party, founded in 1980). The former is a religio-cultural organisation that strives to achieve a universal Hinduism. Various scholars have written that the nationalist discourse is centred on conservative gendered ideals about women's potential as the saviours of the Indian nation through their conformity to a domestic mothering role.[3] Whilst secular feminists find the strength of the nationalist movement worrying, it remains hugely popular with women and men across caste groups.

The ideology of the nationalist movement is highly pervasive, and it is not always obvious whether an organisation subscribes to *Hindutva*.

Case study of a nationalist organisation

One such example is the Sadhu Vaswani 'Mira Movement' based in Pune, Maharashtra (also home to the Gandhi Memorial Society discussed in Chapter Five). Hyderabad, where the mission began, became part of Pakistan under partition and so the origins of the anti-British sentiment running through the mission are easily traced to its origins: 'Ancient is the history of Sind. The Indus valley civilisation is at least 7,000 years old. The Sindis are a highly civilized and cultured people – enterprising, hardworking and industrious, full of the spirit of faith and courage'.[4]

The Sadhu Vaswani Mission has a presence in Southeast Asia, the UK and the USA. According to research I conducted in 2008, the organisation receives money from Hindu diasporas in the countries where it works. The mission is founded on a lineage that began with Sadhu Vaswani, and is now led by his nephew Dada Vaswani. The main mission complex consists of a kindergarten, a primary and secondary school for around 1,400 girls, huge meeting halls, an administration block and Dada Vaswani's residence. The mission also has its own publishing house (Gita Publishing). The mission's educational activities extend beyond the central complex and include Mira College and a nursing college. In total, the mission claims to be educating 4,000 girls at one time. The mission is planning to extend its activities further by building a college of commerce, again exclusively for girls. There is also a large Sadhu Vaswani hospital, which is where the nursing students carry out their practical training and where many of them later find employment.

As my research revealed, the mission, perhaps deliberately, predominantly projects its social welfare activities and highlights its work empowering girls through education.[5] It does not openly claim to be pursuing a politically-orientated goal of uniting India through a singular culture and religion. The organisation's insistence on being called secular further obscures its second goal. The use of the term 'secular' is interesting; the most senior figure I interviewed in the organisation insisted that Sadhu Vaswani Mission was secular because it 'served all faiths'. Even when probed, he refused to admit the organisation was at least predominantly Hindu, claiming instead that it celebrates all faiths and is active in interfaith dialogue and collaboration. Deeper analysis of the teachings that underlie the organisation clearly reveals commitment to a Hindu nationalist agenda. In audiences, I witnessed Dada Vaswani talking about the need to emancipate India from the clutches of British colonialism. The mission concentrates on educating women as the bearers and nurturers of Indian culture and religion, and stresses the need to heal India by strengthening its spiritual foundations. Scholars of Hindu nationalism such as Chiriyankandath, as well as Jaffrelot and Blom Hansen, recognise themes that advocate a singular Indian culture and religion, that lay stress on women as the bearers and nurturers of culture and religion, and express anti-British sentiments as common to the discourses of many organisations. The passage below details the origins of the movement outside Maharashtra in Sind and offers a reason for the nationalist tone that runs through its discourse:

> What we know as the Sadhu Vaswani Mission today was started by Sadhu T.L Vaswani in 1929, at Hyderabad (Sind). Kumari Shanti Maghanmal was a devoted disciple of Sadhu T.L. Vaswani. At her behest, her father offered a hall where Sadhu Vaswani could hold his *satsang* (fellowship meetings). In those days it was known as *Sakhi Satsang*. In the early days of the *Sakhi Satsang*, it was largely composed of women.[6]

The Mission emerged largely as a social-welfare organisation that focused on educating women so they could adopt a more public role influencing and shaping society. The ideas of Sadhu Vaswani were not dissimilar to those of Gandhi, who also saw great potential in women as activists in the nationalist struggle. However, as has been already highlighted Gandhi did not challenge the underlying gendered ideology that associates and restricts women's actions to a concept of 'nurturing'. This is a critique that can also be directed at the philosophy of the Sadhu Vaswani Mission: Sadhu Vaswani regarded female empowerment as about the elevation of women's nurturing nature into community building and nationhood. In other words: 'empowerment' is an extension of the domestic mothering role that feminists see as denying rights rather than respecting them.

The focus on girls seems to be driven by a desire to embed a sense of appropriate female behaviour and pursuits into the mind-sets of young girls; by the time they graduate from the Mira system, many may well be happy to comply with its underlying patriarchal gendered ideology. This, for example, can be seen in a quote from Dada Vaswani:

> Now woman gets her chance. She is called upon to build a New World. She is a symbol of Shakti in the Hindu scriptures. And Shakti is not a force. Shakti is integration. This includes intelligence. Education, more education, is needed. But is must be education of the right character.[7]

The mission, then, believes that the stability of the Indian nation depends on women's willingness to embrace motherhood – hence the statement by a senior devotee that appears in the mission's literature: 'Educate women and you educate a whole country.' So, whilst claims are made by the mission that it is empowering women, its model is far from that projected by feminists. The conservative and nationalist side of the organisation's ideology came to the fore during an annual questions-and-answers session for students held with Dada Vaswani at the Mira college for girls in Pune in 2008, which I witnessed.[8] The quotes I noted on this occasion clearly brought home that the girls are being taught to absorb a specific gender role that prescribes their place in the world as mothers and home-makers: the country is still 'emasculated by the British'; 'It is your duty to complete its India's emancipation'; 'We are not truly free yet'.

Education at the Mission is characterised by a daily sanctuary period in which the girls are asked to reflect on nature and take part in activities that demonstrate their respect for it (e.g. bird watching). The curriculum is divided into seven pillars:

- reverence for life;
- reverence for spirit of education;

- life and nature;
- character building;
- spiritual unfolding;
- love of Indian ideals;
- living for others.

These pillars demonstrate a focus on building a specific mind-set, arguably geared towards the wider goals of the mission rather than empowering girls as independent free-thinking individuals. However, what isn't clear is how these ideas about gender feed into and promote gender-based violence. Obviously, the Sadhu Vaswani Mission and other such organisations are not overtly or even covertly advocating the use of violence, so what is the link?

The link between conservative ideas of gender and violence against women

Violence against women often emerges through tight controls placed over women's lives through practices such as dowry and son-preference, as well as through the general legitimisation of male control over women, which sanctions violence as a means of ensuring women do not transgress their domestic and mothering role. In South Asia specifically (where research has been conducted almost exclusively in India and Bangladesh), various studies have demonstrated a positive correlation between women's economic empowerment and violence against women and girls. This indicates that when women step out of their traditionally defined gender roles and begin to acquire income of their own, this can lead to violent backlash as men try to recalibrate traditional power hierarchies.[9] The common observation that more 'gender-conservative' countries/regions/villages/households are more likely to produce backlash against women's economic empowerment is undoubtedly correct.[10] The importance therefore of raising the visibility of organisations such as the Sadhu Vaswani Mission is precisely because of the way in which they advocate conservative views of gender. These ideals weave into and help construct a wider environment that uses violence to maintain the status quo.

Feminists actively involved in the movement since the 1970s have raised concerns over the increasing rather than decreasing influence of religious conservatism on the lives of women. This, they claim, feeds into and perpetuates the oppression of women within a narrow domestic-mothering role. For example, one prominent feminist activist and publisher stated:

> We have seen a shift to the right both nationally in India but also globally that has given rise to more and more religious groups who pursue an ideology which sees women's role as purely domestic and will go to any lengths to ensure they remain locked into the private sphere.[11]

The case study given in the previous section is further evidence of this shift but also highlights how invisible this process has been. Organisations that advocate conservative and regressive views on women carefully hide their ideology, often masking it in the language of spiritual freedom and personal growth. This masking is further effectively assured through the adoption of familiar and global terms such as 'empowerment'. These terms are co-opted and reinterpreted through a right-wing reading of gender.

As discussed in Chapter Five, some activists express concern that the focus has shifted away from issues of marriage and dowry and onto other forms of violence that are receiving global attention and campaign money; for example, trafficking and prostitution. Yet, for feminist activists and scholars such as Gaytri, whose views have been shared throughout this volume, the 'old' issues are still at the foundations of the systematic abuse of women: namely, marriage and related practices such as dowry, which act to ensure continued violence against women and marginalisation. This reality has not shifted despite women's gains in other areas such as employment and education:

> Women are the target for many forms of violence especially if they are at home, this has not changed, I think that we can see it is a backlash because more women are speaking out, for someone like me I really have to be jolted to see how things have changed.[12]

In trying to explain the continuing prevalence of violence against women, it is important to highlight the increased prominence and influence of conservative religious groups. As already acknowledged in the interview with members of the Sadhu Vaswani Mission, religious teachings are heavily gendered and often project images of femininity that link women to the domestic sphere.

Many religious leaders in India (and indeed across the globe) refuse to acknowledge the ways in which religion can legitimise practices that are in themselves violent or lead to violence. They often employ the artificial division between religion and culture to argue that religion does not endorse the use of violence against women and abusive practices are identified as culture so as to exonerate religion. This can be seen in the current discourses surrounding FGM, in which religious leaders sidestep responsibility; for example, in the case of Islam, by stating there is no mention of female circumcision in the Qur'an.[13] This reading, however, ignores the ways in which religious teachings promote male dominance, rendering women passive and subservient and ultimately vulnerable to violence.[14] Religious leaders often promote patriarchal discourse, which, although challenged in different ways by groups of religious women as well as secular feminist groups, still prevails in shaping and weaving the fabric of the social, cultural and political environment.

In the case of Hinduism, religious leaders who promote women's subservience to their husbands often present Sita as an ideal role model (neatly avoiding interpretations of the Ramayana that highlight Sita's suffering at the hands of a cruel husband), and in doing so endorse female inferiority and male dominance as the norm. Ironically, Gandhi also used the image of Sita to argue that women had a naturally self-sacrificing character, which served the nationalist movement well. He argued for the increased involvement of women in the political and public sphere, something that some right-wing organisations today also endorse for similar reasons (see case study above). However, in terms of eradicating violence from the lives of women this volume has argued throughout that this is not enough. The very structures of gendered identities that render a strict division of labour between men and women must be reshaped according to principles of social justice and equality. Only once this is done will we see a radical transformation in human relationships and an end to violence as a means to police divisions and hierarchies.

Patriarchy is shaped then through and by religious values projected in visions of how we should live our lives that are gendered and then further enforced by and through specific cultural practices such as dowry.[15] In turn, these practices depend on the threat or actual use of violence in order for them to be maintained and to secure the continuation of the heterosexual model of marriage and motherhood. The practices that should be seen as the apparatus of patriarchy may be in themselves violent (e.g. FGM, female infanticide) or act as a trigger for harassment and abuse (e.g. dowry). So, whilst religion may not sanction violence against women directly it does so covertly by rigidly projecting a narrow and ultimately misogynistic system.

The brutal impact of this Hindu-Right ideology on and for the lives of women is spilling out onto the street. Women are less safe in public, yet feminist consciousness-raising has successfully convinced them that they are entitled to occupy space in public places, from bars to buses, and that they should do so with confidence. The tension between the feminist (mostly secular) standpoint and that of *Hindutva* groups is playing itself and reported for the world to see. For example, the Hindu Right has been behind numerous brutal attacks on women who challenge the oppressive and constraining parameters of womanhood prescribed by *Hindutva* ideology.[16] These attacks have targeted women who transgress the conservative religious codes of female modesty and subservience, including women who drink alcohol in pubs and bars or go to nightclubs, wear Western clothes, and have numerous sexual partners. As documented in the section on rape, *Nirbhaya* did none of these things and so the use of brutal violence against her was, in the eyes of the *Hindutva* movement, illegitimate. It is important that support for campaigns against violence against women voiced by Hindu-Right groups must not be misunderstood as a plea for wider gender justice; applying the spectrum introduced in Chapter Two, decrying instances of violence operates to remind the public of when it is legitimate to use violence. Violence is an apparatus for the maintenance of the gender status quo and must not be used against women who are not obviously transgressing. It is important therefore to highlight these responses as falling far short of what is needed to see society reshaped in a more gender-equal model.

Conservative discourses demonstrate how control over female sexuality is crucial in ensuring women conform to their role as procreators and nurturers of the next generation. In *Hindutva* ideology women's role in raising stable children committed to maintaining the unity of the Hindu nation is critical. Ensuring women do not stray from this focus is critical in the quest to achieve this nationalist vision of India; violence is therefore legitimised as a means of ensuring this happens. Feminist campaigning in recent decades has clashed perhaps more directly than ever with this right-wing religious ideology. Feminists, despite their differences as mapped in the previous chapter, challenge the underlying gendered ideology that renders women vulnerable to control and violence. Blame is placed at the root of society in its male-centric and hierarchal structures, and the way forward has to be a radical reshaping of the day-to-day patterns of human behaviours. It is perhaps not surprising that this approach is being met with aggression from the right, who see their role increasingly as maintaining and preserving the status quo. Feminist groups have for a few decades now focused on improving women's lives in a holistic sense, creating employment and educational opportunities for women in the hope that with greater independence, women would challenge the structural constraints that have limited their choices. Research presented in this volume highlights that these shifts have not entirely taken place and patriarchal values and beliefs projecting rigid gender roles continue to hold firm. It is not a coincidence, but rather directly linked, that as conservative religious groups (such as the Sadhu Vaswani Mission) increasingly assert their presence through strict gender codes, practices such as dowry and related violence have become further embedded into the fabric of Indian society.

Evidence of this can be seen in the commonly accepted statements that endorse the use of violence against women. For example, the UNIFEM directory of NGOs working in Jaipur, Rajasthan, on domestic violence suggests that women internalise female religious role models: 'The awareness of gender identity begins with deliberate training on how to be a good woman.' Commonly held beliefs include the sayings 'husbands will beat' and a 'husband has the right to beat his wife.' Similar sentiments can be heard across India and continue to shape the mind-sets of many across professions. For example, in Chapters One and Two I presented the views of members of the ruling BJP as well as lawyers, all of whom fail to problematise the use of violence in circumstances when a woman is seen to challenge traditional gender norms.

Contextualising this link globally is important for emphasising that what is happening in India is not unique. Pearson and Tomalin make a compelling argument when they express a concern that in the rush to include religion in development, it is the dominant view of religion that is getting heard.[17] This dominant view excludes women's voices and unique expressions of spirituality. There is a tendency in many texts examining religion and development to assume that religious traditions speak as one voice. Tomalin and Pearson give the example of the World Bank's interfaith paper on the Millennium Development Goals (MDGs). Their analysis of this document highlights how it reflects the views of particular male religious leaders, which then come to represent the views of all adherents from that tradition. Male religious leaders represent traditions and typically marginalise and essentialise women's roles. In other words, religious leaders are being given a platform by Western development institutions to represent and further promote their essentialist views about women. The authors state: 'This danger is particularly acute in countries and contexts where the political rise of both fundamentalist and conservative religious forms has challenged the movement towards the acceptance of universal rights for women.'[18]

In short, the resurgence of religious identities across the globe is often played out through women's lives, emphasising the need for them to return to their traditional role of reproducers and nurturers. Those that emphasise the need for women to return to this traditional mothering role attack the women's rights agenda.[19] This in turn seriously undermines the significant inroads into promoting social equality made by gender development activists.

The Challenge for Indian Feminists

So it is against this backdrop of increased conservatism that Indian feminists are now having to locate their activism. Ironically, feminists are also having to respond to the adverse impact that globalisation has brought to the lives of women. I use the word ironically, because globalisation has forced open labour markets and presented new opportunities for women to engage with the economy, which should go hand-in-hand with a renewed era of female empowerment. However, as has been pointed out at various points already in this volume and will be picked up again later, this increased public visibility that neoliberal ideas have encouraged has not been well received.

For many feminists the backlash was inevitable because work on gender inequality concentrated too much on providing women with the same life choices as men, but paid insufficient attention to whether these shifts in the role of women would trigger a restructuring of gender norms. As scholars such as Basu and Palriwala have highlighted frequently in their work, the root of women's marginalisation and vulnerability to violence is the institution of heterosexual marriage enshrined in and by patriarchal religious ideology, such as that propounded by *Hindutva* groups outlined above. Globalisation has done little to even dent this underlying ideology. When measuring the progress of the liberal end of the gendered spectrum in challenging the structures that have limited women's expression of their sexuality, it is depressingly clear that the situation in some areas is in fact worsening. Palriwala in her work on sex-selective technologies and female infanticide notes that rates are on the increase.[20] Globalisation, she argues, and the emergence of a richer middle class have enabled India to develop better technologies which can now be afforded in a way they were not before. In my work on dowry I note that the practice has been decried by feminists for decades as both a symbol and cause of marital oppression, yet it has spread across caste groups and religious communities. It was once the preserve of rich upper-caste Hindus, but the impact of Sanskritisation means that lower and Dalit castes see the giving of dowry as a way of demonstrating their increased wealth and social status. The debts that families accrue are breathtaking, but such is the drive to publically project a high level of family honour. In Chapter Eight, on dowry, I present research conducted in Kerala which reveals a second parallel set of reasons for the practice's widespread observance. It is commonly acknowledged that if sufficient dowry is not given the bride is vulnerable to harassment and violence in her married life. So, even in families that believe the system is wrong, they see no alternative: if they do not give dowry they cannot marry their daughters; if they do not give enough dowry they are almost guaranteeing an unhappy future for their daughter.

The argument of scholars such as Palriwala, Srinivasan and Bedi is borne out in this research: liberalisation has increased women's vulnerability to violence.[21] Families have got richer as better-paid employment opportunities have increased, but a stronger economic position has increased pressure on families to produce larger dowries. There is a clear motivation to have a son: sons bring money into a household, hence the rise in cases of female infanticide. Scholars are clear that the heterosexual marriage system operates as a system of economic exchange, ensuring the flow of money between families whilst simultaneously ensuring that a woman's social status in marriage remains inferior to that of her husband. Whilst debates have ensued as to how best to combat dowry, no course of action has been successful despite anti-dowry legislation being in place since the 1960s. Kishwar changed her view that campaigns should focus on the eradication of dowry; instead, she switched to supporting a revision of inheritance rights for women, her argument being that women support the dowry system as it represents the only means through which they gain wealth from their natal family.[22] Feminist campaigning from the 2000s has focused on improving women's lives in a holistic sense, creating employment and educational opportunities for women in the hope that, with greater independence, women would challenge the structural constraints that limited their choices. In my research in Kerala, a state where women's access to education and employment are significantly improved, it is clear that this empowerment has not resulted in a decline of either dowry practice or violence against women.

Despite the gloom of what I present in this volume it is also important to acknowledge the dynamics of change that are also bubbling away at the heart of Indian society. Symbols of female power, for example *Shakti*, used and arguably manipulated by nationalist discourses to subvert their radical potential (see the way in which the Sadhu Vaswani Mission distort and subdue the meaning of *Shakti*), are being reclaimed and used by different feminist groups in India. The application of a gender spectrum to the diversity of Indian culture and society enables us to highlight the diversity of ways in which radical voices are offering powerful narratives that present a socially just and equal vision of India. Goddesses such as Kali and Durga have been used by some feminist groups as symbols of women's *Shakti*, harnessed in order to mobilise women and consciousness raise into political action (for example Shakhi in Kerala). A growing network of organisations exists across India – including for example Sahayatrika, Sahodaran, SANGAMA and the Alternative Law Forum – all of which work to promote different sexualities, forcing open a space for peoples of different sexual identities to co-exist without the fear of violet repercussions. The legislative structure is beginning to catch up, and as the voices of younger activists captured in Chapter Five revealed, there is optimism that the constant campaigning and use of social media is beginning to have effect in terms of changing the mind-sets of men and women.

Conclusion

Much of the campaigning undertaken by the current women's movement has been related to eradicating violence against women in its multiple forms. Whilst violence against women continues to be a persistent problem, various groups have emerged across India that are campaigning against conservative, patriarchal and homophobic ideologies. Success can be seen in the passage of new anti-rape legislation following the release of the Verma Report in 2013,[21] but understandings of the root of this violence and oppression are still limited. This chapter has attempted to chart the threat posed by right-wing ideologies and to demonstrate how this threat has grown, in part aided by globalisation. The transnationalisation of *Hindutva* organisations has been enabled through global technologies that support the transfer of funds and ideas in ever more pervasive and powerful means. However, there is hope that these same technologies may support the growth of a movement motivated to combat fundamentalism.

PART IV

HARMFUL CULTURAL PRACTICES

CHAPTER 7

THE PERSISTENCE AND INVISIBILITY OF HARMFUL CULTURAL PRACTICES

Introduction

The label 'harmful cultural practices' (HCPs) is increasingly being used by global bodies such as UN Women to describe ritualised behaviours that bring violent harm to women.[1] Globally, practices such as 'female genital mutilation' (FGM) and 'forced marriage' (FM) have received the most attention. In India, arguably an array of harmful practices can be identified and linked by an underpinning misogynistic gendered ideology highlighted throughout this volume as being responsible for violent abuse against women and girls. In this section, and through applying the spectrum outlined in Chapter Two, I distinguish between two types of 'harm', or rather two ways in which a practice can cause 'harm'. First, the practice itself may be violent, involving psychological abuse, cutting, scarring or even death. For example, female infanticide and FGM both bring immediate harm. However, there are also practices that in themselves are not harmful but often act as a trigger for physical, emotional and/or financial abuse. It is perhaps harder to argue the harm caused by trigger practices because the violence is less direct but, as I argue here, they must be seen as such. Dowry is an example of just such a practice; whilst the giving of dowry does not guarantee abuse, in a very high number of instances it becomes the cause of ongoing violence suffered by young brides. Some practices cross into both types of harm. Child marriage often causes immediate psychological abuse and lasting trauma, but it also often triggers more or different forms of violence as the girl grows into her marriage. Understanding the ways in which certain cultural practices cause women and girls harm is important but it is also necessary to interrogate why we are seeing a worrying increase in many cases. Some HCPs in India (e.g. sex-selective abortion and dowry) have increased despite legislation and decades of feminist campaigning designed to eradicate them. Neoliberal economics is a large part of the problem, as access to new technologies and rising income levels have made some practices more accessible.

In addition to developing this critique of neoliberalism, the current chapter will argue that the extent of violent practices against women and girls is still largely unknown, with some forms maintaining themselves under the radar of activism and state legislation. For example, female genital mutilation in India is still practised by the Bora Muslim community. This community of Muslims trace their origins to Yemen, where the most brutal type of FGM is practised (see details below). Whilst they may represent a relatively small portion of India's huge population (around 1.4 million Bora Muslims in Mumbai, Delhi and Ahmedabad), this is nevertheless a significant number of people among whom women and girls continue to undergo FGM. The way in which this practice is performed in India is not widely known and FGM has not featured in any of the public campaigns against gender-based violence. This chapter, then, is in part about raising the visibility of FGM in India, arguing that, given the global attention this specific practice is receiving, there is potential for feminist groups in India to tap into the broader publicity it has received. This chapter will also explore the category of harmful cultural practices, particularly in light of the post-colonial feminist critiques already explored in Chapters One and Two. Once again, a delicate balance is needed between identifying the violence and abuse that these practices represent, and avoiding falling into an essentialist and reductionalist description of passive victims of a backward culture. The key questions explored in this chapter include: how and why do these practices continue?; whilst these practices are products of a particular cultural and patriarchal environment, what other factors come into play to support and sustain their continued presence in women's lives?; and how can we talk and write about them as activists committed to eradicating them without reproducing racialised and culturally problematic narratives?

This chapter is divided into four parts. It begins by unpacking the category 'harmful cultural practices', explaining where and when it emerged and asking if it is useful in helping us understand the context of HCPs in India. The second section considers how HCPs may be analysed, and in particular how cross-cultural analysis might be approached, whilst the third looks specifically at FGM in India, arguing that it has largely been ignored and that little is understood about the dynamics of how it plays out in the lives of women and girls in the communities that observe it. The final part theorises the concepts of victimhood and suffering, digging into the politicised environment in which certain HCPs gain press and funding attention, whilst others remain invisible. This last section argues that the construction of a victim is still dependent on a power hierarchy, resting on the usual binary of the oppressed and the liberated. The conclusion to this chapter argues that deconstructing this binary is an important layer in the overall fight to see GBV eradicated in India but also globally.

Unpacking the category of 'harmful cultural practices'

The concept of 'harmful traditional practices' originated in United Nation circles as early as the 1950s. Resolutions were adopted by the General Assembly, such as a referral to 'customs, ancient laws and practices relating to marriage and the family' considered inconsistent with the principles set forth in the Universal Declaration of Human Rights in 1954. The resolution called on all states to abolish such 'customs, ancient laws and practices'

> by ensuring complete freedom in the choice of a spouse; abolishing the practice of the bride-price; guaranteeing the right of widows to the custody of their children and their freedom as to remarriage; eliminating completely child marriages and the betrothal of young girls before the age of puberty and establishing appropriate penalties where necessary.

In 1958 and 1961, the United Nations Economic and Social Council (ECOSOC) invited the World Health Organization (WHO) to study 'customs subjecting girls to ritual operations', making FGM/C into the HCP gaining the most attention, as it remains so today.[2] However, the concept of HCP started to gain more currency in the 1980s and 1990s, following the 1979 Convention on the Eradication of All Forms of Discrimination Against Women, considered a hallmark achievement of the second-wave feminist movement in the West.

Developed by the UN Commission on the Status of Women, CEDAW can still today be seen as one of the most important documents defending the human and equal rights of women. As discussed in Chapter Five, the treaty was ratified by some 188 countries: it demands states undertake actions against all forms of discrimination against women, including 'laws, regulations, customs and practices'.[3] The reference to discrimination embedded in cultural traditions is elaborated further in Article 5a, which stipulates that states must see to it that changes take place in the

> social and cultural patterns of conduct of men and women, with a view to achieving the elimination of prejudices and customary laws and all other practices which are based on the idea of the inferiority or the superiority of either of the sexes or on stereotyped roles for men and women.

As is well known, CEDAW was an important breakthrough in the implementation of a gender perspective in human rights, where, next to legal equality and civil rights for women, demands were also formulated pertaining to the 'private' sphere of reproductive rights and the 'impact of cultural factors in gender relations.'

Since the convention was adopted in different working groups, consultations and reports by the UN and related institutions (e.g. UNFPA, UNICEF, WHO), the tendency towards grouping together phenomena such as FGM and honour-related violence increased. Many organisations dedicated to the eradication of HCPs often focus on one particular HCP, such as FGM, launching global campaigns to eradicate it. This approach could be seen as strategically essentialist; launching coherent campaigns across all forms of violence against women and girls is unrealistic and to be effective a campaign needs unity, which is best mustered through a shared focus. Individual country-level movements then opt in or out of global campaigns, depending on how well they chime with the contextual problems faced in that region.

Initially, HCPs were most often treated under the rubric of either 'health' or 'violence against women and girls', themes that related to the specifically gendered way in which the human rights of women and children were violated. Reports were then produced by new organs such as the UN working group dedicated to the study of 'traditional practices affecting women's and children's health', which was launched in 1985 in Geneva. Since 1994, there have also been periodic reports by the Special Rapporteur on violence against women, its causes and consequences.[4]

In the South, organisations such as the Inter-African Committee (IAC) on traditional practices affecting the health of women and children were formed at the initiative of African delegates at the UN working group sessions. In 1995, UN Fact Sheet No. 23 was published, *Harmful Traditional Practices Affecting the Health of Women and Children*, in which a direct reference is made to the CEDAW treaty. In this document HCPs are described as follows:

> Traditional cultural practices reflect values and beliefs held by members of a community for periods often spanning generations. Every social grouping in the world has specific traditional cultural practices and beliefs, some of which are beneficial to all members, while others are harmful to a specific group, such as women. These harmful traditional practices include female genital mutilation (FGM); forced feeding of women; early marriage; the various taboos or practices which prevent women from controlling their own fertility; nutritional taboos and traditional birth practices; son preference and its implications for the status of the girl child; female infanticide; early pregnancy; and dowry price. Despite their harmful nature and their violation of international human rights laws, such practices persist because they are not questioned and take on an aura of morality in the eyes of those practising them.[5]

What follows in the document is a clear and strong condemnation of HCPs, by no means eschewing feminist critique, noting that the 'bleak reality' is that such practices exist for male benefit: 'Female sexual control by men, and the economic and political subordination of women, perpetuate the inferior status of women and inhibit structural and attitudinal changes necessary to eliminate gender inequality.'[6] Governments and the international community are held accountable for not having challenged the 'sinister' implications of these practices, among which violating rights to 'health, life, dignity and personal integrity'. 'Sensitive cultural issues' such as FGM have wrongly been avoided, it is claimed, and relegated to the 'spheres of women and the family'. The practices listed above are discussed in the following order: female genital mutilation, son preference and its implications for the status of the girl child, female infanticide, early marriage and dowry, early pregnancy, nutritional taboos and practices related to child delivery and violence against women.

The religion–culture nexus in global politics

In measuring shifts in attitudes it has become clear that in some contexts practices have in fact become further embedded as the wider social-cultural-religious contexts have become more conservative. Actors in the global context in which development-security policies are being framed seem unaware of the negative knock-on impact for the lives of women, and specifically for the prevalence of HCPs. Ironically, the development agenda is fast becoming reinvented as one of 'human security', which, according to the UN post-2015 MDG position paper,[7] must respond to and eradicate gender-based violence, including all HCPs; however, in reality, global policy has at times made the situation worse. For example, Siddiqui argues[8] that diaspora women are becoming more marginalised in many European countries by the secular state's engagement with 'faith communities' led by men. Engagement with so-called faith communities now represents a key strategy in the war against terror in many parts of the world in an attempt to appease and bring on side potentially radical and violent groups. Echoing the argument made in Chapter Six, Bradley and Kirmani argue in the context of Pakistan and India that this global terror agenda has sparked a shift to the right, with the emergence of more conservative religious groups that in turn advocate traditional and often harmful practices as a means of disciplining women who transgress gender norms.[9]

In India we are seeing: the emergence of honour crimes previously for the most part observed only in Pakistan, linked to marriage practices that become harmful when family wishes are not followed; a sharp rise in sex-selective abortions associated with the increased availability and affordability of the technology used to determine the sex of a foetus; and dowry practices acting as a trigger for harassment and abuse that are deeply entrenched across Hindu, Christian, Muslim and Sikh communities, with ever greater pressure placed on parents to produce high dowries for their daughters in order to guarantee their safety in marriage (see Chapter Eight).[10] Religious leaders and organisations actively campaign for the maintenance of what they see as traditional values, which are played out through practices that serve to control and regulate women's bodies. Governments and bi-lateral and multi-lateral agencies have made commitments to reduce gender-based violence, but the way agencies operate does not always reflect this commitment or acknowledge the reality of the situation as evidenced by feminist activists and academics. On the contrary, they often collude with patriarchal violence by raising the visibility of male patriarchs who advocate strict gender codes enforced through HCPs.[11] An example of this contradiction can be seen in the multi-million pound global FGM eradication programmes which exist alongside initiatives to promote and engage with male leadership, religious and political (e.g. programmes to increase funding to faith-based, predominantly male-led organisations by UNFPA's Culture Matters Programme, the Tony Blair Faith Foundation, and the UK Department for International Development). Whilst religion and culture are not the only dimensions that promote and sustain patriarchy, and in turn HCPs, I argue here that they do feed into the construction of a wider social-political and economic environment that devalues women, reducing them to passive objects, and that this is in part achieved through HCPs.[12] Religion and culture therefore need to form aspects of a wider analytical frame through which to interrogate HCPs.

How to analyse HCPs

In a publication I co-edited with Chia Longman,[13] considerable attention was given to various frameworks for analysing why HCPs exist and continue, and why approaches to evaluating and identifying triggers for long-term mind-set change have been slow to emerge. We proposed two frames/approaches that together enable complex insight into 'why' and 'how' HCPs are sustained generation after generation, and a method for monitoring shifts in attitudes. These approaches are summarised here and then tested out in the context of HCPs in India both below in this chapter and in Chapter Eight, on dowry. To begin, monitoring attitude change is crucial when assessing the success of interventions designed to eradicate HCPs. In Chapter Two I outlined an attitude spectrum/continuum, which I argue is a valuable tool for capturing cross- and intergenerational differences in individual perceptions. The continuum should be used alongside an intersectional analysis of qualitative data. In combination, the intersectional approach and the attitude continuum act as an effective way of drawing out patterns and nuances in how people retell their experiences of, for example, FGM and dowry, identifying the influence of class, ethnicity, and other social constructs in the shaping of specific narratives around the practice. But most significantly in terms of measuring the impact of eradication programmes, it challenges the assumption that people's views remain static throughout their lives. As research in relation to dowry in Chapter Eight shows, it is common for a woman to hold radically different views as a young married woman and later as an older mother-in-law. A frame is therefore needed to capture any shifts in attitudes; eradication programmes can only claim to have worked if people hold their 'anti' views throughout their life-cycle. As found in relation to dowry in India, young women are more likely to be opposed to harmful practices, as their experiences of trauma are still very strong in their memory; however, as women get older, and if they bear a son, their status changes and they acquire greater authority within the family and wider community. In line with this more assured positioning, many women become more conservative in their views and often switch to supporting practices they once saw as problematic.

The research presented in this section highlights this by using an attitude continuum in the analysis of women's responses to HCPs;

specifically, attitudes to dowry and FGM (Figure 7.1). At one end are women who hold firm to the need to maintain the practice, because it is an expression of cultural identity and carries practical-economic functions enabling, as they see it, a smooth transition for women into marriage; and at the other are those women who fervently believe that these practices must be eradicated. The research found that many women place themselves at the mid-point: they know the practices to be harmful and abusive, but they also say that as yet they feel unable to challenge them. From an activist standpoint, views clearly have to shift to the liberal end of the spectrum if HCPs are to disappear, and measuring the shift (or not) in attitudes is vital in the fight to influence such change.

Culture remains an important part of the analytical web helping to unpack 'why' HCPs remain embedded in the lives of women even as other aspects of their lives change; for example, as they access education and employment. However, explanations for 'why' HCPs continue cannot be reduced to cultural accounts: instead, the frame used to analyse them must reflect a web of interlocking factors. Crenshaw coined the term 'intersectionality' to describe the various social factors that produce the social inequalities women experience.[14] In the critical analysis of HCPs, a gendered lens is the most useful perspective, but intersectionality does much more than just pinpoint the root of oppression: it explores the interrelationships of various dimensions such as gender, age, class, race and ethnicity, which come together in varying ways to shape the differing forms of discrimination to which women find themselves subjected. Culture and religion have to be placed alongside these factors, which in turn shape a person's positioning, identity and experiences in relation to HCPs.

Intersectionality as an analytical concept is used by bodies such as the UN and many NGOs; for instance, the 58th session of the UN Commission on Human Rights in its first paragraph states that the body

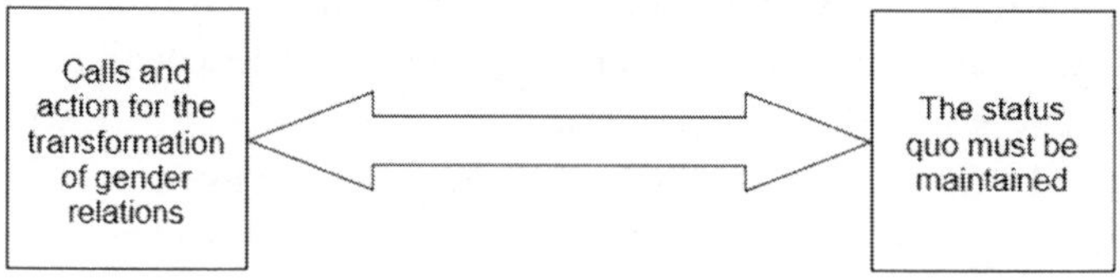

Figure 7.1 Attitude continuum on HCPs.

recognises 'the importance of examining the intersection of multiple forms of discrimination including their root causes from a gender perspective.'[15] Yuval-Davis has compared different definitions and practical translations of intersectionality, and highlights a level of confusion in its application.[16] Intersectionality is sometimes used to explain structural inequalities, whilst at other points – or sometimes even in the same analysis – also used to discuss issues of identity and personhood. What often comes through in stories, such as those recorded in my earlier research, is that culture, tradition and religion are not in themselves the problem; rather, it is the way that in certain contexts they feed into and help to perpetuate misogynistic values that produce and sustain abusive and violent practices against women.[17] The most important application of intersectionality, as Essed states,[18] is to understand the structural inequalities underpinning oppression – in the case of this volume, HCPs. So, applying intersectionality to HCPs will support an emergence of a web-like structure drawing out, in different contexts, the threads that weave together to support their continuance. It is highly likely that this intersectional web will look different across the countries in which a particular practice is observed.

As already argued in this chapter, and also as is evident by the increase in right-wing religious ideologies in India (see Chapter Five of this volume), this intersectional approach needs to contain a focus on religion. Religion, as argued above and previously,[19] is an area of much debate in terms of its role in relation to HCPs, but its influence on them is little understood and there are misunderstandings around to what extent (if any) religious teachings promote these practices. Questions rarely asked but already broached in this volume include: what impact do religious teachings, values and beliefs have in shaping attitudes to HCPs?; what role does religious leadership have in influencing public debate and local attitudes towards HCPs?; and how useful might religious leaders be within eradication campaigns?

Key research questions in relation to other intersectional dimensions include: what are the cultural dynamics that feed into HCPs?; what are the gender norms that shape the life expectations of men and women?; are there perceptions that these have changed at all over time?; what perceptions are there in relation to the education of girls and boys?;

in what ways does ethnicity shape HCPs?; what beliefs and practices specific to different ethnicities act to perpetuate these practices?; and what are the similarities and differences between different ethnic and sub-ethnic groups which might help to explain the prevalence of HCPs (e.g. why some ethnicities observe certain HCPs, while others do not)? Whilst I will not be able to answer these questions in any comprehensive way here, I draw attention to the importance of thinking about them for the rectification of the invisibility of HCPs.

So far I have looked at different approaches to understanding HCPs and the dynamics that maintain them. But how can different HCPs be compared, and is this even a useful exercise? I have already distinguished at the start of this chapter between practices that cause obvious and immediate harm (such as FGM) and those that act as a trigger for harm in the future (such as dowry). As highlighted above, gender and culture are two aspects that should form part of a broader intersectional approach; here, gender is the primary lens of cross-cultural analysis, although I also consider generational attitudes towards cultural tradition and gender, as well the concept of 'honour'.

'Honour' has throughout this volume been identified as a justification for continuing violence against women and girls in all its forms. As noted above, younger women are often vocal in expressing their abhorrent disgust for the practices of FGM and dowry, recounting the raw abuse they suffered or the concerns they have about what awaits them. However, research on dowry and FGM shows that it is often women who actively protect and perpetuate these practices. Despite the significant acknowledgement among women in the younger generation that these practices are wrong, resistance is difficult, not least because the practices are so embedded into the cultural and social system and carry economic as well as status value. Concepts of honour also help ensure a woman's emotional submission, as they do not want to dishonour those closest to them by refusing to conform.

Safe passage into womanhood, motherhood and married life is clearly woven into the fabric of each practice, and these practices will continue unless each strand is unravelled and challenged. Given generational shifts in attitude, activism needs to be positioned at points along a continuum, responding to a woman's changing experience and perceptions of these practices. However, analysis focusing on women's active participation has a tendency to reduce male involvement, even suggesting that they are not complicit. The gendered frame employed here shows the need to rethink this 'myth', and to look at the ways in which men act to ensure compliance or, through their silence, passively endorse HCPs.

The complex issue of agency, resistance and consent in relation to HCPs is addressed from the perspective of feminist anthropology and feminist post-colonial theory. Questions to be discussed include: where can lines be drawn between a woman feeling pressured into a practice and feeling that resistance is not an option because the repercussions are too extreme?; and to what extent can Western human rights and liberal and post-modernist frames of autonomy, agency and subjectivity be applied to the analysis and tackling of non-Western practices?

Making the invisible visible: Female genital mutilation/ cutting in India

Global background information on FGM/C

FGM/C is practised among a variety of ethnic and religious communities in at least 28 countries in Sub-Saharan and North-east Africa, Asia and the Middle East, with a prevalence rate between 0.6 per cent and 98 per cent. The practice is also increasingly found among migrant populations originating from these areas in other countries. An estimated 125 million[20] girls and women aged nine years or above have undergone FGM/C and 3.3 million girls are at annually at risk of undergoing the practice.[21] The World Health Organisation (WHO) classifies FGM/C into four types as below:

Type 1: Involves the removal of the prepuce with or without excision of all or part of the clitoris.
Type 2. Excision of the clitoris with partial or total excision of the labia minora (FGM types 1 and 2 constitute 80 per cent of FGM/C performed world-wide).
Type 3. Excision of part or all of the external genitalia (the clitoris, labia minora and labia majora) with stitching/narrowing of the vaginal opening (infibulation). This is the most extreme form of

FGM/C, involving removal of almost two thirds of the female genitalia. This type constitutes 15 per cent of all FGM performed world-wide.

Type 4. Unclassified, includes pricking, piercing, incising of the clitoris and/or labia, cauterisation by burning of the clitoris and surrounding tissue, scraping of tissue surrounding the vaginal orifice or cutting into the vagina, introduction of corrosive substances or herbs into the vagina to cause bleeding or for the purpose of tightening or narrowing it.[21]

State apparatus often fail to understand and respond to instances of abuse that fall under the banner of 'cultural' unless a 'moral panic' is stirred and then a sudden rush of concern is expressed across state services.[22] To give an example, and as already unpacked, FGM has risen to the surface in Europe and also globally as the latest practice nation states are panicked about. In the UK, FGM has arguably here replaced forced marriage, which was given significant policy and press attention from the early 2000s. Policy around FGM is fast being drawn up, but investment in collecting quantitative and qualitative research on the prevalence and impact of the practice is only just emerging. Funding is being directed towards training and awareness raising, but without complex knowledge of the practice and how it manifests in different diaspora communities as well as in those countries where is widely practised. I argue here that similarly in India, certain HCPs and types of violence rise to prominence and demand action because of lobbying and wider pressures from global/international bodies. Rape, for example, has become a key focus in India because of the horrific Delhi case already covered in this volume. Arguably, types of violence that impact on smaller, more marginal communities will get less attention, but it is necessary if GBV is to be stamped out in India to face the realities of how far reaching and varied violence affecting women and girls is. However, although documenting women's experiences of violence is essential to understanding the breadth and impact of violence, there is a point at which this can become voyeuristic; it is vital to find a balance that includes giving voice, because ultimately it is those that suffer who must be in control of the activist discourse and path to eradication. This is discussed further in the next section.

Capturing the views of those affecting by HCPs such as FGM is not easy, not least because of how secretly such practised are observed. Below is just one interview with Mehzabin, a young woman (in her early thirties) from the Bora community, conducted in October 2014.

Do you think the oppressive acts against women in the Bora community are due to society's pressure or do they have religious reasons?

I think it is a mix of both. Some things are restricted for women due to religious reasons, and sometimes society or the community pressurises a family. I think it also depends from family to family. In more developed areas like Mumbai, which is metropolitan, the Bora community tends to be more closely associated. Because ours is a smaller community compared to other communities, so we tend to stick close together.

So we know each and everything about each other and the family. Which makes it restrictive.

But that does not stop people from doing what they want. I know young girls who would leave their houses in burqas and hijab, but the moment they reached college, they would change into casual wear. Or guys will go out to drink.

There is also lot of hypocrisy within the community.

Did you ever feel obliged to talk to these people, or about these people who broke these rules?

No, I never bothered. I understood that sometimes the pressure of the families is too much. And kids/young people did it only to please their parents, but never really believed in any of these rules/restrictions. Also, it is common to see that normally parents of these kids enforced these rules without really understanding them. It was more to show off in the community they follow and believe in everything but in reality they did not care that much at all. It was done more to preserve their image within the community.

Ok. So can we talk about FGM, now?

FGM? What is that?

FGM – Female Genital Mutilation.

Oh, you mean circumcision?

Yeah. Sorry, I didn't know it was called circumcision.

It's ok. Yeah we call it circumcision. There is no mutilation or anything. It is not like girls' parts are mutilated or damaged. If done properly, it is a simple circumcision.

Circumcision is performed in both boys and girls. In boys it is normally done at a very young age. And medically it is said that it helps. That it needs to be done.

In girls however it is done at a later age. Sometime after 4–5 years of age. And maximum age at which it can be done is 8 years. However, medically it is said that it is not really needed. So I am against it. Because it is unnecessarily putting a child through pain.

My Mum believes the same thing. She said after she got mine done, she got to know that it does not really help with anything. Nor is it needed. So she told me that she will make sure it does not happen with my daughter if I ever have one. She asked me to make sure that I do not put my daughter through it.

I have a cousin, who did not get it done for her daughter. Even though her mother-in-law wanted. But my cousin was against it and refused. So now women have started saying no to it. And stopped supporting it.

And it is not just younger generation that is against it. My mother tells me that lot of her friends are also against it. They say they will not let their granddaughters go through it. So views are changing.

Why is circumcision practised in your community? Is there any specific reason? Are there any religious directives?

Well medically we know there is no significance in girls. But for boys, it is medically said it should be done. But circumcision is practised to control sexual desires. It is said that when we hit puberty, we can become sexually active. That we have a desire for it. To curb that desire, circumcision is practiced.

There is no religious significance behind it. It is not like our leader asks us to do it. But it is also not something we talk about. If I am against it, I won't go around and talk about it with other people in my community. I will only talk about it with my close friends.

Like, I am friends with this guy who is my neighbour. But I won't be able to discuss this or my views with him or his family because

I do not know what they think about it. And I don't know if they support it or are against it. I do not know how they will react. So it is better I do not talk to them about it.

Why did you choose to talk to me about it? And why do you want to be anonymous? Do you expect some form of backlash?

Yes, there is a chance that people will not be happy that I am talking about this issue. They will talk about me. They will say that Mehzabin says stuff like this against the community.

I am talking to you because I think more young people should talk about change. And progress. We should not be regressive. There is a gap in our community, where young people do not express their opinions and views. I think we need to fill that gap.

Circumcision does not achieve anything. It is unnecessary putting a child through pain. Within my family, my Mum and I have decided that we will not get it done for my niece, my brother's daughter.

Have you had circumcision done?

Yes. My mother said she got it done for me when I was 5–6 years old. But I do not remember. But when I grew up and she talked to me about it, she told me: 'Mehzabin, do not get it done to your daughter. I do not want you to put your daughter through that pain.'

Do you resent it?

I do not remember anything from my experience. My mother says it is a simple procedure. But she did say that I had nightmares for some time after that. I couldn't sleep and I used to cry at night. So she asked our family doctor about it. And he told my Mum that there is no medical reason that supports circumcision.

Since then she has been against it.

Did you know that circumcision is not performed on girls outside your community?

No. This is something we do not talk about. It is not only personal, but also awkward to talk about. We are normally very uncomfortable. I have only talked about it with my closest friends, who all belong to my community. So they understand and we share our experiences.

I have never had close friends outside the community. So I never got to talk about it with them. When I became older and my mother talked to me about it, she told me not to talk about it outside the community. She said that other girls will not understand because it is not done for them.

So I never talked about it. Plus, unless you choose to talk about it, no one ever knows who has got circumcision done. There is no way to tell unless you look for it specifically.

Are there any problems for girls after marriage who have not had circumcision?

No, that's the thing. No one knows if you have been circumcised or not unless you say it. Even after marriage, the husband doesn't get to know about the circumcision. And if you don't tell anyone, there will not be a problem.

Do men in the family have any say in such cases? Like fathers?

Men do sometimes take a stance. And it can be orthodox. Usually men are not involved. It is mostly women who take these decisions. My dad never said anything. Now in my niece's case as well he doesn't say anything. But my brother is like, if there is really no problem then she should get it done. But my mother and I are against it.

He is worried that someone will get to know that she has not had it done. But we told him that if we tell my niece not to talk about it and not to tell anyone, then no one will know. We are just waiting for it to be June, because then she will turn 8 years old, and circumcision is not done after that age.

Why?

Because girls' bodies start changing for puberty. And it is not considered good or safe to do it after that. Ideal age is between five and seven years.

Do you know anyone who does circumcision?

These days lot of people get it done by a doctor. They go to doctors belonging to the Bora community. Because it is safe and in a controlled and healthy environment. And they are trained. So there are less chances of something going wrong.

> I used to know an old lady who used to do it. But she has passed away. There are fewer women who do it in houses now. Almost everyone now goes to a doctor.
>
> *Do you know if any doctors turn the parents away and suggest against circumcision?*
>
> No. I have never heard of doctors recommending against female circumcision or refusing to do it. Unless asked if it is necessary, they do not say anything and perform the procedure.
>
> *Do you know if anyone has ever had problems due to circumcision?*
>
> We do hear cases of it going wrong. Personally I knew some girl in my family's village. She was my cousin's friend. We got to know that hers was not done properly and she had bled a lot. Since then she has had constant problems.

This interview confirms much of what is already known in terms of the motivations and reasoning for continuing with the practice, in particular two recent studies that draw attention to the tensions and contradictions in how women from different communities talk about the practice.[23] Those who link pain and medical complications to the practice are more likely to be against it and to prevent their own daughters from going through it. Those who feel that the cultural or religious requirements have strong links to identity and personhood are more likely to remain firm, arguing for the continued necessity of the practice. This woman expresses understanding of why FGM continues, but also seems adamant she will not put her own daughter through it. However, one interview is not enough to give insight into the dynamics of a community and the tensions between those who hold to FGM as an important part of their tradition and those who feel it is no longer needed. What this interview does show is that FGM is a reality for women in this community. Feminists I have spoken with and asked about FGM admit it happens but locate its prevalence within tribal/rural communities rather than in India's most urban metropolises.

Theorising victimhood

The problem of 'voyeurism' when conducting qualitative research that involves 'giving voice' to difficult and personal topics such as FGM needs further consideration. Within anthropology we have a significant body of work that looks at the 'politics of suffering' and 'victimhood'; these discourses have been helpful in unravelling and presenting a narrative on how and why moral panics erupt around some particular practices but not others. Suffering and victimhood are approached within such works as social and cultural constructs; the various examples of violence looked at in the current volume highlight the extent to which particular tropes in fact emerge in different ways. As Kleinman states: 'Cultural representations of suffering – images, prototypical tales, metaphors, models – can be (and frequently are) appropriated in the popular culture or by particular social institutions for political and moral purposes.'[24] Returning to the discourse analysis in Part Two of this volume, in which newspaper reporting of rape was the focus, I argued that the image of the female victim is constructed in relation to the supposed backwardness of a culture that condones the violence she has suffered. The reporting rendered rape victims silent, maintaining a subaltern position reminiscent of colonial portrayals of *sati*. Frequently, articles reporting HCPs carry a single photograph of a 'victim' followed by a gruesome account of their experiences of the practice and its lasting trauma.

Anthropology has recast suffering in part as a social object rather than solely an individual or natural experience: suffering is learned, used and represented, and this we see in the emergent public narratives of HCPs. These narratives are of course highly politicised. As Jeffery and Candea observe, 'victimhood establishes a space for a specific kind of politics',[25] and this space is characterised in this instance by moral outrage which then has a determining role in the response that surfaces from the various stakeholders: 'Grass-roots research on victims often involves co-construction that is moral and analytical engagement with subaltern subjects in the field of study which becomes the medium through which moral and social or political support is administered.'[26] The process of co-construction is fraught with pitfalls and the likelihood of actual responsive equal engagement is dependent on each other's attention. Unfortunately, the politics of movements is often such that actors within them use the construction of a victim as a way of leveraging power, and so a subaltern is maintained as necessary in order to mobilise the masses around the cause. Jeffery, drawing on Ferguson's 'Anti-politics Machine', argues that victimhood can negate the political with victims deliberately positioned as 'apolitical' so as to appeal to a wider pool of patrons.[27] In the context of global feminism, this is in part about capturing funds to eradicate particular instances of violence: images of suffering help to generate a moral obligation that draws funds. The politicisation of victimhood also helps us understand a little more of why it is that certain types of violence receive a disproportionate amount of attention at any given time. The line between victim and agent is also blurry: Werbner (following Levinas) has pointed out that perpetrators can 'violently enforce silence';[28] but in the case of HCPs the victims are also often the perpetrators. For example, women perform FGM on girls; mothers-in-law may harass their daughters-in-law if they believe they have brought insufficient dowry into the household. In both examples the perpetrators may hold raw memories of their own suffering linked to the practices they continue to uphold.

How does this theorising help researchers navigate away from voyeuristic depictions of victims? Ethnography and qualitative approaches more widely cannot just be about recording different voices and experiences, constructing a narrative out of them that is often subversive and radical; they also need to weave between competing discourses, highlighting how one viewpoint emerges as dominant and enabling the emergence of critical questions as to the marginalised treatment of subaltern voices. Throughout this volume, and in this section specifically, the intention has been both to give voice to different groups of women involved in GBV – from activists to survivors and both – and to draw attention to problematic discourses that may be well intentioned but that assert power over those best placed to eradicate violence. In particular, the macro critique has argued that neoliberal ideology has served to entrench violence, making it easier for certain practices to continue whilst maintaining a false binary between liberated and oppressed that adds yet another power dynamic that must be challenged in an already toxic mix of conservatism and misogyny.

Conclusion

In summary, in this chapter I have argued that there is no definitive 'solution' to these controversies. I maintain that 'HCPs' is a viable category of analysis, and I have offered an analytical, comparative frame through which HCPs across the globe may be usefully studied. This frame takes the form of a spectrum along which practices are placed according to the extent to which they display various intersectional characteristics, factors and dimensions. The results raise a number of questions, including: to what extent is a practice used as a means to maintain a particular view of social order and to the benefit of whom or what?; are HCPs limited to longstanding 'traditions' through which cultural complexes such as family and group honour are maintained?; in what way are modern institutions such as the state and the media involved in the emergence and reproduction of HCPs?; how do patterns of colonialism, decolonisation, migration, globalisation and transnational flows and exchange impact on the dissolution or spread of HCPs and the emergence or adaption of new forms, such as diminishing FGM or the globalisation of the beauty and cosmetic surgery industry?; what is the relationship between an HCP and constructions of female, class and ethnic identity?; what are the psychological and physical dimensions of HCPs and how physically intrusive and violently painful is a particular form?; and what is the likelihood that one practice will lead to other forms of abuse and harassment (e.g. domestic violence)? Each question listed here to end this chapter requires careful unravelling and contemplation. The interrogation of the category 'HCP' is a useful starting point but only if it is taken as a tool for a much wider critique.

The wider critique must include an analysis of the negative impact of global neoliberal economics on the prevalence of HCPs, but also of how they are observed. As stated at junctures through this volume, India's embrace of neoliberalism has resulted in an endorsement of consumerism as a new means to acquire status, even for those born into a low caste. This is particularly evident in the case of dowry, as outlined in the next chapter. Modernisation has woven a path through India's traditions and cultures in such a way that a crude binary between those that 'fit' the vision and those that 'do not fit' is stark. In a society where status is everything, being seen to 'have' is a matter of honour and women's bodies remain an asset in the commodity market, used by families to gain more through the gift-giving rituals attached to marriage.

CHAPTER 8

DOWRY, MARRIAGE AND VIOLENCE

Introduction

It is now a decade since the All India Democratic Women's Association (AIDWA) conducted its important national survey exploring the breath and impact of dowry. The resulting report, *Expanding Dimensions of Dowry*, published in 2003,[1] has been well-referenced and analysed by leading dowry scholars. The conclusions were shocking: dowry had spread and was no longer predominantly observed in the north of India, it was also no longer the preserve of the upper castes. As the benefits of India's economic liberalisation were increasingly felt by lower-caste groupings, so they had begun to practise dowry. Muslim families also adopted dowry, instead of or in addition to *mehr*. With the spread of dowry came a rise in dowry harassment. In particular, newly married women were increasingly tormented by in-laws expressing dissatisfaction at the amount of money, gold and/or consumer goods they brought in dowry. In other cases commonly reported, husbands turned violent towards their wives once their perceived economic usefulness had passed; in other words, once the dowry had been given and spent. AIDWA's survey, as its title suggests, highlighted the complexities of dowry both in relation to how it is practised but also in terms of the impact it has on women's lives. One of the main objectives behind AIDWA's survey was to measure the impact that women's organisations and movements across the country have had on challenging dowry. Prior to the survey, the eradication of dowry had been a main focus for many feminist campaigns for two decades. The key question therefore was: could any decline in the practice be seen? Palriwala analysed AIDWA's findings and concluded that dowry operates within a complex web.[2] She claims that dowry feeds into a gendered ideology committed to ensuring that women remain inferior to men. Dowry, she argues, will only be removed once the misogynistic values that it promotes are destabilised and no longer represent the norms of family life. It is a mistake, she asserts, to see dowry harassment and violence as the only forms of abuse women suffer: instead, dowry needs to be seen in the context of a deep-rooted patriarchal system that leads to an array of oppressions against women. The survey revealed that anti-dowry legislation had failed to have any real impact on halting the practice, and that dowry was more deep-rooted than originally thought. According to Palriwala: 'If dowry is to be tackled its multi-structural links and the network of relationships in which it is embedded have to be broken.'[3] The current chapter tests in one field site the extent to which dowry is still practised and why, to see if anything has changed ten years after the AIDWA report and a further decade of feminist campaigning.

My approach involves examining the relationship between dowry and the wider abuses and inequalities that women experience; in addition to the vibrant women's movement in India, there is a heightened global awareness that gender inequality, and specifically violence against women, represents, across the world, a key barrier to social equality. The data was collected through qualitative fieldwork in a rural location in Kerala; the findings represent one of the most recent studies on attitudes towards dowry and critical examinations of the relationship between the practice and forms of abuse against women. It starkly highlights that the dowry problematic continues, with an ongoing detrimental impact on the lives of women. Dowry is shown to shape a marriage system that limits women's opportunities as well as subjecting them to high instances of abuse, and the study also exposes an interesting contradiction. The women interviewed, across educational levels and caste background, expressed a heightened awareness of the impact of dowry. Many directly identified dowry as the trigger for the abuse and unhappiness they experienced as married women. However, despite this acknowledgement of dowry as a problem, very few women stated that they would not give dowry at their daughter's wedding. Dowry was necessary if women were to acquire any degree of protection from abuse in marriage, and was also required if a high-status marriage was to be secured. Our research exposes the impact of two dominating discourses on dowry: the feminist view, expressed by highly active women's organisations in the state, that pushes women to resist dowry; and that of male community leaders and marriage brokers, who continue to deny that dowry is a problem. The women interviewed for this study stand between these views, understanding through their experiences the accuracy of the feminist interpretation of dowry, but influenced in their immediate lives by the patriarchal status quo perpetuated through dowry, which is endorsed by key local figures. The research highlights the importance of continuing, even increasing, anti-dowry campaigning, focusing on those views that recognise the need for the marriage system to change.

The following section outlines the methodology adopted in the study. This in turn is followed by a review of research conducted on dowry in India, and specifically Kerala. In the third section, the data is summarised and a detailed analysis given. The conclusion offers some thoughts on the way forward for activists working to end dowry and improve gender equality in India and beyond.

Methodology

Kerala in south India was selected because it presents very positive development indicators, particularly in regard to gender, and as such is of particular interest. For example, many women access education at secondary and university levels and state-provided healthcare is freely accessible, with positive impacts on mortality rates and quality of life. It is reasonable to infer that if dowry is still highly prevalent in this state, and a link could be made between the practice and forms of harassment, this would suggest that improving women's lives in other areas had failed to significantly reduce violence triggered by dowry. Low levels of violence against women, alongside access to education, healthcare and employment, is a key indicator of women's empowerment. The key research question therefore focused on whether a link can be evidenced between dowry, violence and gender inequalities more widely.

Qualitative data was collected from Engandiyour Village, in Kerala's Trichur district. It was selected because it is representative of other villages across the state: it is a mixed village with families from a range of castes including Dalits, there is no segregation of Scheduled-Caste housing and although untouchability was prevalent until the 1930s, it is less noticeable now. The population in 2001 was 22,449 (2001 census), across an area of 14.12 sq km. The sex ratio was reported as 86 men for every 100 women. Religious groups in the village break down as follows: Hindus, 65 per cent; Muslims, 15 per cent; and Christians, 20 per cent. Inter-caste and religious interactions increased from the 1970s, when migration from the village to the Middle East began. The village is and has always been patrilineal. Maternal and infant deaths are very uncommon, at less than two deaths per year. The majority of the houses now have concrete roofs, whereas in the 1950s coconut-thatched houses were the norm. There are ten government schools in the village (both primary and secondary), which is thought adequate for the number of school-age pupils. Literacy is almost 100 per cent among both males and females. Agriculture has declined since the 1970s, when coconut plantations and rice cultivation was prevalent. Labour shortages due to migration to the Middle East and high wages are thought to have resulted in the decline of this sector. There is no hunger or malnutrition in the village. This demographic information clearly paints a picture of a well-developed and reasonably prosperous village.

The literature reviewed below indicates that across India, despite increased prosperity and less caste distinction, wealth has not curbed gender inequality, and that dowry practice and related harassment have increased. In the case of Engandiyour Village, local informants commented that the average income of villagers has increased dramatically, but in line with this so has the amount families must raise in dowry, with every family practising it regardless of caste background. Kerala is exceptional in that in some areas (although not Engandiyour Village) used to practise matrilocality or matriliny. However, dowry is now widespread, and there are no differences in the nature of the practice or its impact as regards caste, religion or formerly matrinilial practice.

Given India's anti-dowry legislation, informants could not be asked directly about the practice. However, given that dowry is a marriage practice and marriage is viewed as a significant moment in a person's life information was likely to come through in how people reflect on and recall their life experiences. I began by conducting structured interviews with married women, the aim of which was to explore links evidenced in previous research (discussed below) which suggests that marital gift giving (dowry) in many cases feeds into different forms of abuse after marriage. However, in line with arguments made by Basu and Parliwala, dowry was not viewed interchangeably with domestic violence;[4] dowry manifests as a trigger for forms of harassment but does not represent the full range of abuse women suffer under the label 'domestic violence'. Further, the research was not premised on the view that removing dowry would result in a reduction of domestic violence; rather, the analysis applied to the data reveals that in challenging and eradicating dowry, deeper-rooted structural changes to gender relations will have to occur, and that it is these changes that will result in a reduction in violence against women. Dowry therefore makes a useful focal point for wider research on women's empowerment and a good measurement when assessing shifts in gender relations, but its eradication is not in itself sufficient to radically equalise the lives of men and women.

I interviewed 47 women aged between 18 and 35, drawn from across religion and caste groupings. The interviews were limited to this group to make the data analysis more focused, but also because the link between dowry and domestic violence is most likely to materialise among the newly married. Arguably, women in this age range have less power to negotiate within their marital home and are therefore more vulnerable to abuse. The data collected also seeks to understand the impact of this powerlessness on how young newly married women understand the impact of dowry on their lives. In other words, how conscious are young women of dowry acting as a trigger for abuse that they and/or others experience? A smaller sample of eight men was also interviewed, again within the same age group and across castes. All of our informants were asked questions about their experiences of married life and the role that gift giving (dowry) had played in it. The women interviewed were also asked further about the problems they face and about whether they had experienced any form of violence.

The structured interview data was then expanded through in-depth interviews at community level. Seven in-depth interviews were conducted with women in the same age group as the survey informants; they were asked to reflect on their experiences or perceptions of marriage and give their views on dowry. Two focus group sessions were held with local women. The first was with a local women's self-help group, the age range of which was 40 to 60, while the second was with a group of women again aged between 18 and 35. The focus session held with the self-help group was particularly helpful. The grassroots nature of these groups means that members are well-placed to give a view on dowry prevalence and its impact.

A similar focus group was held with a group of male community leaders, who were asked similar questions to the women's self-help group. An in-depth interview was conducted with a prominent marriage broker in the area. Finally, members of an active and high-profile women's organisation in Kerala, who themselves have conducted research on gender-based violence in Kerala, were interviewed.

The dowry problematic in India: What the literature says

Across India

Studies, beginning with the survey conducted by AIDWA in 2003,[5] show that dowry is increasingly the trigger for some forms of domestic violence. It should not be seen simply as a symptom or factor propping up and supporting violence, but rather as the starting point for an array of exclusionary and violent practices against women. Studies have found that the practice of dowry makes it twice as likely that a woman will suffer domestic violence.[6] Even more troubling is that dowry giving has increased over the years, involving more and more caste groupings.

According to authors such as Srinivasan, Dalmia and Lawrence, the surge in dowry giving has been caused by India's shift in economic policies toward liberalisation from the 1990s.[7] As people gradually saw their wages increase, particularly in the agricultural sector as a result of the Green Revolution, so lower castes and Dalits could afford to give dowry. As Srinivasan has articulated:

> From being a symbolic practice, dowry has become a coercive transaction in which the woman's value is determined by the amount of dowry her parents will pay. Although there are differences among different castes and classes on each/all of the three dimensions discussed here, the general perception is that it is increasingly becoming impossible for a woman to be married without a sizable dowry. What was once a scattered phenomenon in south India, limited to some castes and classes, has now become pervasive.[8]

Economic modernisation and liberalisation has also increased women's employment opportunities and earning potential. Dowry is seen as an important means through which a family can both display its status and attempt to raise it, and giving dowry is linked to household reputation.[9] Further, for the lower castes and Dalits, giving dowry is a means of emulating the upper castes (Sanskritisation). If all groupings give dowry the practice is no longer the preserve of the wealthier and thereby a marker of their superior position.[10]

However, according to scholars such as Srinivasan the giving of dowry is not just about social status; it is also about preserving family honour. Daughters mirror the family's status and so must be well presented both in terms of their physical appearance, expensive clothes and jewellery but also increasingly in terms of educational attainment. Pressure has increased on families to not only present daughters at marriage with a large dowry; daughters should also be well-educated, with the potential to earn money and increase the wealth of their new family.

Links between different forms of gender inequalities

Dowry and forms of violence against women, including domestic violence, can be linked. It therefore follows that other gender inequalities will also affect a woman's life, including restricted access to health services. AIDWA in their survey show how dowry is part of a series of linkages (Figure 8.1).

A number of studies in which men were interviewed about whether they beat their wives revealed some shocking findings. In 2002 a survey conducted by ICRW in four states – Rajasthan, Tamil Nadu, Punjab and Delhi – found that 85 per cent of the men reported engaging in at least

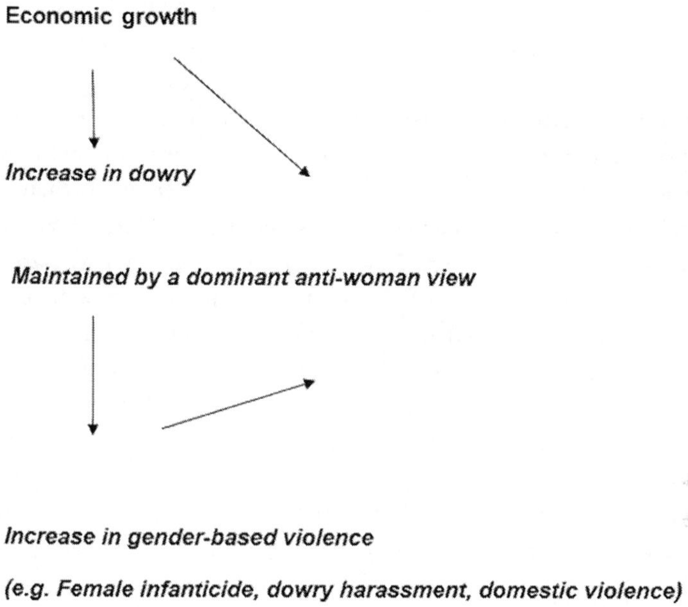

Figure 8.1 Dowry and gender-based violence.

one form of violent behaviour in the past twelve months. Breaking down that figure to types of violence, 72 per cent reported engaging in emotional violence, 46 per cent reported control, 50 per cent reported sexual violence and 40 per cent reported physical violence. Narayana in a similar study examining five districts in Uttar Pradesh found that 30 per cent of the men reported beating their wives.[11]

There is agreement among feminist scholars such as Palriwala and Basu that at the root of the problem is the social construction of gender and women's position in the family.[12] The significant force of women's movements in India seems unable to transform patriarchal constructions of gender identities; Bush in the early 1990s argued that despite the anti-dowry legislation in India and widespread activism, the practice had increased along with domestic violence.[13] Explanations for the rise in domestic violence have focused on the impact that modernisation and Westernisation have had in improving women's economic productivity, making them more independent. This shift in women's employment status has placed pressure on men to maintain their position as the breadwinner. This, so Bush claims, has led to increases in domestic violence as a backlash against the perceived greater autonomy of women. As Srinivasan explains, the Green Revolution increased the demand for women as agricultural labourers; however, women's improved financial independence did not translate into a more equal social status.[14] A contradiction emerges: there is no correlation between women's level of economic productivity and their social status. Women, regardless of their earning potential, are still viewed as an economic burden. As Agnihotri states, it will only be when women are valued for their economic contribution that their social status will improve.[15] The more recent analysis of the Youth Study data discussed in Chapter Two found that women who continued to work after marriage were twice as likely to suffer forms of physical domestic violence than those women who did not work for wages.[16] Whilst this research collectively supports the link between increases in women's economic participation and rising levels of violence against women, this cannot explain the underlying reason, which still remains under-researched.

The development context in Kerala

In 1997, the United Nations Development Programme (UNDP) listed Kerala among Indian states as having both the highest position on the Human Development Index (HDI) and the highest position on the Gender-related Development Index (GDI). Basic demographic indicators such as life expectancy are almost on par with those of the developed world:

> Superior physical health indicators and high levels of education among Kerala's women are not accompanied by commensurately high levels of social development in other areas. The persistence of social practices such as dowry and women's lack of empowerment works against their physical, psychological, and financial well-being.[17]

The glowing social development statistics hide a picture of increasing levels of domestic violence: the social situation in Kerala is deeply patriarchal and strong gender stereotypes prevail which prevent freedom, mobility and independence among women.[18]

Sakhi is a feminist organisation based in Trivantrum. In the early 2000s it conducted research for the state government on gender-based violence and found that almost 40 per cent of women had experienced some type of violence during their lifetime. It identified physical and psychological violence as the most common types experienced (rather than sexual or economic), and disputed assumptions about some groups of women being more vulnerable to violence than others: 'Women experienced domestic violence across all educational strata almost equally, and in fact women with a university degree reported a slightly higher level of violence than others without any education.'[19]

Sakhi claim that the full extent of gender-based violence in Kerala has been hidden by the positive focus commentators and politicians have placed on high literacy and health provision. In the early 2000s there was a growing uneasiness with Kerala's social development outcomes; research carried out by Eapen and Kodoth revealed that across several indicators women suffered low status – for example, political participation.[20] Sakhi's report concluded that cases of dowry-related violence, rape and other atrocities against women in Kerala were increasing. About 34 cases of dowry deaths were registered in the state in 2000, but the cases of dowry harassment by either the husband or family members stood at 2,653, compared with 380 in 1993. The organisation explained:

> The review of studies on Kerala present a complex picture of a state with high levels of literacy and high life expectancy for women coexisting with a relative lack of autonomy. The few studies on gender-based violence and the state's crime statistics indicate a potentially high level of gender-based violence against women, with its many negative health and developmental consequences.[21]

In Sakhi's survey, 41 per cent of married women had been subjected to demands for dowry from their husbands' families. Although about 60 per cent of the women reported that their husbands' families were satisfied with the dowry received, a very large number preferred to not comment. According to Sakhi, 'it may not be out of place to interpret this as a not very positive situation.'[22] For 6 per cent of women, their husbands' families were clearly not satisfied with the dowry they had brought, and 8 per cent of the women stated that demands for dowry continued also after marriage. Sakhi's survey also captured women's views on violence, with one third of the women feeling that a husband has the right to beat his wife. At the same time, the majority (74 per cent) believed that it was also right for women to react against or not put up with GBV. Out of the 900 women surveyed, 347 (38.6 per cent) had at some time in their lives experienced physical and/or sexual violence, or mental and/or economic abuse.

Of all the variables considered as a trigger for violence, Sakhi found demand for dowry to be most significantly associated with experience of lifetime violence. Women whose husbands or their families had demanded dowry before marriage were twice as likely to experience violence as those who did not face such a demand. However, this study is now more than ten years old, and Sakhi cautions that it is now too old to reflect the current situation. Our data therefore is significant, as it offers insight into the current impact of dowry on women's lives and conclusively reinforces much of the findings from the research of the early 2000s. Our findings and accompanying analysis depressingly show that dowry remains a fundamental problem in women's lives.

The 'dowry is necessary'–'dowry is a problem' continuum

In total, taking all the various interviews, surveys and focus groups into account, 73 per cent of the women interviewed were clear that dowry results in forms of harassment and abuse, even if they themselves had not directly experienced it. Around 34 per cent of the women interviewed talked about their own experiences of harassment, although the abuse suffered was, in most cases, described as not physical, but rather mental. The women with direct experience of harassment all talked openly about the profoundly negative impact it had on their lives, and specifically their sense of wellbeing. One informant talked about the mental/emotional abuse she suffered from her mother-in-law, who, she stated, 'restricts my freedom and does not regard me as a daughter.

My mother-in-law demands more dowry, and I have not got any, the harassment is unrelenting.'

Ninety-five per cent of the informants talked about how important dowry was for securing a good marriage for women. When asked what they meant by a 'good' marriage, female informants interviewed in the two focus groups described it in terms of 'no harassment'; most also went on to describe it as a match that brings high status. This statistic is particularly significant as it helps us to understand why dowry remains so persistent: dowry is seen as necessary, and while this remains the case clearly there is little chance of reducing the practice. We see in our findings an inherent contradiction, with 72 per cent of informants linking dowry to a reduction in women's freedom and increased vulnerability to harassment; an even higher percentage – 95 per cent – felt that dowry was an important part of marriage and therefore life. For example, when asked how important gift giving is at marriage, one informant replied: 'Yes very important it is the responsibility of the parents, without such gifts the wellbeing of the daughter is vulnerable. So gifts secure her happiness in marriage.' Yet this same informant also responded to the question 'what is the main problem women face in life?' by saying 'dowry is the main problem women face.' Another respondent revealed a similarly contradictory view within the same answer: 'Dowry is a problem, but marriage is a necessary part of life and so dowry is necessary because it is the parents responsibility to secure good marriage.'

So whilst it is clearly acknowledged, particularly by younger women, that dowry triggers harassment, it is also seen as part of the wider social system, and that to reject dowry will bring graver consequences for women. This confirms Parliwala's argument that the underlying problem is not dowry itself but the gender ideology on which it rests.[23] Removing dowry will not automatically improve women's lives; however, as stated previously, dowry does provide a useful focus in wider campaigns on women's lives and in the fight to eradicate GBV. This wider acceptance of dowry by women, who understand, through direct experience, the negative impact the practice has on women's lives, can be also explained through quantitative analysis conducted in the Youth Study. This analysis found that women's ability to use dowry reduced the risk of domestic violence by 30 per cent compared to women who did not have the ability to use dowry.[24] Fear of harsher repercussions if dowry expectations are not met is one reason why the system remains so impenetrable. However, fear alone cannot explain the situation; indeed, if this were the sole explanation it perhaps would not be too great an obstacle to overcome. Rather, power emerges a key determinate of a woman's vulnerability to violence. If a woman has autonomy over her dowry then she is unlikely to be harassed in her marital home. She is also less likely to experience wider gender inequalities, being free to work and to continue with education without fear of violent repercussions.

Theories of patriarchy, in particular those that attempt to understand its impenetrability, tend to argue that women utilise a considerable amount of agency in their daily lives. Kandyoti, in her much-cited article 'Bargaining with patriarchy',[25] states that women, rather than rejecting patriarchy outright, instead manipulate the system for their own benefit and exercise agency in order to bargain their way into a better position. Other scholars, such as Basu,[26] agree with this but go further, stating that many women operate with a dual position, on the one hand acknowledging and rejecting the oppression of patriarchy whilst at the same time conforming to the system. Gold, in her work with rural women in Rajasthan, argues that women are critically reflective of the realities of their lives and the oppression they suffer. They exercise agency in often highly creative, but publically invisible ways. Gold and Raheja, and also Bradley, add that it is both inaccurate and patronising to assume that the lack of gender equality evident in high levels of harassment and domestic violence exists hand-in-hand with a lack of consciousness.[27] The situation and the positions women occupy in relation to inequalities and violence are highly complex and multi-layered.

The data in the current study clearly distinguishes between two narratives: 'dowry is a necessary part of life' and 'dowry is a problem'; informants can be placed on a continuum depending on the extent to which they endorse either or both narratives. Few informants stood clearly at one end or the other; most occupied a space in between moving between these two viewpoints, without experiencing them as contradictory: dowry is both a problem and a necessary part of their lives. Many women express these seemingly opposing views, even when they themselves have been subjected to dowry harassment and/or violence.

However, it should be emphasised that their views are not reflective of a lack of consciousness, but instead reveal the extent to which they find themselves caught within a web of interlocking factors that the eradication of dowry on its own cannot transform. What holds the web together is patriarchal power, a much more complex force to challenge.

Digging down into the qualitative data makes it hard for outsiders to comprehend why the 'dowry is necessary' narrative especially is expressed by younger women. In the focus group discussion with the younger women, they talked about emotional and psychological distress being used as a smokescreen for violence. They said women are unwilling to talk directly about the violence they may suffer at home because of the impact it would have on their families and specifically their children. Instead, women focus their testimonies on the mental trauma they experience. The nature of the harassment, so the focus group women agreed – and which is also backed up by the survey – is characterised by accusations that a woman is unworthy because she failed to provide adequate dowry. It is common for a family to make comparisons between the amounts of dowry brought by its various daughters-in-law. The women surveyed who had experienced this form of harassment often admitted that it affected their self-esteem and confidence, but once again this does not reflect a lack of consciousness or understanding of why they suffer abuse.

In some interviews, women talked about mental trauma and harassment as worse than violence. As one woman in the focus group shared: 'When you are physically beaten the pain is short, the wound will heal, with psychological and emotional abuse it is constant and never goes away.' However, in the same session the group seemed to agree that it is highly likely that when psychological abuse occurs violence is also there. This view is also supported by the director of Sakhi, who stated: 'It is hard to get women to talk about physical violence and many see psychological violence as worse, but we know it is there, in most cases where psychological abuse is recorded we expect women to also suffer forms of physical abuse.'

In conducting this research we found young women willing to talk about dowry, much more so than the eight men interviewed. The women surveyed were very up-front in linking dowry to the forms of harassment they suffer or that they have knowledge of other women experiencing.

This level of consciousness may well be evidence of the impact of local- and state-level women's organisations such as Sakhi, that continue to highlight dowry as a problem. It may also be due to the existence of various forums and networks within which women talk to their peers and share experiences, for example the local network of self-help groups. Scholars such as Bradley and Erndl[28] have offered ethnographic examples of the adeptness with which women, particularly younger women who find it hard, because of domestic demands, to meet with peers, make use of all available space to share problems and solutions. As already cited, Gold argues that creative expression and reflection in these spaces enables women to acknowledge oppression and think about how to respond to it; Erndl refers to these spaces as 'cracks in patriarchy'.[29] The most strongly expressed 'dowry is a problem' narratives in our research represent cracks in the still dominant patriarchal worldview. Our findings certainly suggest that younger women share similar views of dowry as a problem and that something of a consensus exists within this age group. Comparing the findings of our two female-only focus groups – one with younger women and the other with an older age group – reveals that they occupy different spaces on the continuum. Although both groups accepted dowry created tensions and was therefore a problem for women, the older women also offered other explanations in relation to the tensions experienced by women. Before analysing the views offered by the older women, we will first take a more in-depth look at the narratives given by the younger women.

The strength of the 'dowry is a problem' narrative expressed by the younger women can be seen in the transcripts of the in-depth interviews, and sections from four of these interviews are given below. Analysed comparatively they also emphasise the usefulness of understanding the views expressed through this continuum of views on dowry, as they each occupy slightly different spaces within it.

The first section is taken from the interview with a middle-class Hindu woman from a middle-high income family:

> In marital house when we have dowry we have prestige, it becomes a status symbol and all they will think she has brought this much money, or that gold, she must be from a great family. Why do

people think about a woman by gold or ornaments is that the only thing, if the person is educated it should certainly matter. Why should a woman be assessed only according to gold?

In the married house without dowry there will be comparisons. In my experiences in my husband's house there are three sons and I brought five lakhs altogether money, half in cash and half in gold, the second daughter-in-law came with less amount of gold and money and the mother-in-law compared us.

She talked with harsh words to the other girls, she used to suffer a lot, they considered me from a well set up family, she had respect for me but later this changed and she began to react serious to us, she did not know how to behave to girls, doesn't know how to speak to girls softly at all.

The more dowry a woman brings the better she is regarded.

Dowry is important to in-laws, and to parents as a way of ensuring daughters do not have any humiliation in her husband's house. Mental violence is more harsh than physical, both happen because of dowry. Mentally harassment creates wounds in our minds, physical violence does happen because of dowry.

In marriage market the more parents give, the better wealthier a husband they will get. It is like going to the market to buy an apple; we look for the export quality sticker. Men are stupid: how can you select a wife like this, dowry does not say anything about a woman's character, how can you select on this basis?

I was pressured to marry at 22, already I was told I was too old, I was not mentally prepared. This is why I now continue with my education. I had an arranged marriage, the families met, I asked to meet with him separately I said to him we can only proceed if I can complete my education after marriage. You have to be self-sufficient and not dependent because you do not know what will happen in the future. Many girls have to stop education when they get married and they do not contest this, I am not a person like this I definitely express my view.

This transcript brings out a number of issues, such as the way in which dowry feeds into and supports notions of family honour and status; the strength of this link is also noted by Srinivasan in her research on dowry in Tamil Nadu.[30] The transcript also highlights the extent to which dowry brings tensions into a household that are intensified when there are differences between the amounts daughters-in-law have brought. The informant has defiant views on dowry, seeing it as deeply problematic. However, when questioned about whether she would give dowry at her daughter's marriage, she replied that she would, for fear of the repercussions if she did not. In terms of the continuum, she sits nearer to the 'dowry is a problem' side but because she does not outrightly reject the system she edges slightly towards the 'dowry is necessary' end.

A second interview was with a middle-class Christian woman from a middle-income family:

> If he is measuring me based on money I will not marry him, I cannot go to public places like church, I can't even go to church because in my age group women are already married with children, they look at me like I am a fool, thinking it's a time for marriage. In the marriage market I will be disposed because I am getting old, right time for marriage not job, I want a job first, I will complete my education first.
>
> I cannot go to church because of the harassment from neighbours, brokers, friends which are married, they look at me she is ready for marriage. They look at me and think 'she is educated, she will get a good job', so the brokers will make more money from the match, I am worth more, so the brokers are chasing me.

This woman is unusual among our informants in her complete rejection of dowry. She sits firmly on the side of the continuum advocating that dowry is a problem and she will not have any part in the system. Her experiences also highlight the implications a woman faces when she projects this view so firmly. She has not chosen an easy path and has been marginalised from her community because of her decisions. She does, however, admit to receiving support from her parents, who believe that her education and career are important. In securing a good career with a comfortable income, she is able to ensure independence and financial resilience from what may come in marriage. Similarly, Srinivasan suggests that parents' investment in their daughter's education is another form of dowry, as it increases her long-term economic value to potential in-laws.[31] This informant, however, did not indicate if this was the view of her parents, and this is certainly not how she saw it.

The experiences of the third informant, a Hindu woman from a poor family are different again:

> I have no parents, my father passed away when I was two, I am 28, I married last year. I have two sisters who are married, in my house the eldest daughter-in-law is now not living in the house. Tensions between her and my mother-in-law were high.
>
> When I got pregnant my mother-in-law did not care, I drank only water the whole day, the neighbours warned me that the other daughter-in-law had to leave because of her.
>
> She controlled my ornaments saying: 'I keep you, so I will take your ornaments so they are not stolen.'
>
> After delivery I had an Ayurvedic treatment, my family had to cover the whole costs, my husband's family would not pay so my sister's husband had to take care of me financially. After three months, still the mother-in-law ignored my crying baby. I was expected to continue with domestic work even after just delivering. I had to show her that I won't put up with her temper.
>
> In some cases my husband is strict, I have no parents so I go to my sister's, my husband challenges me: 'why do you go to your sister's, it is not your home?' Now he is working abroad in the Gulf, sometimes he doesn't call because we argue and this makes me upset. Because I have no parents or brother I am very dependent on him. I worked hard to get an education so I can get a job and not be so dependent on my husband.
>
> Dowry is a problem in our society, so many elder sisters waiting for marriage because of lack of dowry; their family background is OK but no money for dowry. Job is necessary for every woman before getting married.
>
> Education and fair skin is what families look for in wives. I have a friend who is working but dowry is a problem, she is 27 and has no dowry, it makes her sad, she says 'I will not marry.'

> Dowry is not good.
>
> In the first few days of my marriage my mother-in-law said 'my son could have got a better wife than you with more dowry.' I feel some tensions, with other daughter-in-laws who brought more dowries, but things got better once my daughter came.

This informant has clearly suffered because of dowry and feels she has not been treated well in her marriage by either her mother-in-law or husband. She also exerts strong views about wanting a good education and securing her own economic position, perhaps as a result of these negative experiences. However, she is worried that if she does not give a dowry to her daughter she will suffer even more harshly than she has done already. This informant stands in an uneasy space along the continuum; she has a heightened critical awareness of her own situation and believes dowry to be the trigger, yet she is fearful of what might happen to her daughter if she does not provide a good dowry. She admits:

> I feel torn I know that my suffering has been caused by dowry, I don't want my daughter to suffer in the same way. If I make sure her dowry is large she can avoid such tensions, yet I know that dowry is the root problem, so what can I do? Also my husband would not agree to no dowry, he will want to show he is successful, I don't care about this.

The fourth woman is from a low-caste and low-income Hindu family:

> A life partner is necessary in this society otherwise it is seen as bad. I am 28, this is very late to get married, but I decided to marry after I secure good education and a job, this is what my father wants. My father is very poor but he will give something at my marriage and if he does so willingly then I will take it. I am not interested in dowry and I expect an educated husband who may not look for a high dowry.
>
> Dowry makes a big problem for poor families who feel pressured to find large dowry. If dowry is not given then there will be mental trauma, mental harassment. Physical harassment is

> happening, when women admit to mental harassment violence will also be there.

This woman again has a critical awareness of the problems dowry causes, yet she contradicts herself by saying that she will let her father give dowry if he so wishes. She is therefore not exercising agency to stop dowry but is hopeful that she will meet a husband who is educated enough to not be bothered if dowry is given or not. As with the second informant, her father's investment in her education may also be viewed by him as a form of dowry that will secure his daughter a better marriage; this, however, was not made clear in this interview.

Out of the seven in-depth interviews, only two of the women – one of whom is the second woman whose views are documented here – stated they would not marry with dowry; they therefore are the only women prepared to reject dowry outright. Each woman stands somewhere along the continuum, in some cases open about the uncomfortable position they occupy in regard to dowry. Using the continuum to analyse their responses again builds a picture of why dowry persists: unless women and men shift wholeheartedly to the view that 'dowry is a problem' and do not also sway towards 'dowry is necessary', the practice will remain even with such an open critique of its repercussions.

The older women in the self-help group talked about dowry causing families pressure and stress because of having to raise such high amounts. They acknowledged that families who were unhappy with the amount they received from a bride's family may direct that frustration towards her. However, they claimed that dowry remains a necessary part of life in the community, a way of ensuring that women secure a good marriage. One woman also talked about how many problems occur because mothers do not prepare their daughters sufficiently for married lives, and how harassment will also emerge when a daughter-in-law does not conform to the behaviour expected of them as wives. In the self-help focus group the following question was posed: what problems do women face in the society?

> Dowry is the most important problem and also lack of education, lack of employment and lack of cooperation from the point of the

> daughter-in-law. Women must cooperate in the in-laws family if these things are lacking then a problem(s) will occur.
>
> Mothers are no longer bringing their daughters up to understand the importance of respecting mother-in-laws. Daughters must be raised with a clear understanding that as young wives they must work alongside and take instructions from mother-in-laws. Girls these days, because they are more educated they seem to enter marriage with higher expectations. They become dissatisfied more quickly and this brings tensions in the family. They find it hard to accept that the dowry they brought into the home is not theirs to spend, that they are part of a family and decisions must be made for the good of the whole family not just them.
>
> Also the problem is that families want to marry up, if they marry at their own status no problems will occur.
>
> Although they don't agree with it they feel that giving dowry will ensure the status of their daughters in their marital home.
>
> The older generation is able to cope with problems the younger generation will not tolerate and as soon as there is a problem they will go to their natal home.

The other women in the group agreed enthusiastically with these views and it sparked an excited discussion in which the women shared experiences of problematic daughters-in-law, either directly or indirectly. This perception of the problem is interesting; dowry is placed as one problem among others. The women focused their discussion on the tensions young women bring to the family because they fail to adapt their behaviour to suit their new role. They blamed these tensions on mothers not raising their daughters to understand what being a daughter-in-law entails. So, on the one hand dowry is seen as a trigger for tension, but in fact they place the practice within a much broader framework of marital behavioural expectations, the focus of which is placed on young brides whose actions and attitude following marriage are under far greater scrutiny than that of their husbands.

Analysing these responses gives us a picture of the complex dynamics within joint family structures, a subject about which a significant amount has been written.[32] It also highlights the extent to which young women who enter the joint home as outsiders are subject to intense observation. The stress this must cause the new bride can be imagined; add to this situation dissatisfaction over dowry, and pressure on a young woman intensifies, spilling over, in some instances, into abuse. Whilst it is not suggested this extreme situation occurs in the homes of the women we spoke with in this focus group, their perceptions help us to understand how such a situation does arise in a significant number of homes. It also helps us appreciate the intrinsic link between dowry, marriage and the behavioural expectations placed on young wives.

The views of these women are interesting because the self-help group, of which the women are a central part, make employment opportunities for women a key activity. They emphasised in the same discussion the importance of women being financially independent; they did not see this independence as a means of breaking with tradition but merely a way of helping to increase women's status and decision-making power within the family. As one woman said: 'earning your own money is important as it means you can make decisions over how to spend it, perhaps saving it for children's education.' These older women therefore support and actively work to secure female autonomy within the family. At the same time they also openly endorse patriarchy, stressing the importance of young women conforming to their role as wives and mothers. Our research highlights that many women, once they reach the status of mother-in-law, are so invested in the patriarchal system that they become the primary harassers and perpetrators of violence against young women. Out of the 34 per cent of informants who talked of their direct experiences of violence, 45 per cent of the perpetrators were mothers-in-law. Although we cannot be confident that women were sharing the full picture, this finding is significant. The older women were not as critically focused as the young women in terms of talking about dowry as the main trigger for abuse.

Our data presented here helps build a picture of what factors feed the impenetrableness of the gendered ideology underpinning dowry. The feminist ideals of organisations such as Sakhi have had a profound impact in terms of offering women opportunities to increase their bargaining power within the family. However, they have not, by their own admission, been able significantly to dislodge the underlying patriarchal values structuring society. Comparing these two all-female focus groups reveals the differing preoccupations and perceptions of two generations. The data taken from the older group reveals that women themselves at certain points of their lives benefit from patriarchal power, which acts as a disincentive to accept any wider structural changes to the system.

The younger women focus much more directly on dowry as the root of women's problems, and make links between the practice and the wider inequalities suffered by women. The older women acknowledge that dowry brings tensions and pressures into the household, and note a rise in these tensions. However, their explanations of why problems arise in a family include the claim that young brides struggle to adjust to the demands of family life. A question that emerges from this analysis, and which cannot be answered from this data, is whether women's views shift along the continuum as they get older, or whether young women who hold very clear perceptions of dowry as problematic now will keep these views into their forties. Understanding how these shifts in perception may occur can help to assess the impact of feminist discourses on women's views of themselves and their place in the world. In other words, if young women towards the 'dowry is a problem' end of the spectrum hold on to those views into later life when they themselves are mothers-in-law, this would provide evidence of the lasting impact of feminist discourses on dowry. If, however, as they get older, their views slide along the continuum towards 'dowry is necessary', it could be argued that feminist discourses have a momentary impact that lessens as a woman's experience of the patriarchal system changes. The challenge for activists continues to be how to harness and hold on to the critique of dowry voiced by many women, and direct it into decisive action. This study suggests that despite increased levels of education for women across castes and religion, women remain vulnerable to violence, for which dowry often acts as the trigger. The reason for this vulnerability is not a lack of consciousness but rather of autonomy and power.

The views of men

Concerns that the younger generation were moving away from traditional values emerged in the male focus group, comprising three

Hindu community leaders aged 45–70, from the middle-castes. However, unlike the women, they did not see dowry generally as a problem, although one man said, 'perhaps in Christian or Muslim families but not among us Hindus'. This was an interesting projection of the problem on to other religious groups, which also came through in the women's self-help group, in which the women agreed that the most extreme cases of dowry resulting in violence against young wives occurred among Muslim families. The male focus group expressed fears that tensions were emerging because women and men no longer valued the joint family structures and the traditional gender roles bound within it. Across both focus groups it seemed that women were blamed more than men for this shift. One of the more vocal community leaders talked about how women's expectations had changed as they had become more educated and many now worked even after marriage.

The men interviewed endorsed the view that dowry was very important, and while none saw its practice as a problem, they certainly did not make any links between dowry and harassment toward women. On the topic of how important it is for parents to give dowry to daughters, the common response was that it was important to give dowry. If dowry is not given, the family will suffer a drop in status. However, views did differ on the wider issue of gender and specifically what women's role should be once married. The male informants did not always support an overtly patriarchal view. Similarly, Jehan, in her study of male views on dowry in Tamil Nadu, concludes that male perceptions and views on dowry and women's roles were far from homogenous.[33] She also talks about the need to recognise the contradictory views that men as well as women hold on dowry.

In this research the most extreme and obviously patriarchal was as follows:

> In community it is very important as there is no marriage without dowry. People give dowry sometimes beyond their ability. Status in the society is important reason for giving dowry for parents and receiving dowry. People ask how much dowry (gold) your daughter-in-law brought. Some people use dowry wisely others use it for alcohol etc.

When this informant was asked whether he thought his wife had any right over her dowry, he replied: 'No direct right. She has to discuss with me before she does anything with that'.

Each male informant was then asked whether women should pursue their education after marriage. Here views diverged; some agreed that they should, and went on to express support for women working once married. However, others shared the view of one informant who replied: 'No. I am not interested in her education', and 'no, women should not work, their job is in the home and a wife must do nothing unless her husband agrees.' Although no men in their responses came out with views located squarely on the 'dowry is a problem' end of the continuum, there were differences in views over women's role, and some seemed ambivalent about dowry, unconcerned at the thought of it not being practised. The continuum proposed to analyse views seems to work just as well in analysing male responses as it does when unpacking those of women.

Conclusion

The findings presented here depressingly show that little has changed since the comprehensive surveys conducted on dowry in the early 2000s. Dowry, and the gendered values it is embedded within, remain all-pervasive and unchallenged by liberalisation, despite increased educational provision for both boys and girls, better healthcare, advances in women's political participation and active local self-help groups and NGOs. Men seem unsure as to whether they should embrace women's entrance into the employment market; in-laws, rather than young wives directly, seem to retain control over the role women pursue in marriage and whether they should work or continue with their education. Women who hold defiant views insisting on a different way of being suffer because of their convictions. Some of the conclusions from the AIDWA survey stated that, rather than continue with anti-dowry campaigning as their central focus, activists needed to broaden their activities. The activities of many women's organisations across the country expanded to include raising women's autonomy and independence through greater access to education and employment. Projects also focused on ensuring women have access to healthcare and reproductive advice. Finally, initiatives have focused on empowering women to take on effective political roles at local, district and state levels. In Kerala the picture analysed through education, healthcare and employment looks positive for women. A significant amount of state funding has been directed at improving women's access to a range of services and opportunities, supported by the work of feminist NGOs like SEWA, Sakhi and AIDWA, which have been active in the state for the past decade. However, in terms of the next decade of campaigning, Sakhi, for example, feel that a lot more work needs to be done developing political leadership training programmes for women, as participation rates for women in local and district councils is still low. Perhaps, given another decade of work promoting women as decision makers we will begin to see shifts in the prevailing views on gender.

What is the way forward? The data analysed through the continuum of 'dowry is a problem'–'dowry is necessary' makes visible cracks in patriarchy, in that a significant number of women express views in line with the 'Dowry is a problem' narrative. Strengthening the audibility of these voices and supporting them in responding to the issues they feel dowry causes is vital; strengthening these voices should include attempts to remove ambiguity in the views expressed. In other words, initiatives should focus on moving the views of women and men across ages more squarely to the 'dowry is a problem' end, rather than hovering around 'but it is still necessary'. It should, however, be stressed that action in shifting opinion in this way must not solely focus on women; this is not a female-only problem that should be solved by more affirmative action on their part. Dowry should be viewed as the starting point for a deep-rooted restructuring of gender relations. As stated at the start of the article, removing dowry will not result automatically in a reduction in violence against women. However, this shift has also not been achieved through a more holistic approach either. Power dynamics underpinning inequalities remain intact and need to be challenged more directly. Shifts in attitudes can be measured by a focus on dowry and how people view it; do women's views change along the continuum as they get older? Or will we now see a significant shift in how dowry is viewed across generations as the young women we surveyed move into the status of mother-in-law?

A decade is far too long to leave such important surveying of views, especially when the practice being analysed acts as a deeper indicator of problematic gender values and inequality. The study here also highlights the importance of engaging men, in particular young men, whose views about marriage and the place of dowry within it could be influenced more heavily by the feminist anti-dowry discourse. If young men have greater exposure to both the arguments against dowry and the evidence which highlights its negative impact their views may also be transformed. If more cracks can be forced in the patriarchal narrative of 'dowry is necessary' then wider transformations to gendered norms may finally happen.

CONCLUSION

THE IMPACT OF NEOLIBERALISM ON VIOLENCE AGAINST WOMEN AND GIRLS

This volume has focused on two central but linked arguments, the first of which is that gender-based violence in India (as elsewhere in the world) remains an embedded and horrifying widespread abuse directed at half the population. This gendered abuse in all its forms has not receded, even with the onslaught of decades of feminist campaigning. Whilst inroads into gender equality have certainly been made – in particular, women's access to education and employment has much improved – violence remains as a constant reminder that the goal of gender equality has not yet been achieved. The second argument is that neoliberalism has not helped to reduce GBV but has in fact made it worse. Although research evidencing a backlash is still emerging, it is a reality in the testimonies of those experiencing it (see the Introduction and Chapter Two). What the backlash clearly tells us is that mind-sets have not shifted and the normalised view remains that women are inferior, and their place is within the domestic sphere, where they should stay. When women stray from the patriarchal demarked space, it is viewed by many (men and women) as legitimate to punish them. This mind-set is evident across the spectrum of class, caste and economic status. In Chapter One I documented numerous articles capturing views of India's male political elite, who continue to endorse GBV. To offer yet another example here: Ramsevak Paikra, the home minister of central Chhattisgarh state, said recently that 'such incidents [rapes] do not happen deliberately. These kind of incidents happen accidentally.' These remarks came just days after Babulal Gaur, the home minister of the BJP-ruled Madhya Pradesh, said about rape: 'Sometimes it's right, sometimes it's wrong.'[1] This has led critics to point to a 'culture of complicity' around GBV.

Neoliberalism has increased women's vulnerability to violence because its model of economic growth demands, in order to expand markets, the involvement of women in the workplace. In short, India needs to mobilise women into factories and offices and ensure they have the right levels of education so they are skilled enough to fulfil their economic role. The motivation, therefore, from this neoliberal economic perspective, is profit and growth, not the realisation of equal human rights for men and women. Of course women's full entry into the workforce is an important component of social equality and empowerment, but it has to be projected as such and not accepted begrudgingly as an economic necessity. What we see in the example that India provides is success in achieving a larger workforce of women has done little to dislodge mind-sets that still hold that public workspaces are no places for women. And so the contradiction emerges, with many women (but not all; for example, poor Dalit women remain outside of India's economic boom) being nurtured into new roles, promised a new-found independence and allowed to dream that their lives may be different. This reality takes us back to where I started this volume: with the brutal case of *Nirbhaya*. She is an example of such a woman who had made a choice that her life would break the mould of what her family in the past had expected. With their support she strove to become a professional and earn her own income. Her rapist-murderers felt justified in their actions because she, as far as they were concerned, was not behaving as she should; she was transgressing the gender line, which they found threatening.

Violence is a reality in the lives of all women, cutting across age, caste/class and wealth boundaries. Global attempts to address it have dented it, but have failed to reshape attitudes and behaviours to the extent needed. However, throughout this volume I have been cautious not to feed into an unhelpful narrative that portrays India as the worst place in the world to be a woman. This is simply not the case: India is a diverse and spectacular country endlessly varied with so many enriching experiences on offer. It is, though, blighted by extremes of violence so horrific most of us close down our minds to them. The hidden (or not so) horror of epidemic violence is a secret many countries harbour. India, because of the success of its women's movement and a new generation of activists, is being forced to come out in the open about the brutality within. In order to highlight the problem without isolating one country as worse than others, I will now offer some limited regional contextualisation, looking at instances of violence against women and girls across other countries in South Asia (Table 9.1 to 9.3), arguably at different stages of the neoliberal project. I will contrast these statistics with the economic opportunities available and national policy environment in place to curb instances of GBV.

The bleak statistics on GBV in India were presented at the start of this volume. In terms of the legal position currently under the Indian Penal Code, crimes against women include rape, kidnapping and abduction, molestation, sexual harassment, torture, homicide for dowry, and the importation of girls. The Criminal Law (Amendment) Act of 2013 expands the scope of sexual and gender-based crimes against women, including recognition of stalking and acid attacks, and removing the 'special permission' requirement to prosecute public servants. The Act however features degenerative elements: marital rape has impunity, it reduces victims' access to healthcare and other services, it fails to recognise the rape of men and it criminalises same-sex consensual relations. Critics (see the work of the Lawyers Collective, summarised in Chapter Five) have raised concerns about the vagueness of the definitions of crimes against women, especially with regard to rape. Perpetrators of severe sexual attacks are frequently charged with criminal assault on a woman with 'intent to outrage her modesty'; this carries a minor penalty which is rarely enforced. It has been suggested that young offenders are often treated too leniently, as regards both the conviction rate and sentencing.

The Indian Constitution still attributes legal rights related to marriage, divorce and inheritance according to an individual's religious background. As such, the judiciary either interprets religious law or accepts the judgments of clergy (male-dominated and largely conservative). However, and as discussed in Chapter One, the problem is not the existence of laws but how they are implemented. Moreover, according to Human Rights Watch, India's progressive laws are stymied

Table 9.1 The situation of women in Pakistan

Violence against Women	Women's Economic Environment	Policy environment
Three quarters of Pakistani women have experienced IPV.[2]	In 2014, women comprise 24.2 per cent of the labour force.[5]	Despite multiple changes to the law in recent years, including valuable secularising steps, effective state protection is unlikely to be available to those fearing VAWG.[8]
Unofficial VAWG data for Punjab province in 2013:[3] 774 murders 217 honour killings 1,569 abductions	Of the 12.1 million women in the labour force, 8.3 million work in agriculture / fisheries, 2.2 million in other elementary occupations, and 1.4 million in crafts and related trades.[6]	Acceded to CEDAW in 1996. The judicial system is still said to be biased against women.[9]
706 rapes 427 driven to suicide 56 women in 2013 were killed for having baby girls.	The Global Gender Gap Index places Pakistan 135th (of 136 countries), including 135th for 'economic participation and opportunity'.[7]	Pakistani law criminalises assault, rape, intimidation, insulting a woman's modesty, trading in women, forced marriages and marrying women to the Qur'an. Spousal rape is not a crime.
International orgs also highlight: forced and child marriage, acid attacks, IPV, marriage to the Qur'an.[4]		Religious organisations maintain significant influence over the law, with negative implications for women.[10] Section 18 of the Constitution grants all citizens the right to conduct lawful trade and business; all formal banking services are available to women.

Table 9.2 The situation of women in Myanmar

VAWG	WEE	Policy environment
No official statistics on VAWG are available,[11] but IPV and trafficking have been noted as increasing concerns.[12]	Women comprise 50 per cent of the labour force.[15]	Acceded to CEDAW in 1997
		No domestic violence laws.
Sexual violence is used by the military with impunity, especially against ethnic minority women.[13]	55 per cent of women workers are in the agricultural sector,[16] and they dominate the garment production sector.	Spousal rape is not a crime if the wife is aged 14 or above. Otherwise rape is illegal, but the law is rarely enforced.[18]
Customary law varies between states and regions; localised research is needed in the fields of family law and family issues.[14]	Wage disparities: for similar job roles, men earned an estimated income of US$1,043 in 2007, while women earned only US$640.48.[17]	Labour unions have recently been permitted; the media reports numerous instances of female garment workers striking.[19]

by entrenched corruption and lack of accountability. Is there real commitment to see VAWG end? Hence the importance of the spectrum introduced in Chapter Two, designed to test the depth of statements and initiatives to reduce VAWG.

In terms of women's economic empowerment, discussed in Chapter Two as responsible for a violent backlash, working Indian women tend to be located in specific industries and occupations, including basic agriculture, sales and elementary services and handicraft manufacturing. The WEF's 2014 Global Gender Gap Report ranked India 134th (of 142 countries) for gender inequality in economic participation and opportunity, and 126th in educational attainment. The Constitution of India prohibits discrimination on the basis of sex, while the Equal Remuneration Act (1976) ensures equal wages and

Table 9.3 The situation of women in Nepal

VAWG	WEE	Policy environment
Official figures on VAWG are not available,[20] but NGO figures for 2012–13 document the prevalence of IPV, rape, murder and trafficking.[21]	Women comprise 51 per cent of the labour force.[24]	Acceded to CEDAW in 1991.
	85 per cent of women workers are in agriculture, compared to 67 per cent of men.[25]	A reasonable legal framework is in place regarding VAWG, but the implementation still requires substantial work.[27]
77 per cent of abused women in Nepal have never sought help and 64 per cent have never told anyone.[22]	The Global Gender Gap Index places Nepal 121st (of 136 countries) overall, and 116th for 'economic participation and opportunity'.[26]	Government economic policy has generally sought women's increased participation in agricultural work.
Women reporting sexual violence are frequently ostracised, leading to vast underreporting.[23]		Women have legal access to bank loans and other types of financial credit,[28] but access to institutional credit remains limited.[29]

equal work for women.[30] However, this is poorly enforced and so does not reflect the situation on the ground: of 142 countries in the Gender Gap Index, India ranks 109th in 'wage equality for similar work'.[31] The Sexual Harassment of Women at the Workplace (Prevention, Prohibition and Redressal) Act was passed in 2013. However, a recent report finds that 97 per cent of companies are unaware of it.[32] A recent UNFPA publication[33] argues that while laws against child-marriage, sex-selective abortion and dowry are also poorly enforced, other laws exist that openly permit discrimination: one example is that sons, as heads of family, but not daughters, are guaranteed a government job if their father dies while in service. The publication also discusses inheritance issues. Upon separation/divorce, Indian women are entitled to maintenance, but have no claim over marital assets, such as a house or commercial property, purchased in the husband's name during the marriage. The picture is clear: as inroads into equality are made, the male-dominated establishment pulls back, helped by other sections of society that fear change or harbour anger that neoliberal modernisation has not transformed their lives as they were promised.

What we see when comparing across these countries is that the collection of official data is patchy, and the full prevalence and overall picture of GBV across the region (and globally) is still not fully known. The first stage to the eradication of GBV is to understand the full extent of the picture, however bleak, and this volume is intended as a contribution to this effort. Even in India, where statistics, legislation and overall empowerment programmes are happening – even if half-heartedly – the impact feels minimal. Clearly, the conservative realities emerging from the Pakistani data also ring true in the context of India. In Pakistan, women are not in great force in the economy, because of the conservative gender ideology under which they live. If women transgress the demarcated gender line, violence is the immediate tool of discipline, perhaps more so than in India (although I say this with caution, as the evidence is flimsy). In Myanmar and Nepal women are participating in larger numbers in the economy in the agricultural sector, which we know usually involves long hours and low pay. We cannot properly correlate instances of GBV to economic activities in these cases because the data simply does not exist. It seems, though, that at some level women's involvement in certain economic activities is tolerated if there is a serious necessity. So, in economies early in the neoliberal project, where subsistence living rather than market engagement is the main means of survival, women work alongside men. The implications this has for the structures of gender relations and instances of GBV is unknown, and I hesitate from claiming that more equal participation in employment activities spells equity in other areas. In India, poor rural women work in the fields along with their husbands but we know that they are particularly vulnerable to rape, for example from higher-caste land-owners who see them as property along with the earth they work. However, the critique I direct at neoliberalism is that it has not delivered on its other promises of empowerment and freedom. To return to the arguments presented in the introduction to this volume made by Harvey and Chomsky, neoliberal advocates promoted their vision with the promise that neoliberalism would not only increase wealth but would promote positive values of human rights and social justice. The universalisation of Western values is of course problematic, but even if we leave that aside, the reality is that neoliberalism has not, for many women, helped them overcome the most fundamental oppression they face: violence. I argue that in the context of India it is the formalisation and professionalisation of women's work that has the most impact in relation to triggering a backlash. This backlash comes in the form of intimate partner violence as well as harmful practices. Neoliberalism has left women more vulnerable than ever and its supporters offer no solution that has had any real effect. India, then, is a stark warning to countries now under pressure to move into the neoliberal way of being (whatever that really is): be wary of what it will deliver and be ready to respond to the violence it unleashes. The ability of states to respond to violence against women is hampered by the patriarchal foundations from which its apparatuses are shaped. Introducing legislation that promotes freedoms and equality means little if there is not the will to implement it and to do so with force and determination. External pressures to recognise the widespread abuse of rape has manifested in more legislation and more public declarations that attempts are being made; time will tell if these efforts actually contribute to the shift in mind-sets needed to eradicate GBV once and for all.

So what am I advocating? Essentially, what is needed is a systematic and sustained exposure of the perilous impact that neoliberalism has brought to the lives of women and girls. We must deconstruct the neoliberal narrative and retell it through the experiences of violence and abuse that women suffer the world over. This has been the objective of this volume, but of course it was never going to be able to achieve this with any comprehension: it has merely pointed at the irony of the prosperity promised by neoliberal economists. I hoped to have gone some small way towards bringing them, through the pages, into dialogue with women who have endured abuse and with those who work so tirelessly to end it, and of course those that represent both. The strongest evidence I have for this critique is the rise of a conservative right that insists that women must not move from the home. Ironically, many factions and organisations on the right are happy to embrace at least aspects of global neoliberalism: for example, the infrastructure that provides the mechanisms to communicate with new supporters and to secure funding. Additionally, access to technologies to kill and control and empire build has an appeal which groups of different political persuasion seem unable to turn their backs on.

The global and local tale of GBV is one of contradiction and side-stepping, but ultimately it remains a story about power and immorality. The web is a tangled mess and women continue to be marginalised and oppressed across the intersectional boundaries. I wish that after 20 years of researching and writing about violence against women and girls I could write a happy ending but I cannot. I can only hope that one day I will . . .

NOTES

Introduction

1. PTI, 'Statistics: 92 women raped in India every day, 4 in Delhi', *India Today*, 4 September 2014. Available at http://indiatoday.intoday.in/story/india-rape-92-women-every-day-4-delhi-statistics/1/380956.html (accessed 12 April 2016).
2. International Center for Research on Women, *Masculinity, Intimate Partner Violence and Son Preference in India: A Study* (Washington, DC, 2014), p. vii.
3. Sohini Paul, *Women Labour Force Participation and Domestic Violence: Evidence from India* (New Delhi, 2014).
4. World Health Organisation, South African Medical Research Council and the London School of Hygiene and Tropical Medicine, *Global and Regional Estimates of Violence against Women: Prevalence and Health Effects of Intimate Partner Violence and Non-Partner Sexual Violence* (Geneva, 2013).
5. UN Population Fund, *UNFPA Strategy and Framework for Action to Addressing Gender-based Violence 2008–2011* (New York, 2009), p. 7.
6. Nancy Chez, 'Helping the victim of domestic violence', *American Journal of Nursing* xciv/7 (1994), pp. 32–7.
7. UNICEF, *Progress for Children: A Report Card on Adolescents*, No. 10 (2012, New York), p. 32.
8. Jean Comaroff and John L. Comaroff, 'Millennial capitalism: First thoughts on a Second Coming', in Jean Comaroff and John L. Comaroff (eds), *Millennial Capitalism and the Culture of Neoliberalism* (Durham, North Carolina, 2001), pp. 1–56, p. 8.
9. Ibid., p. 4.
10. Ibid., p. 7.
11. Noam Chomsky, *How The World Works* (London, 2011), p. 3.
12. David Harvey, *A Brief History of Neoliberalism* (Oxford, 2005), p. 3.
13. Ibid.
14. See also Robin Truth Goodman, *Gender Work: Feminism after Neoliberalism* (London 2013).

15. Kristin Bumiller, *In an Abusive State: How Neoliberalism Appropriated The Feminist Movement Against Sexual Violence* (Durham, North Carolina, 2009).
16. Mary E. Hawkesworth, 'Knowers, knowing, known: Feminist theory and claims of truth', *Signs* xiv/3 (1989), pp. 533–57.
17. Nancy Fraser, *Fortunes of Feminism: From State Managed Capitalism to Neo-Liberal Crisis* (London, 2013).

Chapter 1 The Politics of Voice: Unravelling the Discourses

1. David Mosse, 'Global governance and the ethnography of international aid', in David Mosse and David Lewis (eds), *The Aid Effect: Giving and Governing in International Development* (London, 2005), pp. 1–36.
2. See, for example, Bill Cooke and Uma Kothari (eds), *Participation: The New Tyranny?* (London, 2004); Marc Edelman and Angelique Haugerud (eds), *The Anthropology of Development and Globalization: From Classical Political Economy to Contemporary Neoliberalism* (Cambridge, 2005); Jean-Pierre Olivier de Sardan *Anthropology and Development: Understanding Contemporary Social Change* (London, 2005); Tamsin Bradley, *Challenging the NGOs: Women, Religion and Western Dialogues in India* (London, 2006).
3. Mosse, 'Global governance', p. 1.
4. Nici Nelson and Susan Wright (eds), *Power and Participatory Development: Theory and Practice* (London, 1995); Emma Crewe and Elizabeth Harrison, *Whose Development? An Ethnography of Aid* (London, 1998); Andrea Cornwall, Elizabeth Harrison and Ann Whitehead (eds), *Feminism in Development: Contradictions, Contestations and Challenges* (London, 2007); Richard Peet, *Geography of Power: The Making of Global Economic Policy* (London, 2014).
5. Chandra Mohanty, *Feminism Without Borders: Decolonizing Theory, Practicing Solidarity* (Durham, North Carolina, 2003).
6. Donna Haraway, *The Companion Species Manifesto: Dogs, People, and Significant Otherness* (Chicago, 2003).
7. Interview conducted in January 2014.
8. Leslee Udwin (dir.), *India's Daughter* (2014). Made by Assassin Films for BBC Four's *Storyville* series.
9. Deutsche Welle, 'Women's rights barely a topic in Indian election', 12 May 2014. Available at http://www.dw.de/womens-rights-barely-a-topic-in-indian-election/a-17629634 (accessed 12 April 2016).
10. Tony Bonnici, 'Rape level shames country, says India leader Modi', *The Times*, 15 August 2014. Available at http://www.thetimes.co.uk/tto/news/world/asia/article4177227.ece (accessed 12 April 2016).
11. See the work of Sulabh International, who have been contracted by the Indian government to work on this issue across India and who make women's safety a key message in all the work they do (www.sulabhinternational.org).

12. UNICEF, *Progress for Children: A Report Card on Adolescents*, No. 10 (2012, New York).
13. Meredeth Turshen, 'A global partnership for development and other unfulfilled promises of the millennium project', *Third World Quarterly* xxxv/3, pp. 345–57.
14. Naila Kabeer, *Women's Economic Empowerment and Inclusive Growth: Labour Markets and Enterprise Development*. SIG Working Paper 2012/1 (London, 2012).

Chapter 2 Interventions, Good (or Not) Intentions and the Reality of the Backlash

1. Natalie J. Sokoloff and Ida Duport, 'Domestic violence at the intersections of race, class and gender: Challenges and contributions to understanding violence against marginalized women in diverse communities', *Violence against Women* xi/1 (2005), pp. 38–64.
2. Liz Kelly, 'Inside Outsiders: Mainstreaming violence against women into human rights discourse and practice', *International Journal of Feminist Politics* vii/4 (2006), pp. 471–95.
3. Chandra Mohanty, 'Under Western eyes: Feminist scholarship and colonial discourses', *boundary 2* xii/3–xiii/1 (1984), pp. 338–58; ead. *Feminism Without Borders: Decolonizing Theory, Practicing Solidarity* (Durham, North Carolina, 2003).
4. Mohanty, 'Under Western eyes', p. 337.
5. Uma Narayan, *Dislocating Cultures: Identities, Tradition and Third World Feminism* (New York, 1997), p. 50.
6. Interview conducted in January 2014.
7. Himika Bhattacharya, 'Performing silence: Gender violence and resistance in women's narratives from Lahaul, India', *Qualitative Inquiry* xv/2 (2009), pp. 359–71; Corinne H. Rocca, Sujit Rathod, Tina Falle, Rohini P. Pande and Suneeta Krishnan, 'Challenging assumptions about women's empowerment: Social, economic resources and domestic violence among young married women in urban South India', *Journal of International Epidemiology* xxxviii/2 (2009), pp. 577–85; International Center for Research on Women, *Solutions to End Child Marriage: What the Evidence Shows* (Washington, DC, 2011); Jennifer L. Solotaroff and Rohini Prabha Pande, *Violence against Women and Girls: Lessons from South Asia* (Washington, DC, 2014).
8. Ibid.
9. Interview conducted in June 2014.
10. Nitya Rao (ed.), *Migration, Education and Socio-Economic Mobility* (London, 2012).
11. Interview conducted in January 2014.
12. Action Aid, *A Theory of Change for Tackling Violence Against Women and Girls* (London, 2013).
13. Banyan, 'Despite being a woman', *Economist*, 13 June 2015. Available at http://www.economist.com/news/asia/21654123-south-asia-one-worst-places-world-be-female-despite-being-woman (accessed 12 April 2016).
14. UN Women, 'UN Women strategy'. Available at http://clientdisplay.com/unwomen/focus-areas/human-rights/un-women-strategy/ (accessed 12 April 2016).

15. UN Women, Asia and the Pacific website, available at http://asiapacific.unwomen.org/en/focus-areas (accessed 12 April 2016).
16. Ajay K. Mehra, *Party System in India: Party System in India: Emerging Trajectories* (Atlanta, Georgia, 2013).
17. UN Women, *Handbook for National Action Plans on Violence Against Women* (New York, 2012).
18. Ibid., p. 34.
19. Ibid., p. 39.
20. Ibid., p. 40.
21. All India Democratic Women's Association, 'Women and violence', available at http://aidwaonline.org/category/issues-concern/women-and-violence (accessed 12 April 2016).
22. All India Democratic Women's Association, 'A note on violence against women and violence', available at http://aidwaonline.org/issues_of_concern/note-violence-against-women (accessed 12 April 2016).

Chapter 3 'Two Feet Forward and One Back': Reflections on the Impact of the Anti-Rape Protests in India

1. Ignatius Pereira, '715 Rape cases registered till September this year', *Hindu*, 4 November 2012. Available at http://www.thehindu.com/news/national/kerala/715-rape-cases-registered-till-september-this-year/article4062700.ece (accessed 12 April 2016).
2. The *Hindu*, 'India's Rape Crisis in 2010'. Available at http://www.thehindu.com/multimedia/archive/00948/India_s_rape_crisis_948146a.pdf (accessed 12 April 2016.
3. Ratna Kapur, 'Rape and the crisis of Indian masculinity', in the *Hindu*, 19 December 2012. Available at http://www.thehindu.com/opinion/op-ed/rape-and-the-crisis-of-indian-masculinity/article4214267.ece (accessed 12 April 2016).
4. Interview conducted in January 2014.
5. Ibid.
6. Interview conducted in July 2013.
7. Ibid.
8. Ibid.
9. Interview conducted in January 2014.
10. Sudipto Mondal, 'The rise and rise of a Hindutva hitman', *Hindu*, 31 July 2012. Available at http://www.thehindu.com/news/cities/Mangalore/the-rise-and-rise-of-a-hindutva-hitman/article3704704.ece (accessed 12 April 2016).
11. Warren Adler, 'The dark underbelly of modern India', *Huffington Post*, 27 March, 2012. Available at http://www.huffingtonpost.com/warren-adler/katherine-boo-indi a_b_1382122.html (accessed 12 April 2016).
12. Tamsin Bradley, *Religion and Gender in the Developing World* (London, 2011).

Chapter 4 The Remaking of Subalterns through Western Newspaper Narratives of Rape in India

1. Gayatri Chakravorty Spivak, 'Can the subaltern speak?', in Cary Nelson and Lawrence Grossberg (eds), *Marxism and The Interpretation of Culture* (Urbana, Illinois, 1988), pp. 271–313, p. 287.
2. Spivak, 'Can the subaltern speak?'; Chandra Talpade Mohanty, *Feminism Without Borders: Decolonizing Theory, Practicing Solidarity* (Durham, North Carolina, 2003).
3. For example, Elizabeth Chacko, 'Marriage, development, and the status of women in Kerala, India', in *Gender and Development* xi/2 (2003), pp. 753–73; Sharada Srinivasan, 'Daughters or dowries? The changing nature of dowry practices in South India', *World Development* xxxiii/4 (2005), pp. 593–615; Tamsin Bradley and Saseendran Pallikadavath, 'Dowry and women's lives in Kerala: What has changed in a decade?' *Contemporary South Asia* xxi/4 (2013), pp. 444–61.
4. Spivak, 'Can the subaltern speak?'
5. See Chapter One, and also United Nations, *The Millennium Development Goals Report* (New York, 2013).
6. Uma Narayan, *Dislocating Cultures: Identities, Tradition and Third World Feminism* (New York, 1997).
7. Suzanne Moore, the *Guardian*, 31 December 2012, emphases added.
8. Narayan, *Dislocating Cultures*, pp. 84–5.
9. Srimati Basu, *She Comes to Take Her Rights: Indian Women, Property and Propriety* (New Delhi, 2001); ead. 'Legacies of the dowry prohibition act in India: Marriage practices and feminist discourse', in Tamsin Bradley, Emma Tomalin and Mangala Subramaniam, *Dowry: Bridging the Gap Between Theory and Practice* (Delhi, 2009), pp. 116–44; Rajni Palriwala and Patricia Uberoi (eds), *Marriage and Migration in Asia*. Special Issue *Indian Journal of Gender Studies* xii/2–3 (2005); Rajni Palriwala, 'The spider's web: Seeing dowry, fighting dowry', in Tamsin Bradley, Emma Tomalin and Mangala Subramaniam, *Dowry: Bridging the Gap Between Theory and Practice* (Delhi, 2009), pp. 144–76.
10. Spivak, 'Can the subaltern speak?', p. 271.
11. Quoted in Paul B. Courtright, 'The iconographies of Sati', in John Stratton Hawley (ed.), *Sati: the Blessing and the Curse* (Oxford, 1994), pp. 27–48.
12. Nicholas B. Dirks 'The invention of caste: Civil society in colonial India', *Social Analysis* 25 (1989), pp. 42–52; id. *Castes of Mind: Colonialism and the Making of Modern India* (Princeton, 2001).
13. Spivak, 'Can the subaltern speak?', p. 286.
14. Gustavo Esteva, 'Development', in Wolfgang Sachs (ed.), *The Development Dictionary: A Guide to Knowledge as Power* (London, 1993), pp. 6–25; Arturo Escobar, *Encountering Development: The Making and Unmaking of the Third World* (New York, 1995); Boaventura de Sousa Santos, 'On oppositional postmodernism', in Ronaldo Munck and Denis O'Hearn (eds), *Critical Development Theory: Contributions to a New Paradigm* (London, 1999), pp. 29–34; Vincent Tucker, 'The myth of development: A critique of a Eurocentric discourse', in Munck and O'Hearn (eds), *Critical Development Theory* (London 1999); Johan Pottier, Alan Bicker and Paul Sillitoe (eds),

Negotiating Local Knowledge: Power and Identity in Development (London, 2003); Marc Edelman and Angelique Haugerud (eds), *The Anthropology of Development and Globalization: From Classical Political Economy to Contemporary Neoliberalism* (Cambridge, 2005).

15. Arundhati Roy and Jon Snow, 'Author says events say a lot about India's inequality', *Channel 4 News* (UK), 21 December 2012. Video of interview available at https://www.youtube.com/watch?v=tjzl4xAhrao (accessed 12 April 2016).
16. Associated Press, 'Six jailed over Swiss tourist gang rape in India', *Independent*, 20 July 2013. Available at http://www.independent.co.uk/news/world/asia/six-jailed-over-swiss-tourist-gang-rape-in-india-8722901.html (accessed 12 April 2016).
17. Joanna Sugden, 'British dentist jumped from window "to avoid rape in India"', *The Times*, 20 March 2013. Available at http://www.thetimes.co.uk/tto/news/world/asia/article3717206.ece (accessed 12 April 2016).
18. Spivak, 'Can the subaltern speak?'; Julia Leslie (ed.), *Roles and Rituals for Hindu Women* (London, 1991); Hawley, *Sati*; Lata Mani, *Contentious Traditions: The Debate on Sati in Colonial India* (Delhi, 1998).
19. Robin Pagnamenta, 'Old problem, new statistics', *The Times*, 20 March 2013. Available at http://www.thetimes.co.uk/tto/news/world/asia/article3717780.ece (accessed 12 April 2016).
20. Lavanya Sankaran, 'The good men of India', *New York Times*, 21 October 2013. Available at http://www.nytimes.com/2013/10/20/opinion/sunday/the-good-men-of-india.html (accessed 12 April 2016).
21. *Business Times*, Singapore, 18 September 2013.
22. Libby Purves, 'Indian women need a cultural earthquake', *The Times*, 31 December 2012. Available at http://www.thetimes.co.uk/tto/opinion/columnists/article3643810.ece (accessed 12 April 2016). Also published in *The Australian* as 'Gang-rape shame could drag India into 21st century', 1 January 2013. Available at http://www.theaustralian.com.au/news/world/gang-rape-shame-could-drag-india-into-21st-century/story-fnb64oi6-1226545829569 (accessed 12 April 2016).
23. Katherine Mayo, *Mother India* (Michigan, 1927), p. 79.
24. Mary Daly, *Gyn/Ecology: The Metaethics of Radical Feminism* (London, 1979).
25. Chandra Mohanty, 'Under Western eyes: Feminist scholarship and colonial discourses' *boundary 2* xii/3–xiii/1 (1984), pp. 338–58.
26. Annie Gowen, 'In wake of gang rape, India sees rise of "women only" taxis, buses and parks', *Washington Post*, 28 September 2013. Available at https://www.washingtonpost.com/world/asia_pacific/in-wake-of-gang-rape-india-sees-rise-of-women-only-taxis-buses-and-parks/2013/09/27/9552caac-25e6-11e3-b3e9-d97fb087acd6_story.html (accessed 12 April 2016).
27. Pagnamenta, 'Old problem'.
28. Purves, 'Gang-rape shame'.
29. Ibid.
30. Jason Burke, 'Delhi rape: How India's other half lives', *Guardian*, 10 September 2013. Available at http://www.theguardian.com/world/2013/sep/10/delhi-gang-rape-india-women (accessed 12 April 2016).

31. Matthew Marosszeky. Letter to the Editor, *Toronto Star*, 19 September 2013. Available at https://www.thestar.com/opinion/letters_to_the_editors/2013/09/19/frosh_chants_just_mirror_society.html (accessed 12 April 2016).
32. *The Times*, 20 March 2013.
33. Mallika Kaur, 'Why hangings won't stop India's rape culture', *Age*, 19 September 2013. Available at http://www.theage.com.au/comment/why-hangings-wont-stop-indias-rape-culture-20130918-2tzkl.html (accessed 12 April 2016).
34. Spivak, 'Can the subaltern speak?', p. 295.
35. Andrew Buncombe, 'Rape in India: Leaders need to prove they want to make their country safe for women', *Independent*, 19 March 2013. Available at http://www.independent.co.uk/voices/comment/rape-in-india-leaders-need-to-prove-they-want-to-make-their-country-safe-for-women-8540783.html (accessed 12 April 2016).

Chapter 5 The Changing Face of the Feminist Movement in India

1. For a detailed account of the All India Women's Conference see Aparna Basu and Bharati Ray, *Women's Struggle: A History of the All India Women's Conference 1927–2002* (New Delhi, 2003).
2. See Chapter Three, also Radh A. Kumar, *The History of Doing* (New Delhi, 1993).
3. Mrinalini Sinha, *Colonial Masculinity: The 'Manly Englishman' and the 'Effeminate Bengali' in the Late Nineteenth Century* (Manchester, 1995).
4. V.C. Joshi, *Rammohun Roy and the Process of Modernization in India* (Delhi, 1975); Meredith Borthwick, *The Reluctant Debutante: The Changing Role of Women in Bengal 1875–1927* (Princeton, 1984); Dagmar Engels, *Beyond Purdah? Women in Bengal 1890–1939* (Oxford. 1996).
5. Rassundari Devi, 'Sashto Rachona (The Sixth Composition)', in Susie Tharu and K. Lalita (eds), *Women Writing in India, Volume I: 600 B.C. to the Early Twentieth Century* (Delhi, 1991), pp. 199–202, p. 199.
6. Samita Sen, *Towards a Feminist Politics? The Indian Women's Movement in Historical Perspective*. World Bank Policy Research Report on Gender and Development Working Paper Series No. 9 (Washington, DC, 2000).
7. Ibid., p. 15.
8. Sen, *Towards a Feminist Politics?*
9. Tamsin Bradley, 'Religion as a bridge between theory and practice in work on violence against women in Rajasthan', *Journal of Gender Studies* xix/4 (2010), pp. 361–75.
10. Ibid., p. 158.
11. Mohandas K. Gandhi, *An Autobiography: The Story of My Experiments with Truth* (London, 1984), p. 123, quoted in Kirk Johnson, 'Media and social change: The modernising influences of TV in rural India', *Media, Culture, Society* xxiii/2 (2001), pp. 147–69, p. 105.
12. Tamsin Bradley, *Challenging the NGOs: Women, Religion and Western Dialogues in India* (London, 2006).

13. Geraldine Forbes, *Women in Modern India* (Cambridge, 1996).
14. Shreeniwas Sudha and S. Irudaya Rajan, 'Female demographic disadvantage in India 1981–1991: Sex selective abortions and female infanticide', *Development and Change* xxx/3 (1999), pp. 585–618.
15. Interviews conducted in October 2014.
16. Interview conducted in July 2013.

Chapter 6 The Religious Right and Violence against Women

1. Liz McKean, *Divine Enterprise: Gurus and the Hindu Nationalist Movement* (Chicago, 1996).
2. Emma Tomalin, 'Thinking about faith-based organisations in development: Where have we got to and what next?' Development in Practice 22 (5–6), 2012 pp. 689–703.
3. Tanika Sarkar and Urvashi Butalia, *Women and Right-wing Movements* (London, 1995); Urvashi Butalia, *The Violence of Development: The Politics of Identity, Gender and Social Inequalities in India* (New Delhi, 2002); Sumit Sarkar, *Beyond Nationalist Frames: Postmodernism, Hindu Fundamentalism, History* (Bloomington, Indiana, 2002).
4. J.P. Vaswani, *Peace or Perish: There is no Other Choice* (Pune, 2007) p. 45.
5. Tamsin Bradley, 'Religion as a bridge between theory and practice in work on violence against women in Rajasthan', *Journal of Gender Studies* xix/4 (2010), pp. 361–75.
6. Vaswani, *Peace or Perish*, p. 42.
7. Ibid. p. 53.
8. Bradley, 'Religion as a bridge'.
9. See, for example, Purna Sen, 'Enhancing women's choices in responding to domestic violence in Calcutta: A comparison of employment and education', *European Journal of Development Research* xi/2 (1999), pp. 65–86; Michael A. Koenig, 'Women's status and domestic violence in rural Bangladesh: Individual and community level effects', *Demography* xl/2 (2003), pp. 269–88; Sunita Kishor and Kiersten Johnson, *Profiling Domestic Violence: A Multi-Country Study* (Calverton, Maryland, 2004); Dallan F. Flake, 'Individual, family, and community risk markers for domestic violence in Peru', *Violence against Women* xi (2005), pp. 353–73; Suneeta Krishnan, 'Do structural inequalities contribute to marital violence? Ethnographic evidence from rural South India', *Violence against Women* xi/6 (2005), pp. 759–75; Corinne H. Rocca, Sujit Rathod, Tina Falle, Rohini P. Pande and Suneeta Krishnan, 'Challenging assumptions about women's empowerment: Social, economic resources and domestic violence among young married women in urban South India', *Journal of International Epidemiology* xxxviii/2 (2009), pp. 577–85; Mukesh Eswaran and Nisha Malhotra, 'Domestic violence and women's autonomy in developing countries: Theory and evidence', *Canadian Journal of Economics* xliv (2011), pp. 1222–63; Sohini Paul, *Women Labour Force Participation and Domestic Violence: Evidence from India* (New Delhi, 2014).

10. Koenig, 'Women's status and domestic violence'; Rocca et al. 'Challenging assumptions'.
11. Interview conducted in July 2013.
12. Interview conducted in January 2014.
13. Tamsin Bradley, *Religion and Gender in the Developing World* (London, 2011).
14. Ibid.
15. Tamsin Bradley, *Women, Violence and Tradition: Bringing FGM and Other Practices to a Secular State* (London, 2011).
16. Sudipto Mondal, 'The rise and rise of a Hindutva hitman', *Hindu*, 31 July 2012. Available at http://www.thehindu.com/news/cities/Mangalore/the-rise-and-rise-of-a-hindutva-hitman/article3704704.ece (accessed 12 April 2016); Gauri Lanikesh, 'The Sene Patis lose their marbles', *Outlook*, 20 May 2013. Available at http://www.outlookindia.com/magazine/story/the-sene-patis-lose-their-marbles/285356 (accessed 12 April 2016).
17. Ruth Pearson and Emma Tomalin, 'Intelligent design?: A gender-sensitive interrogation of religion and development', in Gerard Clarke and Michael Jennings (eds), *Development, Civil Society and Faith Based Organisations* (London, 2008), pp. 46–71.
18. Ibid., p. 47.
19. Maxine Molyneux and Shahra Razavi, *Beijing Plus 10: An Ambivalent Record on Gender Justice*. UNRISD Occasional Paper 15 (Geneva, 2006), cited in Pearson and Tomalin, 'Intelligent design?', pp. 115–16.
20. Palriwala, Rajni, 'The spider's web: Seeing dowry, fighting dowry', in Tamsin Bradley, Emma Tomalin and Mangala Subramaniam, *Dowry: Bridging the Gap Between Theory and Practice* (Delhi, 2009), pp. 144–76.
21. Ibid; Sharada Srinivasan, 'Daughters or dowries? The changing nature of dowry practices in South India', *World Development* xxxiii/4 (2005), pp. 593–615; Sharada Srinivasan and Arjun S. Bedi, 'Domestic violence and dowry: Evidence from a South Indian village', *World Development* xxxv/5 (2007), pp. 857–80.
22. Madhu Kishwar (ed.), *Off The Beaten Track* (New Delhi, 2002).
23. *The Justice JS Verma Committee Report on Amendments to Criminal Law relating to Sexual Violence in India* (2013). Available at http://www.prsindia.org/uploads/media/Justice%20verma%20committee/js%20verma%20committe%20report.pdf (accessed 12 April 2016).

Chapter 7 The Persistence and Invisibility of Harmful Cultural Practices

1. Chia Longman and Tamsin Bradley (eds), *Interrogating Harmful Cultural Practices* (London, 2015).
2. Jane Cottingham and Eszter Kismodi, 'protecting girls and women from harmful practices affecting their health: Are we making progress?', *International Journal of Gynecology and Obstetrics* cvi/2 (2009), pp. 128–31.
3. UN Convention on the Elimination of All Forms of Discrimination Against Women, Article 2ff.

4. In 1980, Halima Embarek Warzazi was elected Rapporteur of the Sub-Commission on the Prevention of Discrimination and Protection of Minorities in Geneva. In 1985, she was elected in Geneva Chairwoman-Rapporteur of the UN Sub-Commission working group, which was in charge of studying the traditional practices affecting women's and children's health.
5. UN Office of the High Commissioner for Human Rights, *Harmful Traditional Practices Affecting the Health of Women and Children*. UN Fact Sheet No. 23 (Washington, DC, 1995).
6. Ibid.
7. UN Women, *A Transformative Stand-Alone Goal on Achieving Gender Equality, Women's Rights and Women's Empowerment: Imperatives and Key Components* (Washington, DC, 2013).
8. Hannana Siddiqui, '"I wish I'd taken her with me": The lives of black and minority ethnic women facing gender-based violence', in Tamsin Bradley (ed.), *Women, Violence and Tradition: Taking FGM and Other Practices to a Secular State* (London, 2011), pp. 161–90.
9. Tamsin Bradley and Nida Kirmani, 'Religion, gender and development in South Asia', in Emma Tomalin (ed.), *Routledge Handbook of Religions and Global Development* (London, 2015), pp. 215–30.
10. See also Tamsin Bradley and Saseendran Pallikadavath, 'Dowry and women's lives in Kerala: What has changed in a decade?', *Contemporary South Asia* xxi/4 (2013), pp. 444–61.
11. See Pragna Patel, 'Flying by the nets of racism, patriarchy and religion', in Sukhwant Dhaliwal and Nira Yuval-Davis (eds), *Women Against Fundamentalism: Stories of Dissent and Solidarity* (London, 2014), pp. 52–66.
12. Longman and Bradley, *Interrogating*.
13. Ibid.
14. Kimberle Crenshaw, 'Demarginalising the intersection of race and sex', *University of Chicago Legal Forum* i (1989), pp. 139–67.
15. Resolution E/CN.4/L.59, quoted by Nira Yuval-Davis, *Gender and Nation* (Thousand Oaks, California, 2006), p. 194.
16. Yuval-Davis, *Gender and Nation*.
17. Bradley, *Religion and Gender*.
18. Philomena Essed, *Everyday Racism: Reports From Women of Two Cultures* (Claremont, California, 1993).
19. Bradley, *Women, Violence and Tradition*.
20. UNICEF report, July 2013.
21. R. Elise B. Johansen, Nafissatou J. Diop, Glenn Laverack and Els Leye, 'What works and what does not: A discussion of popular approaches for the abandonment of FGM', *Obstetrics and Gynaecology International* Article ID 348248 (2013), p. 1 of 10.
22. World Health Organization, 'Female genital mutilation'. Available at http://www.who.int/mediacentre/factsheets/fs241/en/ (accessed 12 April 2016).

23. See Erica Burman, Sophie L. Smailes and Khatidja Chantler, '"Culture" as a barrier to service provision and delivery: Domestic violence services for minoritized women', *Critical Social Policy* xxiv/3 (2004), pp. 332–57.
24. Tamsin Bradley, *Women, Violence and Tradition* (London, 2011); Longman and Bradley, *Interrogating*.
25. Arthur Kleinman, Veena Das and Margaret Lock, 'Introduction', in id. (eds), *Social Suffering* (Berkeley, California, 1997), pp. ix–xxvii, p. xi.
26. Laura Jeffery and Matei Candea, 'The politics of victimhood', *History and Anthropology* xvii/4 (2006), pp. 287–96, p. 289.
27. Iris Jean-Klein and Annelise Rile, 'Introducing discipline: Anthropology and human rights administrations', *Political and Legal Anthropology Review* xxviii/2 (2005), pp. 175–202, p. 176.
28. Patricia Jeffery and Roger Jeffery, *Confronting Saffron Demography: Religion, Fertility and Women's Status in India* (New Delhi, 2006).
29. Pnina Werbner, 'Introduction' in Pnina Werbner and Tariq Modood (eds), *Debating Cultural Hybridity: Multi-Cultural Identities and the Politics of Anti-racism* (London, 1997), p. 245.

Chapter 8 Dowry, Marriage and Violence

1. All India Democratic Women's Association, *Expanding Dimensions of Dowry* (New Delhi, 2003).
2. Rajni Palriwala, 'The spider's web: Seeing dowry, fighting dowry', in Tamsin Bradley, Emma Tomalin and Mangala Subramaniam, *Dowry: Bridging the Gap Between Theory and Practice* (Delhi, 2009), pp. 144–76.
3. Ibid., p. 150.
4. Srimati Basu, 'Legacies of the dowry prohibition act in India: Marriage practices and feminist discourse', in Tamsin Bradley, Emma Tomalin and Mangala Subramaniam, *Dowry: Bridging the Gap Between Theory and Practice* (Delhi, 2009), pp. 144–176; Palriwala, 'The spider's web'.
5. All India Democratic Women's Association, *Expanding Dimensions*.
6. Sakhi, *A Study on Gender Based Violence in Kerala* (Trivandrum, 2004).
7. Sharada Srinivasan, 'Daughters or dowries? The changing nature of dowry practices in South India', *World Development* xxxiii/4 (2005), pp. 593–615; Sonia Dalmia and Pareena Lawrence, 'Trends and patterns in dowry transactions: Evidence from North and South India', in Tamsin Bradley, Emma Tomalin and Mangala Subramaniam, *Dowry: Bridging the Gap Between Theory and Practice* (Delhi, 2009), pp. 115–43.
8. Srinivasan, 'Daughters or dowries?', p. 14.
9. Judith Heyer, 'The role of dowries and daughters' marriages in the accumulation and distribution of capital in a south Indian community', *Journal of International Development* iv/4 (1992), pp. 419–36.
10. Sanjay Kumar, Anthony Heath and Oliver Heath, 'Changing patterns of social mobility: Some trends over time', *Economic and Political Weekly* xxxvii/40 (2002),

pp. 4091–6; Srinivasan, 'Daughters or dowries'; Karin Kapadia, 'Marrying money: Changing preference and practice in Tamil marriage', *Contributions to Indian Sociology* xxvii/1 (1993), pp. 25–51.

11. G. Narayana, 'Family violence, sex and reproductive health behaviour among men in Uttar Pradesh, India', in *Women in South-East Asia: A Health Profile* (New Delhi, 2000), pp. 55–64.
12. Rajni Palriwala and Patricia Uberoi (eds), *Marriage and Migration in Asia.* Special Issue *Indian Journal of Gender Studies* xii/2–3 (2005); Palriwala, 'The spider's web'; Basu, 'Legacies of the dowry'.
13. Diane Mitsch Bush, 'Women's movements and state policy reforms aimed at domestic violence against women: A comparison of the consequences of movement mobilization in the US and India', *Gender and Society* vi/4 (1992), pp. 587–608.
14. Srinivasan, 'Daughters or dowries'.
15. Satish Balram Agnihotri, *Sex Ratio Patterns in the Indian Population: A Fresh Exploration* (New Delhi, 2000).
16. Saseendran Pallikadavath and Tamsin Bradley, '"Dowry autonomy" and domestic violence among young married women in India' India' (forthcoming in the *Journal of South Asian Development*).
17. Elizabeth Chacko, 'Marriage, development, and the status of women in Kerala, India', in *Gender and Development* xi/2 (2003), pp. 753–73.
18. Sundara Rajan Ramanatha Iyer and Stewart MacPherson, *Social Development in Kerala: Illusion or Reality* (Farnham, UK, 2000).
19. Sakhi, *Study on Gender Based Violence* (2003), pp. 14–23.
20. Mridul Eapen and Praveena Kodoth, 'Demystifying the "High Status" of women', in *Kerala: An Attempt to Understand the Contradictions in Social Development* (Thiruvananthapuram, 2001).
21. Sakhi, *Study on Gender Based Violence*, p. 34.
22. Ibid., p. 35.
23. Palriwala, 'The spider's web'.
24. This is discussed further in Pallikadavath and Bradley, '"Dowry autonomy"'.
25. Deniz Kandiyoti, 'Bargaining with patriarchy', *Gender and Society* ii/3 (1988), pp. 274–90.
26. Srimati Basu, *She Comes to Take Her Rights: Indian Women, Property and Propriety* (New Delhi, 2001).
27. Goodwin Raheja and Ann Grodzins Gold, *Listen to the Heron's Words: Re-imagining Gender and Kinship in North India* (Berkeley, California, 1996); Tamsin Bradley, 'Religion as a bridge between theory and practice in work on violence against women in Rajasthan', *Journal of Gender Studies* xix/4 (2010), pp. 361–75.
28. Kathleen M. Erndl, *Victory to the Mother: The Hindu Goddess of North West India in Myth, Ritual and Symbol* (New York, 1992); Tamsin Bradley, *Challenging the NGOs: Women, Religion and Western Dialogues in India* (London, 2006); ead. 'Religion as a bridge'.
29. Kathleen M. Erndl, 'The play of the mother: Possession and power in Hindu Women's Goddess rituals', in Tracy Pintchman (ed.), *Women's Lives, Women's Rituals in the Hindu Tradition* (Oxford, 2007), pp. 149–58.

30. Srinivasan, 'Daughters or dowries?'
31. Ibid.
32. Tulsi Patel, *The Family in India: Structure and Practice* (New Delhi, 2005).
33. Kate Jehan, 'Heroes or Hondas? Analysing men's dowry narratives in a time of rapid social change', in Tamsin Bradley, Emma Tomalin and Mangala Subramaniam, *Dowry: Bridging the Gap Between Theory and Practice* (Delhi, 2009), pp. 59–86.

Conclusion The Impact of Neoliberalism on Violence against Women and Girls

1. Gottipati, Sruthi, 'MP minister Babulal Gaur says rape "sometimes right, sometimes wrong"', *Reuters*, 5 June 2014. Available online: http://in.reuters.com/article/uk-india-rape-idINKBN0EG1EX20140605 (accessed 12 April 2016).
2. USAID Knowledge Services Center, *Pakistan: Gender Overview* (Washington, DC, 2013).
3. Cited in UK Foreign and Commonwealth Office, 'Human rights and democracy report 2012 – Pakistan' (London, 2013). Available at https://www.gov.uk/government/news/human-rights-and-democracy-report-2012-pakistan--2 (accessed 12 April 2016).
4. UN Committee on the Elimination of Discrimination against Women, 'Concluding observations on the fourth periodic report of Pakistan adopted by the Committee at is fifty fourth session (11 February – 1 March 2013)', available at http://www2.ohchr.org/english/bodies/cedaw/docs/co/CEDAW.C.PAK.CO.4.doc (accessed 12 April 2016); Human Rights Watch, 'World report 2015: Pakistan'. Available at https://www.hrw.org/world-report/2015/country-chapters/pakistan (accessed 12 April 2016).
5. Data from World Bank's World DataBank, World Development Indicators. Available at http://databank.worldbank.org/data/reports.aspx (accessed 12 April 2016).
6. Shahnaz Wazir Ali, 'Economic empowerment of rural women in Pakistan'. Presented at the 56th Session of the UN Commission On the Status of Women (New York, 2012). Available at http://www.un.org/womenwatch/daw/csw/csw56/panels/panel1-presentation-Shanaz-Wazir-Ali.pdf (accessed 12 April 2016).
7. World Economic Forum, *The Global Gender Gap Report 2013* (Geneva, 2013), pp. 306–07.
8. Freedom House, 'Freedom in the world report: Pakistan' (2012). Available at https://freedomhouse.org/report/freedom-world/2012/pakistan (accessed 12 April 2016); UK Home Office, *Country Information and Guidance Pakistan: Women Fearing Gender-Based Harm / Violence* (London, 2014). Available at https://www.gov.uk/government/uploads/system/uploads/attachment_data/file/331642/Pakistan_CIG.Women2014.07.16v1.0.pdf (accessed 12 April 2016); International Crisis Group, *Women, Violence and Conflict in Pakistan*. Asia Report No. 265 (Brussels, 2015).
9. International Refugee Board of Canada, *PAK104261.E: Pakistan Domestic Violence Including Effectiveness of the Protection of Women (Criminal Laws Amendment) Act, 2006; State Protection and Services Available to Victims* (Ottawa, 2013). Available at

http://irb-cisr.gc.ca/Eng/ResRec/RirRdi/Pages/index.aspx?doc=454350 (accessed 12 April 2016).

10. USAID Knowledge Services Center, *Pakistan: Gender Overview.*
11. UN Committee on the Elimination of Discrimination against Women, 'Information provided in follow up to the concluding observations of the Committee: Myanmar. Response by Myanmar to the recommendations contained in the concluding observations of Committee following the examination of the combined second and third periodic report of Myanmar on 3 November 2008'. Committee on the Elimination of Discrimination against Women Fiftieth Session 3–21 October 2011. Available at http://www.refworld.org/publisher,CEDAW,,MMR,4ef8338a2,0.html (accessed 12 April 2016); US Department of State, *Burma 2012 Human Rights Report* (Washington, DC, 2013). Available at http://www.state.gov/documents/organization/204400.pdf (accessed 12 April 2016).
12. Austrian Red Cross and ACCORD, *Myanmar: COI Compilation* (Vienna, 2011). Available at http://www.refworld.org/publisher,ACCORD,,,4e9291912,0.html (accessed 12 April 2016); Freedom House, 'Freedom in the world report: Burma' (2011) Available at https://freedomhouse.org/report/freedom-world/2011/burma (accessed 12 April 2016);
13. Women's League of Burma, *In the Shadow of the Junta: CEDAW Shadow Report* (Chiang Mai, 2008). Available at http://womenofburma.org/Report/IntheShadow-Junta-CEDAW2008.pdf (accessed 12 April 2016); Organisation for Economic Co-operation and Development, 'Social Institutions and Gender Index: Myanmar'. Available at http://www.genderindex.org/country/myanmar (accessed 12 April 2016); Gender Equality Network, *Myanmar Laws and CEDAW: The Case for Anti-Violence against Women* (Yangon, 2013). Available at http://www.burmalibrary.org/docs20/MyanmarLaw+CEDAW-en-red.pdf (accessed 12 April 2016); id., *Behind the Silence: Violence against Women and their Resilience Myanmar* (Yangon, 2014). Available at http://www.burmalibrary.org/docs20/GEN-2014-11-Behind_the_Silence-en-ocr-tpo.pdf (accessed 12 April 2016).
14. Women's League of Burma, *In the Shadow of the Junta*; Organisation for Economic Co-operation and Development, 'Social Institutions and Gender Index: Myanmar'.
15. Data from World Bank's World Data Bank, World Development Indicators.
16. UN Women, 'Myanmar'. Available at http://asiapacific.unwomen.org/en/focus-area/cedaw-human-rights/Myanmar (accessed 12 April 2016).
17. Ibid.
18. UK Home Office, *Burma (Myanmar): Country of Origin Information Report* (London, 2012). Available at https://www.gov.uk/government/uploads/system/uploads/attachment_data/file/311393/Burma_COI_report_2012.pdf (accessed 12 April 2016); US Department of State, *Burma 2014 Human Rights Report* (Washington, DC, 2014). Available at http://www.state.gov/documents/organization/236640.pdf (accessed 12 April 2016).
19. See e.g. Spike Johnson, 'The rising power of Burma's women's workforce', *Irrawaddy*, 2 October 2014. Available at http://www.irrawaddy.com/feature/rising-power-burmas-womens-workforce.html (accessed 12 April 2016).

20. Organisation for Economic Co-operation and Development, 'Social Institutions and Gender Index: Nepal'. Available at http://www.genderindex.org/country/nepal (accessed 12 April 2016).
21. Ibid.
22. Ibid.
23. Ibid.
24. Ibid.
25. Ibid.
26. World Economic Forum, *The Global Gender Gap Report 2013* (Geneva, 2013), pp. 292–3.
27. US Department of State, *Burma 2012*; id. *Burma 2014*; UK Aid, UN Population Fund, UN Women, UCL and CREHPA, *Tracking Cases of Gender-Based Violence in Nepal 2013: Individual, Institutional, Legal and Policy Analyses* (New York, 2013). Available at http://asiapacific.unfpa.org/sites/asiapacific/files/pub-pdf/TrackingCasesofGBV.pdf (accessed 12 April 2016); Organisation for Economic Co-operation and Development, 'Social Institutions and Gender Index: Nepal'.
28. Organisation for Economic Co-operation and Development, 'Social Institutions and Gender Index: Myanmar'.
29. CEDAW 2010. Website. http://web.archive.org/web/20101223222814/http://cedaw2010.org/ (accessed 12 April 2016).
30. Durba Ghosh, *Sex and The Family in Colonial India: The Making of Empire* (Cambridge, 2006).
31. World Economic Forum, *The Global Gender Gap Report 2014* (Geneva, 2014), pp. 206–07.
32. Ibid.
33. UN Population Fund, *UNFPA Strategy and Framework for Action to Addressing Gender-based Violence 2008–2011* (New York, 2009).

BIBLIOGRAPHY

Action Aid, *A Theory of Change for Tackling Violence Against Women and Girls* (London, 2013).

Adler, Warren, 'The dark underbelly of modern India', *Huffington Post*, 27 March 2012. Available at http://www.huffingtonpost.com/warren-adler/katherine-boo-india_b_1382122.html (accessed 12 April 2016).

Agnihotri, Satish Balram, *Sex Ratio Patterns in the Indian Population: A Fresh Exploration* (New Delhi, 2000).

Ali, Shahnaz Wazir, 'Economic empowerment of rural women in Pakistan'. Presented at the 56th Session of the UN Commission On the Status of Women (New York, 2012). Available at http://www.un.org/womenwatch/daw/csw/csw56/panels/panel1-presentation-Shanaz-Wazir-Ali.pdf (accessed 12 April 2016).

All India Democratic Women's Association, *Expanding Dimensions of Dowry* (New Delhi, 2003).

———, 'A note on violence against women and violence', available at http://aidwaonline.org/issues_of_concern/note-violence-against-women (accessed 12 April 2016).

———, 'Women and violence', available at http://aidwaonline.org/category/issues-concern/women-and-violence (accessed 12 April 2016).

Associated Press, 'Six jailed over Swiss tourist gang rape in India', *Independent*, 20 July 2013. Available at http://www.independent.co.uk/news/world/asia/six-jailed-over-swiss-tourist-gang-rape-in-india-8722901.html (accessed 12 April 2016).

Austrian Red Cross and ACCORD, *Myanmar: COI Compilation* (Vienna, 2011). Available at http://www.refworld.org/publisher,ACCORD,,,4e9291912,0.html (accessed 12 April 2016).

Banyan, 'Despite being a woman', *Economist*, 13 June 2015. Available at http://www.economist.com/news/asia/21654123-south-asia-one-worst-places-world-be-female-despite-being-woman (accessed 12 April 2016).

Basu, Aparna and Bharati Ray, *Women's Struggle: A History of the All India Women's Conference 1927–2002* (New Delhi, 2003).

Basu, Srimati, *She Comes to Take Her Rights: Indian Women, Property and Propriety* (New Delhi, 2001), pp. 145–77.

———, 'Legacies of the dowry prohibition act in India: Marriage practices and feminist discourse', in Tamsin Bradley, Emma Tomalin and Mangala Subramaniam (eds), *Dowry: Bridging the Gap Between Theory and Practice* (Delhi, 2009), pp. 145–77.

Bhattacharya, Himika, 'Performing silence: Gender violence and resistance in women's narratives from Lahaul, India', *Qualitative Inquiry* xv/2 (2009), pp. 359–71.

Bonnici, Tony, 'Rape level shames country, says India leader Modi', *The Times*, 15 August 2014. Available at http://www.thetimes.co.uk/tto/news/world/asia/article4177227.ece (accessed 12 April 2016).

Borthwick, Meredith, *The Reluctant Debutante: The Changing Role of Women in Bengal 1875–1927* (Princeton, 1984).

Bradley, Tamsin, *Challenging the NGOs: Women, Religion and Western Dialogues in India* (London, 2006).

———, 'Religion as a bridge between theory and practice in work on violence against women in Rajasthan', *Journal of Gender Studies* xix/4 (2010), pp. 361–75.

———, *Women, Violence and Tradition: Bringing FGM and Other Practices to a Secular State* (London, 2011).

———, *Religion and Gender in the Developing World* (London, 2011).

Bradley, Tamsin and Nida Kirmani 'Religion, gender and development in South Asia', in Emma Tomalin (ed.), *Routledge Handbook of Religions and Global Development* (London, 2015), pp. 215–30.

Bradley, Tamsin and Saseendran Pallikadavath, 'Dowry and women's lives in Kerala: What has changed in a decade?' *Contemporary South Asia* xxi/4 (2013), pp. 444–61.

Bumiller, Kristin, *In an Abusive State: How Neoliberalism Appropriated The Feminist Movement Against Sexual Violence* (Durham, North Carolina, 2009).

Buncombe, Andrew, 'Rape in India: Leaders need to prove they want to make their country safe for women', *Independent* 19 March 2013. Available at http://www.independent.co.uk/voices/comment/rape-in-india-leaders-need-to-prove-they-want-to-make-their-country-safe-for-women-8540783.html (accessed 12 April 2016).

Burke, Jason, 'Delhi rape: How India's other half lives', *Guardian*, 10 September 2013. Available at http://www.theguardian.com/world/2013/sep/10/delhi-gang-rape-india-women (accessed 12 April 2016).

Burman, Erica, Sophie L. Smailes and Khatidja Chantler, '"Culture" as a barrier to service provision and delivery: Domestic violence services for minoritized women', *Critical Social Policy* xxiv/3 (2004), pp. 332–57.

Bush, Diane Mitsch, 'Women's movements and state policy reforms aimed at domestic violence against women: A comparison of the consequences of movement mobilization in the US and India', *Gender and Society* vi/4 (1992), pp. 587–608.

Butalia, Urvashi, *The Violence of Development: The Politics of Identity, Gender and Social Inequalities in India* (New Delhi, 2002).

CEDAW (2010). Website. http://web.archive.org/web/20101223222814/http://cedaw2010.org/ (accessed 12 April 2016).

Chacko, Elizabeth, 'Marriage, development, and the status of women in Kerala, India', in *Gender and Development* xi/2 (2003), pp. 753–73.

Chez, Nancy, 'Helping the victim of domestic violence', *American Journal of Nursing* xciv/7 (1994), pp. 32–37.

Chomsky, Noam, *How The World Works* (London, 2011).

Comaroff, Jean and John L. Comaroff, 'Millennial capitalism: First thoughts on a Second Coming', in Jean Comaroff and John L. Comaroff (eds), *Millennial Capitalism and the Culture of Neoliberalism* (Durham, North Carolina, 2001), pp. 1–56.

Cooke, Bill and Uma Kothari (eds), *Participation: The New Tyranny?* (London, 2004).

Cornwall, Andrea, Elizabeth Harrison and Ann Whitehead (eds), *Feminism in Development: Contradictions, Contestations and Challenges* (London, 2007).

Cottingham, Jane and Eszter Kismodi, 'Protecting girls and women from harmful practices affecting their health: Are we making progress?', *International Journal of Gynecology and Obstetrics* cvi/2 (2009), pp. 128–31.

Courtright, Paul B., 'The iconographies of Sati', in John Stratton Hawley (ed.), *Sati: The Blessing and the Curse* (Oxford, 1994), pp. 27–48.

Crenshaw, Kimberle, 'Demarginalising the intersection of race and sex', *University of Chicago Legal Forum* i (1989), pp. 139–67.

Crewe, Emma and Elizabeth Harrison, *Whose Development? An Ethnography of Aid* (London, 1998).

Dalmia, Sonia and Pareena Lawrence, 'Trends and patterns in dowry transactions: Evidence from North and South India', in Tamsin Bradley, Emma Tomalin and Mangala Subramaniam, *Dowry: Bridging the Gap Between Theory and Practice* (Delhi, 2009), pp. 115–43.

Daly, Mary, *Gyn/Ecology: the Metaethics of Radical Feminism* (London, 1979).

Deutsche Welle, 'Women's rights barely a topic in Indian election', 12 May 2014. Available at http://www.dw.de/womens-rights-barely-a-topic-in-indian-election/a-17629634 (accessed 12 April 2016).

Devi, Rassundari, 'Sashto Rachona (The Sixth Composition)', in Susie Tharu and K. Lalita (eds), *Women Writing in India, Volume I: 600 B.C. to the Early Twentieth Century* (Delhi, 1991), pp. 199–202.

Dirks, Nicholas B., 'The invention of caste: Civil society in colonial India', *Social Analysis* 25 (1989), pp. 42–52.

———, *Castes of Mind: Colonialism and the Making of Modern India* (Princeton, 2001).

Eapen, Mridul and Praveena Kodoth, 'Demystifying the "High Status" of women', in *Kerala: An Attempt to Understand the Contradictions in Social Development* (Thiruvananthapuram, 2001), pp. 23–38.

Edelman, Marc and Angelique Haugerud (eds), *The Anthropology of Development and Globalization: From Classical Political Economy to Contemporary Neoliberalism* (Cambridge, 2005).

Engels, Dagmar, *Beyond Purdah? Women in Bengal 1890–1939* (Oxford, 1996).

Erndl, Kathleen M., *Victory to the Mother: The Hindu Goddess of North West India in Myth, Ritual and Symbol* (New York, 1992).

———, 'The play of the mother: Possession and power in Hindu Women's Goddess rituals', in Tracy Pintchman (ed.), *Women's Lives, Women's Rituals in the Hindu Tradition* (Oxford, 2007), pp. 149–58.

Escobar, Arturo, *Encountering Development: The Making and Unmaking of the Third World* (New York, 1995).

Essed, Philomena, *Everyday Racism: Reports from Women of Two Cultures* (Claremont, California, 1993).

Esteva, Gustavo, 'Development', in Wolfgang Sachs (ed.), *The Development Dictionary: A Guide to Knowledge as Power* (London, 1993), pp. 6–25.

Eswaran, Mukesh and Nisha Malhotra, 'Domestic violence and women's autonomy in developing countries: Theory and evidence', *Canadian Journal of Economics* xliv (2011), pp. 1222–63.

Flake, Dallan F., 'Individual, family, and community risk markers for domestic violence in Peru', *Violence against Women* xi (2005), pp. 353–73.

Forbes, Geraldine, *Women in Modern India* (Cambridge, 1996).

Fraser, Nancy, *Fortunes of Feminism: From State Managed Capitalism to Neo-Liberal Crisis* (London, 2013).

Freedom House, 'Freedom in the world report: Burma' (2011) Available at https://freedomhouse.org/report/freedom-world/2011/burma (accessed 12 April 2016).

———, 'Freedom in the world report: Pakistan (2012) Available at https://freedomhouse.org/report/freedom-world/2012/pakistan (accessed 12 April 2016).

Gandhi, Mohandas K., *An Autobiography: The Story of My Experiments with Truth* (London, 1984).

Gender Equality Network, *Myanmar Laws and CEDAW: The Case for Anti-Violence against Women* (Yangon, 2013). Available at http://www.burmalibrary.org/docs20/MyanmarLaw+CEDAW-en-red.pdf (accessed 12 April 2016).

———, *Behind the Silence: Violence against Women and their Resilience Myanmar* (Yangon, 2014). Available at http://www.burmalibrary.org/docs20/GEN-2014-11-Behind_the_Silence-en-ocr-tpo.pdf (accessed 12 April 2016).

Ghosh, Durba, 2006. *Sex and The Family in Colonial India: The Making of Empire* (Cambridge, 2006).

Gold, Ann and Gloria-Raheja. *Listen to the Heron's Words: Reimagining Gender and Kinship in North India* (1994 California).

Goodman, Robin Truth, *Gender Work: Feminism after Neoliberalism* (London, 2013).

Gottipati, Sruthi, 'MP minister Babulal Gaur says rape "sometimes right, sometimes wrong"', *Reuters*, 5 June 2014. Available online: http://in.reuters.com/article/uk-india-rape-idINKBN0EG1EX20140605 (accessed 12 April 2016).

Gowen, Annie, 'In wake of gang rape, India sees rise of "women only" taxis, buses and parks', *Washington Post*, 28 September 2013. Available at https://www.washingtonpost.com/world/asia_pacific/in-wake-of-gang-rape-india-sees-rise-of-women-only-taxis-buses-and-parks/2013/09/27/9552caac-25e6-11e3-b3e9-d97fb087acd6_story.html (accessed 12 April 2016).

Haraway, Donna, *The Companion Species Manifesto: Dogs, People, and Significant Otherness* (Chicago, 2003).

Harvey, David, *A Brief History of Neoliberalism* (Oxford, 2005).

Hawkesworth, Mary E., 'Knowers, knowing, known: Feminist theory and claims of truth', *Signs* xiv/3 (1989), pp. 533–57.

Hawley, John Stratton (ed.), *Sati: The Blessing and the Curse* (Oxford, 1994).

Heyer, Judith, 'The role of dowries and daughters' marriages in the accumulation and distribution of capital in a south Indian community', *Journal of International Development* iv/4 (1992), pp. 419–36.

The Hindu, 'India's Rape Crisis in 2010'. Available at http://www.thehindu.com/multimedia/archive/00948/India_s_rape_crisis_948146a.pdf (accessed 12 April 2016).

Human Rights Watch, 'World report 2015: Pakistan'. Available at https://www.hrw.org/world-report/2015/country-chapters/pakistan (accessed 12 April 2016).

International Center for Research on Women, *Solutions to End Child Marriage: What the Evidence Shows* (Washington, DC, 2011).

———, *Masculinity, Intimate Partner Violence and Son Preference in India: A Study* (Washington, DC, 2014).

International Crisis Group, *Women, Violence and Conflict in Pakistan*. Asia Report No. 265 (Brussels, 2015).

International Refugee Board of Canada, *PAK104261.E: Pakistan Domestic Violence Including Effectiveness of the Protection of Women (Criminal Laws Amendment) Act, 2006; State Protection and Services Available to Victims* (Ottawa, 2013). Available at http://irb-cisr.gc.ca/Eng/ResRec/RirRdi/Pages/index.aspx?doc=454350 (accessed 12 April 2016).

Jean-Klein, Iris and Annelise Rile, 'Introducing discipline: Anthropology and human rights administrations', *Political and Legal Anthropology Review* xxviii/2 (2005), pp. 175–202.

Jeffery, Laura and Matei Candea, 'The politics of victimhood', *History and Anthropology* xvii/4 (2006), pp. 287–96.

Jeffery, Patricia and Roger Jeffery, *Confronting Saffron Demography: Religion, Fertility and Women's Status in India* (New Delhi, 2006).

Jehan, Kate, 'Heroes or Hondas? Analysing men's dowry narratives in a time of rapid social change', in Tamsin Bradley, Emma Tomalin and Mangala Subramaniam, *Dowry: Bridging the Gap Between Theory and Practice* (Delhi, 2009), pp. 59–86.

Johansen, R., Elise B., Nafissatou J. Diop, Glenn Laverack and Els Leye, 'What works and what does not: A discussion of popular approaches for the abandonment of FGM', *Obstetrics and Gynaecology International* Article ID 348248 (2013).

Johnson, Kirk, 'Media and social change: The modernising influences of TV in rural India', *Media, Culture, Society* xxiii/2 (2001), pp. 147–69.

Johnson, Spike, 'The rising power of Burma's women's workforce', *Irrawaddy*, 2 October 2014. Available at http://www.irrawaddy.com/feature/rising-power-burmas-womens-workforce.html (accessed 12 April 2016).

Joshi, V.C., *Rammohun Roy and the Process of Modernization in India* (Delhi, 1975).

Justice JS Verma Committee Report on Amendments to Criminal Law relating to Sexual Violence in India (2013). Available at http://www.prsindia.org/uploads/media/Justice%20verma%20committee/js%20verma%20committe%20report.pdf (accessed 12 April 2016).

Kabeer, Naila, *Women's Economic Empowerment and Inclusive Growth: Labour Markets and Enterprise Development*. SIG Working Paper 2012/1 (London, 2012).

Kandiyoti, Deniz, 'Bargaining with patriarchy', *Gender and Society* ii/3 (1988), pp. 274–90.

Kapadia, Karin, 'Marrying money: Changing preference and practice in Tamil marriage', *Contributions to Indian Sociology* xxvii/1 (1993), pp. 25–51.

Kapur, Ratna, 'Rape and the crisis of Indian masculinity', in *Hindu*, 19 December 2012. Available at http://www.thehindu.com/opinion/op-ed/rape-and-the-crisis-of-indian-masculinity/article4214267.ece (accessed 12 April 2016).

Kaur, Mallika, 'Why hangings won't stop India's rape culture', *Age*, 19 September 2013. Available at http://www.theage.com.au/comment/why-hangings-wont-stop-indias-rape-culture-20130918-2tzkl.html (accessed 12 April 2016).

Kelly, Liz, 'Inside Outsiders: Mainstreaming violence against women into human rights discourse and practice', *International Journal of Feminist Politics* vii/4 (2006), pp. 471–95.

Kishor, Sunita and Kiersten Johnson, *Profiling Domestic Violence: A Multi-Country Study* (Calverton, Maryland, 2004).

Kishwar, Madhu (ed.), *Off The Beaten Track* (New Delhi, 2002).

Kleinman, Arthur, Veena Das and Margaret Lock, 'Introduction', in id. (eds), *Social Suffering* (Berkeley, California, 1997), pp. ix–xxvii.

Koenig, Michael A., 'Women's status and domestic violence in rural Bangladesh: Individual and community level effects', *Demography* xl/2 (2003), pp. 269–88.

Krishnan, Suneeta, 'Do structural inequalities contribute to marital violence? Ethnographic evidence from rural South India', *Violence against Women* xi/6 (2005), pp. 759–75.

Kumar, Radha, *The History of Doing* (New Delhi, 1993).

Kumar, Sanjay, Anthony Heath and Oliver Heath, 'Changing patterns of social mobility: Some trends over time', *Economic and Political Weekly* xxxvii/40 (2002), pp. 4091–6.

Lanikesh, Gauri, 'The Sene Patis lose their marbles', *Outlook*, 20 May 2013. Available at http://www.outlookindia.com/magazine/story/the-sene-patis-lose-their-marbles/285356 (accessed 12 April 2016).

Leslie, Julia (ed.), *Roles and Rituals for Hindu Women* (London, 1991).

Longman, Chia and Tamsin Bradley (eds), *Interrogating Harmful Cultural Practices* (London, 2015).

Mani, Lata, *Contentious Traditions: The Debate on Sati in Colonial India* (Delhi, 1998).

Marosszeky, Matthew, Letter to the Editor, *Toronto Star*, 19 September 2013. Available at https://www.thestar.com/opinion/letters_to_the_editors/2013/09/19/frosh_chants_just_mirror_society.html (accessed 12 April 2016).

Mayo, Katherine, *Mother India* (Michigan, 1927), p. 79.

McKean, Liz. *Divine Enterprise: Gurus and the Hindu Nationalist Movement* (Chicago, 1996).

Mehra, Ajay K., *Party System in India: Party System in India: Emerging Trajectories* (Atlanta, Georgia, 2013).

Mohanty, Chandra, 'Under Western eyes: Feminist scholarship and colonial discourses' *boundary 2* xii/3–xiii/1 (1984), pp. 338–58.

Mohanty, Chandra Talpade, *Feminism Without Borders: Decolonizing Theory, Practicing Solidarity* (Durham, North Carolina, 2003).

Molyneux, Maxine and Shahra Razavi, *Beijing Plus 10: An Ambivalent Record on Gender Justice*. UNRISD Occasional Paper 15 (Geneva, 2006).

Mondal, Sudipto, 'The rise and rise of a Hindutva hitman', *Hindu*, 31 July 2012. Available at http://www.thehindu.com/news/cities/Mangalore/the-rise-and-rise-of-a-hindutva-hitman/article3704704.ece (accessed 12 April 2016).

Mosse, David, 'Global governance and the ethnography of international aid', in David Mosse and David Lewis (eds), *The Aid Effect: Giving and Governing in International Development* (London, 2005), pp. 1–36.

Narayan, Uma, *Dislocating Cultures: Identities, Tradition and Third World Feminism* (New York, 1997).

Narayana, G., 'Family violence, sex and reproductive health behaviour among men in Uttar Pradesh, India', in *Women in South-East Asia: A Health Profile* (New Delhi, 2000), pp. 67–83.

Nelson, Nici and Susan Wright (eds), *Power and Participatory Development: Theory and Practice* (London, 1995).

Olivier de Sardan, Jean-Pierre, *Anthropology and Development: Understanding Contemporary Social Change* (London, 2005).

Organisation for Economic Co-operation and Development, 'Social Institutions and Gender Index: Myanmar'. Available at http://www.genderindex.org/country/myanmar (accessed 12 April 2016).

——— 'Social Institutions and Gender Index: Nepal'. Available at http://www.genderindex.org/country/nepal (accessed 12 April 2016).

Pagnamenta, Robin, 'Old problem, new statistics', *The Times*, 20 March 2013. Available at http://www.thetimes.co.uk/tto/news/world/asia/article3717780.ece (accessed 12 April 2016).

Pallikadavath, Saseendran and Tamsin Bradley, '"Dowry autonomy" and domestic violence among young married women in India' (forthcoming in the *Journal of South Asian Development*).

Palriwala, Rajni, *Dowry in Contemporary India: An Overview in Expanding Dimensions of Dowry* (Delhi, 2003).

Palriwala, Rajni, 'The spider's web: Seeing dowry, fighting dowry', in Tamsin Bradley, Emma Tomalin and Mangala Subramaniam, *Dowry: Bridging the Gap Between Theory and Practice* (Delhi, 2009), pp. 144–76.

Palriwala, Rajni and Patricia Uberoi (eds), *Marriage and Migration in Asia*. Special Issue *Indian Journal of Gender Studies* xii/2–3 (2005).

Patel, Pragna, 'Flying by the nets of racism, patriarchy and religion', in Sukhwant Dhaliwal and Nira Yuval-Davis (eds), *Women Against Fundamentalism: Stories of Dissent and Solidarity* (London, 2014), pp. 52–66.

Patel, Tulsi, *The Family in India: Structure and Practice* (New Delhi, 2005).

Paul, Sohini, *Women Labour Force Participation and Domestic Violence: Evidence from India* (New Delhi, 2014).

Pearson, Ruth and Emma Tomalin, 'Intelligent design?: A gender-sensitive interrogation of religion and development', in Gerard Clarke and Michael Jennings (eds), *Development, Civil Society and Faith Based Organisations* (London, 2008), pp. 46–71.

Peet, Richard, *Geography of Power: The Making of Global Economic Policy* (London, 2014).

Pereira, Ignatius, '715 Rape cases registered till September this year', *Hindu*, 4 November 2012. Available at http://www.thehindu.com/news/national/kerala/715-rape-cases-registered-till-september-this-year/article4062700.ece (accessed 12 April 2016).

Pottier, Johan, Alan Bicker and Paul Sillitoe (eds), *Negotiating Local Knowledge: Power and Identity in Development* (London, 2003).

PTI, 'Statistics: 92 women raped in India every day, 4 in Delhi', *India Today*, 4 September 2014. Available at http://indiatoday.intoday.in/story/india-rape-92-women-every-day-4-delhi-statistics/1/380956.html (accessed 12 April 2016).

Purves, Libby, 'Indian women need a cultural earthquake', *The Times*, 31 December 2012. Available at http://www.thetimes.co.uk/tto/opinion/columnists/article3643810.ece (accessed 12 April 2016). Also published in *The Australian* as 'Gang-rape shame could drag India into 21st century', 1 January 2013. Available at http://www.theaustralian.com.au/news/world/gang-rape-shame-could-drag-india-into-21st-century/story-fnb64oi6-1226545829569 (accessed 12 April 2016).

Raheja, Goodwin and Ann Grodzins Gold, *Listen to the Heron's Words: Re-imagining Gender and Kinship in North India* (Berkeley, California, 1996).

Ramanatha Iyer, Sundara Rajan and Stewart MacPherson, *Social Development in Kerala: Illusion or Reality* (Farnham, UK, 2000).

Rao, Nitya (ed.), *Migration, Education and Socio-Economic Mobility* (London, 2012).

Rao, V. 1997. 'Wife beating in rural south India: A qualitative and econometric analysis', *Social Science and Medicine 8:4* (1997). pp. 1169–80.

Rocca, Corinne H., Sujit Rathod, Tina Falle, Rohini P. Pande and Suneeta Krishnan, 'Challenging assumptions about women's empowerment: Social, economic resources and domestic violence among young married women in urban South India', *Journal of International Epidemiology* xxxviii/2 (2009), pp. 577–85.

Roy, Arundhati and Jon Snow 'Author says events says a lot about India's inequality'. *Channel 4 News* (UK), 21 December 2012. Video of interview available at https://www.youtube.com/watch?v=tjzl4xAhrao (accessed 12 April 2016).

Sakhi, *A Study on Gender Based Violence in Kerala* (Trivandrum, 2004).

Sankaran, Lavanya, 'The good men of India', *New York Times*, 21 October 2013. Available at http://www.nytimes.com/2013/10/20/opinion/sunday/the-good-men-of-india.html (accessed 12 April 2016).

Sarkar, Sumit, *Beyond Nationalist Frames: Postmodernism, Hindu Fundamentalism, History* (Bloomington, Indiana, 2002).

Sarkar, Tanika and Urvashi Butalia, *Women and Right-wing Movements* (London, 1995).

Sen, Purna, 'Enhancing women's choices in responding to domestic violence in Calcutta: A comparison of employment and education', *European Journal of Development Research* xi/2 (1999), pp. 65–86.

Sen, Samita, *Towards a Feminist Politics? The Indian Women's Movement in Historical Perspective*. World Bank Policy Research Report on Gender and Development Working Paper Series No. 9 (Washington, DC, 2000).

Siddiqui, Hannana, '"I wish I'd taken her with me": The lives of black and minority ethnic women facing gender-based violence', in Tamsin Bradley (ed.), *Women Violence and Tradition: Taking FGM and Other Practices to a Secular State* (London, 2011), pp. 161–90.

Sinha, Mrinalini, *Colonial Masculinity. The 'Manly Englishman' and the 'Effeminate Bengali' in the Late Nineteenth Century* (Manchester, 1995).

Sokoloff, Natalie J. and Ida Duport, 'Domestic violence at the intersections of race, class and gender: Challenges and contributions to understanding violence against marginalized women in diverse communities', *Violence against Women* xi/1 (2005), pp. 38–64.

Solotaroff, Jennifer L. and Rohini Prabha Pande, *Violence against Women and Girls: Lessons from South Asia* (Washington, DC, 2014).

de Sousa Santos, Boaventura, 'On oppositional postmodernism', in Ronaldo Munck and Denis O'Hearn (eds), *Critical Development Theory Contributions to a New Paradigm* (London, 1999), pp. 29–34.

Spivak, Gayatri Chakravorty, 'Can The Subaltern Speak?', in Cary Nelson and Lawrence Grossberg (eds), *Marxism and The Interpretation of Culture* (Urbana, Illinois, 1988), pp. 271–313.

Srinivasan, Sharada, 'Daughters or dowries? The changing nature of dowry practices in South India', *World Development* xxxiii/4 (2005), pp. 593–615.

Srinivasan, Sharada and Arjun S. Bedi, 'Domestic violence and dowry: Evidence from a South Indian village', *World Development* xxxv/5 (2007), pp. 857–80.

Sudha, Shreeniwas and S. Irudaya Rajan, 'Female demographic disadvantage in India 1981–1991: Sex selective abortions and female infanticide', *Development and Change* xxx/3 (1999), pp. 585–618.

Sugden, Joanna, 'British dentist jumped from window "to avoid rape in India"', *The Times*, 20 March 2013. Available at http://www.thetimes.co.uk/tto/news/world/asia/article3717206.ece (accessed 12 April 2016).

Tomalin, Emma. 'Thinking about faith-based organisations in development: Where have we got to and what next?' *Development in Practice* 22:5–6 (2012), pp. 689–703.

Tucker, Vincent, 'The myth of development: A critique of a Eurocentric discourse', in Munck and O'Hearn (eds), *Critical Development Theory* (London, 1999).

Turshen, Meredeth, 'A global partnership for development and other unfulfilled promises of the millennium project', *Third World Quarterly* xxxv/3, pp. 345–57.

Udwin, Leslee (dir.), *India's Daughter* (2014). Made by Assassin Films for BBC Four's *Storyville* series.

UK Aid, UN Population Fund, UN Women, UCL and CREHPA, *Tracking Cases of Gender-Based Violence in Nepal 2013: Individual, Institutional, Legal and Policy Analyses* (New York, 2013). Available at http://asiapacific.unfpa.org/sites/asiapacific/files/pub-pdf/TrackingCasesofGBV.pdf (accessed 12 April 2016).

UK Foreign and Commonwealth Office, 'Human rights and democracy report 2012 – Pakistan' (London, 2013). Available at https://www.gov.uk/government/news/human-rights-and-democracy-report-2012-pakistan–2 (accessed 12 April 2016).

UK Home Office, *Burma (Myanmar): Country of Origin Information Report* (London, 2012). Available at https://www.gov.uk/government/uploads/system/uploads/attachment_data/file/311393/Burma_COI_report_2012.pdf (accessed 12 April 2016).

———, *Country Information and Guidance Pakistan: Women Fearing Gender-Based Harm / Violence* (London, 2014). Available at https://www.gov.uk/government/uploads/system/uploads/attachment_data/file/331642/Pakistan_CIG.Women 2014.07.16v1.0.pdf (accessed 12 April 2016).

UN Committee on the Elimination of Discrimination against Women, 'Information provided in follow up to the concluding observations of the Committee: Myanmar. Response by Myanmar to the recommendations contained in the concluding observations of Committee following the examination of the combined second and third periodic report of Myanmar on 3 November 2008'. Committee on the Elimination of Discrimination against Women Fiftieth Session 3–21 October 2011. Available at http://www.refworld.org/publisher,CEDAW,,MMR,4ef8338a2,0.html (accessed 12 April 2016).

——— 'Concluding observations on the fourth periodic report of Pakistan adopted by the Committee at is fifty fourth session (11th February – 1st March 2013)', available at http://www2.ohchr.org/english/bodies/cedaw/docs/co/CEDAW.C.PAK.CO.4.doc (accessed 12 April 2016).

UN Convention on the Elimination of All Forms of Discrimination Against Women.

UN Office of the High Commissioner for Human Rights, *Harmful Traditional Practices Affecting the Health of Women and Children*. UN Fact Sheet No. 23 (Washington, DC, 1995).

UN Population Fund, *UNFPA Strategy and Framework for Action to Addressing Gender-based Violence 2008–2011* (New York, 2009).

UN Women, *Handbook for National Action Plans on Violence Against Women* (New York, 2012).

——— *A Transformative Stand-Alone Goal on Achieving Gender Equality, Women's Rights and Women's Empowerment: Imperatives and Key Components* (Washington, DC, 2013).

——— Asia and the Pacific website, available at http://asiapacific.unwomen.org/en/focus-areas (accessed 12 April 2016).

——— 'Myanmar'. Available at http://asiapacific.unwomen.org/en/focus-area/cedaw-human-rights/Myanmar (accessed 12 April 2016).

——— 'UN Women strategy'. Available at http://clientdisplay.com/unwomen/focus-areas/human-rights/un-women-strategy/ (accessed 12 April 2016).

UNICEF, *Progress for Children: A Report Card on Adolescents*, No. 10 (New York, 2012).

United Nations, *The Millennium Development Goals Report* (New York, 2013).

US Department of State, *Burma 2012 Human Rights Report* (Washington, DC, 2013). Available at http://www.state.gov/documents/organization/204400.pdf (accessed 12 April 2016).

——— *Burma 2014 Human Rights Report* (Washington, DC, 2014). Available at http://www.state.gov/documents/organization/236640.pdf (accessed 12 April 2016).

USAID Knowledge Services Center, *Pakistan: Gender Overview* (Wastington, DC, 2013).

Vaswani, J.P., *Peace or Perish: There is no Other Choice* (Pune, 2007).

Werbner, Pnina, 'Introduction: The dialectics of cultural hybridity', in Pnina Werbner and Tariq Modood (eds), *Debating Cultural Hybridity: Multi-Cultural Identities and the Politics of Anti-racism* (London, 1997).

Women's League of Burma, *In the Shadow of the Junta: CEDAW Shadow Report* (Chiang Mai, 2008). Available at http://womenofburma.org/Report/IntheShadow-Junta-CEDAW2008.pdf (accessed 12 April 2016).

World Bank World DataBank, *World Development Indicators*. Available at http://databank.worldbank.org/data/reports.aspx (accessed 12 April 2016).

World Economic Forum, *The Global Gender Gap Report 2013* (Geneva, 2013), pp. 306–7.

———, *The Global Gender Gap Report 2014* (Geneva, 2014), pp. 206–7.

World Health Organisation, South African Medical Research Council and the London School of Hygiene and Tropical Medicine, *Global and Regional Estimates of Violence against Women: Prevalence and Health Effects of Intimate Partner Violence and Non-Partner Sexual Violence* (Geneva, 2013).

———, 'Female genital mutilation'. Available at http://www.who.int/mediacentre/factsheets/fs241/en/ (accessed 12 April 2016).

Yuval-Davis, Nira, *Gender and Nation* (Thousand Oaks, California, 2006).

INDEX